Alex Rzomp
525-7

MULTIPLE-CHOICE AND FREE-RESPONSE QUESTIONS IN PREPARATION FOR THE AP ENGLISH LANGUAGE AND COMPOSITION EXAMINATION

(SEVENTH EDITION)

By

DR. RICHARD VOGEL

Edited and Introduced by Sally Pfeifer

D&S MARKETING SYSTEMS, INC.
1205 38th Street Brooklyn, NY 11218

w w w . d s m a r k e t i n g . c o m

ISBN # 978-1-934780-20-6 / 1-934780-20-0

INTRODUCTION

I began using D&S Marketing's *Multiple-Choice Questions in Preparation for the Advanced Placement English Language & Composition Examination* in the early 1990s. At that time, as a relatively new AP English teacher, I was looking for some concrete help with the multiple-choice section of the exam, a section that seemed to baffle and frustrate teachers and students alike. I quickly discovered that practice with multiple-choice samples was limited by the few practice tests and sample passages available. D&S Marketing's AP English texts helped fill that void. As the years progressed and I gained experience, I learned that teaching my students close reading skills and giving them practice with the types of multiple-choice questions that appear on the exam proved a good tool. My subsequent experiences as a Reader and Table Leader at the exam grading and as a member of the Test Development Committee helped me to understand the construction of the exam and the skills it assesses. Thus, when fellow AP colleague Rich Vogel asked me to review and edit his latest edition, I was excited to use my experience and knowledge to help make this text the most dynamic and usable tool for students and teachers of AP English Language.

With that in mind, I would like to suggest some ideas or methods for using this edition in the AP classroom. This new edition features not only sample exams with multiple-choice and free-response questions, but extremely useful explications, rubrics, student samples and assessments of student responses. Rich has worked diligently to deliver great pieces of nonfiction with solid and provocative questions, and though you may or may not agree with the answer to a given question, you will be able to see and understand the thought process behind it. I suggest that you try not to criticize a particular question, but instead come to an understanding of it with your students, enjoying a "teachable moment."

Though there are many ways to use this wealth of materials and expertise in your classroom, here are a few suggestions:

1. Don't ask your students to take every test "cold." Rather, work backward on a few of the samples first. Read the piece, than the explication, and, in the case of the essays, review the scoring guide and student samples if included. Discuss the piece, then try the questions as a class, in small groups or individually.

2. Try small "chunks" at first; then work up to the "whole exams" slowly — there are six complete exams included in this edition with over three hundred multiple-choice questions to practice on in addition to prompts that address the three disparate language tasks: the essay analysis, the response to a citation, and the synthesis essay.

3. Read a nonfiction passage together and speculate about questions that might be asked; then, see what questions actually appear.

In other words, let this book "work" for you and incorporate the selections and questions into your syllabus. Remember: if you bring your students your "best game" — a love of literature and the skills of reading and responding to it — this book will serve you well.

Thank you to Rich Vogel and David Lederman for the opportunity to play a small part in this edition.

Sally Pfeifer

ACKNOWLEDGMENTS

No work of literature is a solitary effort, even if it is written by a single author, and the 7th edition of *Multiple-Choice and Free-Response Questions in Preparation for the Advanced Placement English Language & Composition Examination* is no exception. I would like to express my gratitude to David Lederman of D&S Marketing who has supported my efforts since the first edition of this text appeared in the mid-1980s. Though I am sure I have on occasion exasperated him with revisions to the text, I think he has grown to understand that the same ambiguity of literature that permits multiple interpretations of *Hamlet* bedevils the creator of multiple choice questions who must try to eliminate all potential challenges to the correctness of a right answer while still creating a choice or two that may serve as a reasonable distractor. And though I doubt he will ever understand that the search for the great passage (one that will yield a dozen or more multiple choice questions) or a great essay prompt often rivals Ahab's search for the white whale, he has nevertheless shown an amplitude of patience in our mutual endeavor to produce the best possible AP English text. Seldom have I been asked to forego a piece that I really thought would add quality to the book despite, I am sure, the considerable royalty some contemporary pieces command. For this unflagging support I am forever grateful.

As for my editor and back-reader, Sally Pfeifer, I cannot begin to express my appreciation for the long hours she has contributed, the literary insights she has shared, and the rigid standards to which she has held me during the arduous gestation of this book. She has provided the most useful feedback whether it be suggesting potential authors or passages, offering an alternate perspective on a particular text, or deterring the wrong-headed foray of which I am sometimes capable. All of these she has done with an admirable mixture of professionalism and affability that has made a process that can easily become turbulent a smooth and enjoyable ride. A comrade and dining companion from my days as a Reader and Table Leader in Daytona and Louisville, Sally has been an invaluable resource and someone whom I have been fortunate to have had working with me on this new edition.

I would be remiss not to mention our typesetter, Chaya Pruzansky, whose patience during the long process of fashioning early drafts into a refined final product, as well as her tolerance for the multiple emendations this process entails, has been boundless. I am deeply appreciative of her efforts in making the presentation of the material on the page both accurate and visually attractive.

I would also like to thank the AP English students at Croton-Harmon High School and at Wilton High School whose essays appear in this book for so generously sharing their time and talent. In joining them in our mutual exploration of literature, I have been humbled daily by their bright minds and engaging personalities.

Lastly, I would like to thank the present and former members of the English Department at Wilton High School. Being surrounded daily by such diverse, fecund and idiosyncratic minds is a continued source of inspiration to me, and the insights you have shared on particular passages and your proffered words of perseverance and encouragement, have provided the last gust to guide this bark into its harbor. I am blessed to call you colleagues, even more so to call you my friends.

Richard Vogel

All communications concerning this book should be addressed to:

D&S Marketing Systems, Inc.
1205 38th Street
Brooklyn, NY 11218
www.dsmarketing.com

TABLE OF CONTENTS

Sample Examination I

Section I

Questions 1-12. Refer to the following passage.

We are told by some ancient authors, that Socrates was instructed in eloquence by a woman, whose name, if I am not mistaken, was Aspasia. I have, indeed, looked upon that
(5) art as the most proper for the female sex.... It has been said in the praise of some men, that they could talk whole hours together upon anything; but it must be owned to the honour of the other sex, that there are many among
(10) them who can talk whole hours together upon nothing. I have known a woman branch out into a long extempore dissertation upon the edging of a petticoat, and chide her servant for breaking a china cup in all the figures of
(15) rhetoric.

Were women admitted to plead in courts of judicature, I am persuaded they would carry the eloquence of the bar to greater heights than it is yet arrived at. If anyone doubts this, let
(20) him be but present at those debates which frequently arise among the ladies of the British fishery.

The first kind, therefore, of female orators which I shall take notice of, are those who are
(25) employed in stirring up the passions, a part of rhetoric in which Socrates' wife had perhaps made a greater proficiency than his above-mentioned teacher.

The second kind of female orators are
(30) those who deal in invectives, and who are commonly known by the name of the censorious.[2] The imagination and elocution of this set of rhetoricians is wonderful. With what a fluency of invention, and copiousness of
(35) expression, will they enlarge upon every little slip in the behavior of another! With how many different circumstances, and with what variety of phrases, will they tell over the same story! I have known an old lady make an unhappy
(40) marriage the subject of a month's conversation. She blamed the bride in one place; pitied her in another; laughed at her in a third; wondered at her in a fourth; was angry with her in a fifth; and in short, wore out a pair of coach-horses in
(45) expressing her concern for her. At length, after having quite exhausted the subject on this side, she made a visit to the new-married pair, praised the wife for the prudent choice she had made, told her the unreasonable reflections
(50) which some malicious people had cast upon her, and desired that they might be better acquainted....

A third kind of female orators may be comprehended under the word gossips. Mrs.
(55) Fiddle-Faddle is perfectly accomplished in this sort of eloquence; she launches out into descriptions of christenings, runs divisions[1] upon an head-dress, knows every dish of meat that is served up in her neighbourhood, and
(60) entertains her company a whole afternoon together with the wit of her little boy, before he is able to speak.

The coquette may be looked upon as a fourth kind of female orator. To give herself
(65) the larger field for discourse, she hates and loves in the same breath, talks to her lap-dog or parrot, is uneasy in all kinds of weather, and in every part of the room....and indeed seems to speak for no other purpose, but as it gives
(70) her an opportunity of stirring a limb, or varying a feature, of glancing her eyes, or playing with her fan....

I have been often puzzled to design a cause why women should have this talent of a ready
(75) utterance in so much greater perfection than men. I have sometimes fancied that they have not a retentive power, the faculty of suppressing their thoughts, as men have, but that they are necessitated to speak everything
(80) they think....But as several are of opinion that the fair sex are not altogether strangers to the arts of dissembling, and concealing their thoughts, I have been forced to relinquish that opinion, and have, therefore, endeavoured to
(85) seek after some better reason. In order to it, a friend of mine, who is an excellent anatomist, has promised me by the first opportunity to dissect a woman's tongue, and to examine whether there may not be in it certain juices
(90) which render it so wonderfully voluble or flippant....

---

[1] entertains diverse opinions

[2] likely meaning censuring, critical

1

1. The first indication of the author's satirical intent is evident in

    (A) lines 8-11
    (B) lines 19-22
    (C) lines 33-36
    (D) lines 53-62
    (E) lines 63-72

2. The author cites the "petticoat" (line 13) and the "china cup" (line 14) to exemplify which of the following?

    I. Chores that dominate a woman's domestic environment.
    II. Trivialities that spawn elaborate orations.
    III. Forums in which women have demonstrated an eloquence that rivals that of the courts.

    (A) I only
    (B) II only
    (C) I and III
    (D) II and III
    (E) I, II and III

3. The salient organizing principle of the passage is

    (A) classification
    (B) comparison-contrast
    (C) a central metaphor
    (D) cause and effect
    (E) inductive reasoning

4. By "stirring up the passions" (line 25), the author is likely referring to this type of orator's

    (A) inspirational rhetoric
    (B) motivational ploys
    (C) marital discord
    (D) amorous words
    (E) feminist bent

5. The author 'compliments' all of the following traits of the "censorious" female orator (lines 29-52) EXCEPT

    (A) her glibness and creativity
    (B) her ability to exaggerate faults
    (C) her diversity of condemnation
    (D) her covetous feelings
    (E) her unabashed hypocrisy

6. In light of the context in which it appears, the phrase "wore out a pair of coach horses" (line 44) should likely be considered

    (A) understated
    (B) metaphorical
    (C) euphemistic
    (D) paradoxical
    (E) clichéd

7. The author stylistically mirrors the mercurial nature of the typical "censorious" female orator as it is depicted in lines 29-52 via which of the following?

    (A) bathos
    (B) parallel action verbs
    (C) inverted syntax
    (D) parody
    (E) colorful invective

8. The most preposterous aspect of Mrs. Fiddle-Faddle's characterization involves her

    (A) singularly appropriate name
    (B) 'accomplished' status as a female orator
    (C) voluble description of christenings
    (D) omniscience of other people's dinner tables
    (E) boasts about the wit of her son

9. Which of the following CANNOT be said to be characteristic of the author's style?

    (A) a witty, first-person perspective
    (B) mildly satirical barbs
    (C) the personification of an archetypal gossip
    (D) misogynistic diction
    (E) pseudo-exclamations of wonder

10. The author's comments about the stereotypical coquette (lines 63-72) depict her as

    (A) sentimental and caring
    (B) effusive and self-absorbed
    (C) pampered and lethargic
    (D) reticent and coy
    (E) discomfited and remote

11. The author's remark about the anatomist who has "promised [him] by the first opportunity to dissect a woman's tongue..." (lines 87-88) reveals which of the following?

    (A) the author's eagerness to examine it as a source of women's volubility
    (B) the author's resignation to never resolving women's capacity for gossip
    (C) the investigative superiority of science over journalism
    (D) the necessity for interdisciplinary cooperation in resolving mysteries
    (E) the subtle but wry culmination of the author's satire

12. Upon completion of the passage, the author's opening allusion to Socrates seems intended to

    (A) provide in Aspasia an example of an influential female orator
    (B) establish Socrates as an exemplar of rhetoric
    (C) camouflage his satirical intent by establishing a mock-serious tone
    (D) challenge the authority of the ancient authors in determining an orator's caliber
    (E) offer a stark historical contrast to the fictional Mrs. Fiddle-Faddle

Questions 13-24. Refer to the following passage.

In the following passage a man who is selling a century-old summer home reflects on the time he spent living in it.

How many Boston Brahmins[1] does it take to screw in a light bulb? Ten: one to put in the new bulb, and nine to reminisce about how great the old one was. If it *used* to be done this
(5) way, it *ought* to be done this way, and, by God, it *will* be done this way. We would never tolerate the Big House's inconveniences in our winter homes, but this is different: we change in the winter, but during the summer—a season
(10) in which we regress to an innocent, Edenic state by replicating the experiences we had as children—change is heresy. We bristle when guests expect, well, something a little more *deluxe*. Were we to stop washing the dishes by
(15) hand, it would mean losing not only the opportunity to watch the boats sail into the harbor, but a precious daily chunk of WASP bonding (which is performed far more adhesively over a mildewed dish towel than
(20) over a beer). Were we to replace the hypersensitive toilets, so aged that their porcelain handles are spiderwebbed with cracks, it would mean taking down the handwritten notes my grandmother
(25) thumbtacked in each of the seven bathrooms, whose words we can recite by heart now, like an affectionate family mantra: NOTHING BUT TOILET PAPER—AND NOT WADS OF THIS—TO GO IN TOILETS. CESSPOOL
(30) TROUBLE POSSIBLE, THOUGH NOT PROBABLE, IF WE WATCH.

Like Plimoth[2] Plantation or Colonial Williamsburg, the Big House is to be preserved intact, uncontaminated either by throwing
(35) anything out or by willingly introducing anything new. Any change is likely the result of serendipity: a book left on a bedside table, a shell on a mantelpiece, a toy car on the kitchen floor. If no one removed them immediately,
(40) they will likely be granted tenure. Several years ago, an iron bedstead in the Little Nursery lost a caster. For two summers the resulting tilt was ignored. This summer we arrived to find that a copy of *Tess of the D'Urbervilles* had been
(45) placed under the shortened leg. We haven't touched it. Recently, sweeping up after a weekend of houseguests, I came across a guitar pick. For the time being, I put it in the wooden dish on the front hall shelf where the key to the
(50) Chelsea clock is kept. I know that if the house were not being sold, that guitar pick would remain there for decades, as immovable as a barnacle. My grandchildren would assume that Ned Atkinson[3] played the guitar, and would
(55) venerate the pick as a holy relic.

Wandering through the old rooms, I have, on occasion, felt as if I were on an archaeological dig. In the bathroom cabinets there are vials of aspirin whose contents
(60) expired more than a decade ago. In the front hall closet, four different eras of life jackets jostle for space. On the utility room shelves, I find five rusty cans of Drano, six cans of lighter fluid (all with prices of less than a
(65) dollar a quart), two cans of weed killer whose toxic contents clearly predate Rachel Carson's *Silent Spring*,[4] and five half-empty tubes of Sea & Ski from the innocent era, before people worried about skin cancer, when it was not
(70) called sunblock but suntan oil. Why have we saved these artifacts? I doubt they will ever be used. And yet when Anne suggests that we throw them out, I cannot bring myself to do it. Not on my watch.
(75) Everything in the house breathes of the past, from the stacks of my grandmother's sheet music on the piano—Gilbert and Sullivan operettas, turn-of-the-century ballads, patriotic World War I tunes—to the globe in the
(80) Playroom whose countries include Palestine, French West Africa, and Tanganyika Territory, to the outdated tide charts under the rusted thumbtacks on the bulletin boards. The photographs in the albums are mostly of long-
(85) dead relatives. The drawers of bureaus and bookcases are lined with old newspapers, their edges yellowed and crinkly; as I retrieve a photo album from the cabinet in the living room, I am confronted by a fading headline
(90) from the May 26, 1969 edition of *The New York Times*: APOLLO 10 AIMS FOR SPLASHDOWN TODAY.

Prospective buyers of the Big House are often stunned into silence by its time-warp
(95) atmosphere. An architect said that when he stepped into the house for the first time, he was reminded of walking into the main hall on Ellis Island after it had been sealed for three decades....

---

[1] term coined by Oliver Wendell Holmes for New England's social aristocracy
[2] original colonial spelling of Plymouth

[3] the children's grandfather
[4] ground-breaking exposé of the environmental hazards of pesticides

13. In the opening paragraph the author reinforces the central theme of the passage—that "change is heresy" (line 12)—by all of the following EXCEPT

    (A) offering a variation on an old joke
    (B) using italics to emphasize the family's commitment to keeping things the same
    (C) alluding to domestic rituals and familiarities
    (D) citing the novelty of their summer behaviors
    (E) chronicling a brusque reaction to the expectancies of others

14. The author's speculations about the consequences of no longer washing dishes by hand or of replacing the antiquated toilets are bolstered MOST by his use of

    (A) the subjunctive mode and the loss it prefaces
    (B) an admonitory tone that foreshadows calamity
    (C) the image of the spiderwebbed porcelain handles
    (D) the simile that compares their grandmother's warnings to a prayer or incantation
    (E) the admonitory upper-case lettering

15. The simile in lines 32-33, "Like Plimoth Plantation or Colonial Williamsburg," implies that the Big House

    (A) is an important national legacy
    (B) needs rehabilitation due to its age
    (C) must be dutifully safeguarded
    (D) has frequent visitors
    (E) deserves landmark status

16. The BEST equivalent for the word "serendipity" (line 37), as it is used in the passage, would be

    (A) indolence
    (B) slovenliness
    (C) absent-mindedness
    (D) indifference
    (E) accident

17. The anecdotes of the iron bedstead and the guitar pick (lines 40-55) do which of the following?

    I. Exemplify the "serendipity" to which the author refers in line 37.
    II. Illustrate how objects that are not immediately removed are quietly "granted tenure" (line 40).
    III. Establish the "pack rat" mentality of the New England family.

    (A) I only
    (B) III only
    (C) I and II
    (D) II and III
    (E) I, II and III

18. The author meticulously details the contents of the bathroom cabinets, front hall closet, and utility room in order to

    (A) enhance the reader's ability to appreciate the setting
    (B) censure the family's wastefulness
    (C) reveal how much prices have inflated since the 1960s
    (D) show how insidiously clutter can accumulate over time
    (E) demonstrate the extent of his emotional ties to the Big House

19. The allusion to the cans of weed killer and the five half-empty tubes of suntan oil (lines 65-70) have MOST in common with which of the following?

    (A) the summertime "regress[ion]" mentioned in lines 9-12
    (B) the "WASP bonding" in lines 17-20
    (C) the grandmother's request to conserve toilet paper in lines 27-31
    (D) the copy of *Tess of the D'Urbervilles* shoved under the leg of the bedstead (lines 43-45)
    (E) the guitar pick placed on the front hall shelf (lines 47-50)

20. Which of the following BEST captures the difference between the objects mentioned in paragraph three (lines 56-74) and those mentioned in paragraph four (lines 75-92)?

    (A) The former are antiquated, the latter more contemporary.
    (B) The former are primarily products, the latter mostly memorabilia.
    (C) The former are utilitarian, the latter impractical.
    (D) The former are well-preserved, the latter deteriorating.
    (E) The former are in concealment, the latter out in the open.

21. Which of the following contributes LEAST towards establishing the "time-warp atmosphere" (lines 94-95) of the Big House in the final three paragraphs?

    (A) the author's comparison of the house to an "archaeological dig" (lines 56-58)
    (B) the personification of the life jackets (lines 61-62)
    (C) participles and adjectives such as "rusty" (line 63), "outdated" (line 82) and "yellowed" (line 87)
    (D) the sheet music, globe and newspaper (lines 76-92)
    (E) the closing allusion to Ellis Island (lines 97-99)

22. The architect's observation (lines 95-99) is likely made in response to which aspect of the house?

    (A) its vast dimensions
    (B) its seaside location
    (C) its sepulchral atmosphere
    (D) its archival lore
    (E) its ubiquitous decay

23. Which BEST establishes the connection between phrases such as "as immovable as a barnacle" (lines 52-53) and "Not on my watch" (line 74)?

    (A) They both reflect the author's reluctance to sell the Big House.
    (B) They both reflect the author's vigilance in preserving the Big House's singular character.
    (C) They both exemplify diction that matches the seaside setting.
    (D) They both imply the author's belief that the Big House would not have fallen into such decrepitude if he had lived in it year-round.
    (E) They both reflect the author's unwillingness to make concessions in pricing to prospective buyers.

24. The tone of the passage is BEST labeled

    (A) resigned
    (B) rueful
    (C) maudlin
    (D) nostalgic
    (E) relieved

Questions 25-36. Refer to the following passage.

In this selection from "The American Scholar" (1837) the author, Ralph Waldo Emerson, discusses the challenges facing the scholar in his time period.

....I have now spoken of the education of the scholar by nature, by books, and by action. It remains to say somewhat of his duties.

They are such as become Man Thinking.
(5) They may all be comprised in self-trust. The office of the scholar is to cheer, to raise, and to guide men by showing them facts amid appearances. He plies the slow, unhonored, and unpaid task of observation. Flamsteed and
(10) Herschel,[1] in their glazed observatories, may catalogue the stars with the praise of all men, and, the results being splendid and useful, honor is sure. But he, in his private observatory, cataloguing obscure and nebulous
(15) stars of the human mind, which as yet no man has thought of as such,—watching days and months, sometimes, for a few facts; correcting still his old records,—must relinquish display and immediate fame. In the long period of his
(20) preparation, he must betray often an ignorance and shiftlessness in popular arts, incurring the disdain of the able who shoulder him aside. Long must he stammer in his speech; often forego the living for the dead. Worse yet, he
(25) must accept—how often!—poverty and solitude. For the ease and pleasure of treading the old road, accepting the fashions, the education, the religion of society, he takes the cross of making his own, and, of course, the
(30) self-accusation, the faint heart, the frequent uncertainty and loss of time, which are the nettles and tangling vines in the way of the self-relying and self-directed; and the state of virtual hostility in which he seems to stand to
(35) society, and especially to educated society. For all this loss and scorn, what offset? He is to find consolation in exercising the highest functions of human nature. He is one, who raises himself from private considerations, and
(40) breathes and lives on public and illustrious thoughts. He is the world's eye. He is the world's heart. He is to resist the vulgar prosperity that retrogrades ever to barbarism, by preserving and communicating heroic
(45) sentiments, noble biographies, melodious verse, and the conclusions of history. Whatsoever oracles the human heart, in all emergencies, in all solemn hours has uttered as its commentary on the world of actions,—these
(50) he shall receive and impart. And whatsoever new verdict Reason from her inviolable seat pronounces on the passing men and events of today,—this he shall hear and promulgate.

These being his functions, it becomes him
(55) to feel all confidence in himself, and to defer never to the popular cry. He and he only knows the world....Let him not quit his belief that a popgun is a popgun, though the ancient and honorable of the earth affirm it to be the crack
(60) of doom. In silence, in steadiness, in severe abstraction, let him hold himself; add observation to observation, patient of neglect, patient of reproach; and bide his own time;—happy enough, if he can satisfy himself
(65) alone, that this day he has seen something truly....

In self-trust all the virtues are comprehended. Free should the scholar be,—free and brave. Free even to the definition
(70) of freedom, "without any hindrance that does not arise out of his own constitution." Brave; for fear is a thing that a scholar by his very function puts behind him. Fear always springs from ignorance. It is a shame to him if his
(75) tranquility, amid dangerous times, arise from the presumption that, like children and women, his is a protected class; or if he seek a temporary peace by the diversion of his thoughts from politics or vexed questions,
(80) hiding his head like an ostrich in the flowering bushes, peeping into microscopes, and turning rhymes, as a boy whistles to keep his courage up....

---

[1] astronomers who made notable discoveries of celestial bodies

25. The persuasiveness of the author's rhetoric is abetted MOST by his

    (A) scientific allusions
    (B) personification of Reason
    (C) strings of adjectives
    (D) loose sentences
    (E) certain and didactic tone

26. Among the deprivations that the author claims a scholar must endure are all of the following EXCEPT

    (A) frequent poverty
    (B) intellectual scorn
    (C) personal isolation
    (D) restricted liberties
    (E) public obscurity

27. Lines 5-8, "The office of the scholar is to cheer, to raise, and to guide men by showing them facts amid appearances," is BEST labeled a(n)

    (A) conjecture
    (B) assertion
    (C) understatement
    (D) fallacy
    (E) paradox

28. The author likely compares the scholar to an astronomer to highlight the

    (A) celebrity and recompense his discoveries yield
    (B) laborious and meticulous observation his work demands
    (C) visionary and anticipatory nature of his research
    (D) controversy and conflict between new discoveries and long-held beliefs
    (E) concrete and pragmatic application of his industry

29. The author describes this "office" in lines 13-19 by using which type of phrase?

    (A) appositive
    (B) participial
    (C) infinitive
    (D) gerundive
    (E) prepositional

30. Which of the following is NOT an object of the verb "takes" (line 28)?

    (A) "cross" (line 29)
    (B) "self-accusation" (line 30)
    (C) "frequent uncertainty" (lines 30-31)
    (D) "nettles" (line 32)
    (E) "state of virtual hostility" (lines 33-34)

31. Of the following, which BEST captures the meaning of "the nettles and tangling vines" mentioned in lines 31-32?

    (A) personal doubts that the scholar must overcome
    (B) intellectual problems that he must surmount
    (C) demands upon his time that conflict with his scholarship
    (D) the poverty and solitude that make him question his career choice
    (E) the burden of imparting wisdom to his fellowman

32. The author effects the major transition in the passage by means of a(n)

    (A) chiasmus
    (B) allusion
    (C) rhetorical question
    (D) shift in verb tense
    (E) personal anecdote

33. The repeated declamations of "He is" in lines 36-46 primarily serve to

    (A) contrast how over-burdened the scholar is due to his limited income
    (B) question the unreasonable diversity expected of the scholar
    (C) stipulate the hours and conditions under which a scholar must complete his work
    (D) celebrate the singular importance of the scholar's contribution to humanity
    (E) clarify the amount of writing a scholar must produce in a given period of time

34. The subsequent "consolation" that the scholar enjoys (lines 36-53) involves all of the following EXCEPT

    (A) performing a selfless humanitarian function
    (B) receiving public patronage to support his labors
    (C) assuming the custodianship of culture and aesthetics
    (D) becoming the spokesperson for human suffering
    (E) becoming, literally, the voice of Reason

35. Lines 57-60—"Let him not quit his belief that a popgun is a popgun, though the ancient and honorable of the earth affirm it to be the crack of doom"—do which of the following?

    I. Bolster the author's stalwart belief in "self-trust" (line 5, lines 67-68).
    II. Confirm "the state of virtual hostility" (lines 33-34) that the true scholar encounters.
    III. Exemplify the "vulgar prosperity that retrogrades ever to barbarism…" (lines 42-43).

    (A) I only
    (B) III only
    (C) I and II
    (D) II and III
    (E) I, II and III

36. The relation of the similes in lines 76-77 and lines 80-81 to the freedom and bravery that are said to be most necessary to the scholar (lines 68-73) is BEST expressed by which of the following?

    (A) They model behavior that the scholar should follow.
    (B) They question the rationality of outright defiance.
    (C) They advise against a particular misconception and course of action.
    (D) They imply that the better course is a policy of neutrality.
    (E) They imply that scholars should avoid political controversy.

Questions 37-45. Refer to the following passage.

In the following passage an author looks back on the landscape of his and his sibling's youth.

The Big Wood we called it. So well we knew it, and for so many years wandered here with weeping like Imogen's[1], and with laughter like Yorick's[2] laughter that when past years
(5) bulk into the likeness of a forest, through which the memory takes its pleasure at eventide…it is really this wood that we see, under a halcyon sky.

It covered two acres in the midst of
(10) ploughland; but we thought of it as enormous, because in it we often lost one another; it had such diversity; it made so genuine a solitude. The straight oaks rising branchless for many feet expanded and then united boughs in a
(15) firmament of leaves. It seemed far enough from London for feelings of security. But even of that our thoughts have changed; for the houses are fearfully close—a recollection of them lingers in the heart of the wood; and
(20) perhaps they will devour it also. . . . Who shall measure the sorrow of him that hath set his heart upon that which the world hath power to destroy, and hath destroyed? Even to-day the circuit of a cemetery is cutting into the field
(25) where we gathered buttercups before the dignity of knickerbockers[3]. . . . And here was a solitude. We cannot summon up any thought or reverie which had not in this wood its nativity. 'Tis we have changed! And if we could paint,
(30) and wished to make a picture of our youth with its seriousness and its folly, we should paint in this wood, instead of in a hostel-yard, another Don Quixote watching his armour all night after the false accolade.[4]

(35) The dark earth itself was pleasant to handle—earth one might wish to be buried in— and had the healthy and special quality of wild earth: upon it you could rest deliciously. (Compare the artificial soil of a London
(40) common with it!) Out of this rose up trees that preserved their wild attitudes. The age-fallen or tempest-uprooted oak tree lay where it dropped, or hung balanced in the boughs of others. Tenderest bramble spray or feeler of
(45) honeysuckle bridged those gaps in the underwood that served as paths. And the winds were husbandmen, reapers and sowers thereof. Though, indeed, the trees were ordered with an incongruous juxtaposition of birch and oak and
(50) elm, it seemed to us a fragment of the primeval forest left by a possible good fortune at the city verge. But it was more than this. With its lofty roof and the mysterious flashes of light in the foliaged clerestory,[5] with its shapely boles in
(55) cluster and colonnade,[6] and the glimpses of bright white sky that came and went among the leaves, the forest had a real likeness to a temple….

---

[1] a faithful wife in Shakespeare's *Cymbeline*, who weeps continuously because her husband suspects her of infidelity
[2] the deceased court jester in Shakespeare's *Hamlet*
[3] baggy pants
[4] an allusion to chapter 3 of Miguel Cervantes' *Don Quixote* in which the delusional protagonist spends the night protecting his armor so that he may be 'knighted' the next day by an inn-keeper he believes is the lord of a castle

[5] the upper part of a church nave, or a wall containing windows
[6] column-like tree trunks

---

37. All of the following are true about the declarative sentence, "The Big Wood we called it," that opens the passage EXCEPT:

(A) Its inverted syntax emphasizes the magnitude of its impression upon the author's childhood perspective.
(B) Its first-person pronoun reveals that the author's experiences in the forest were shared ones.
(C) Its vagueness suggests the author's present inability to determine the name of the exact locale.
(D) Its simple structure mirrors the unencumbered world of the author's childhood.
(E) Its reputation is later debunked by the revelation of its mere two acre scope.

38. The author's statement, "It seemed far enough from London for feelings of security" (lines 15-16), is likely prompted by his fear of

   (A) rampant crime
   (B) real-estate development
   (C) industrial pollution
   (D) population growth
   (E) moral corruption

39. The rhetorical question, "Who shall measure the sorrow of him that hath set his heart upon that which the world hath power to destroy, and hath destroyed?" (lines 20-23), suggests which of the following?

   I. That the sorrow the author feels is beyond comprehension.
   II. That humans have already displayed a capacity for destruction.
   III. That the author resents being judged by others.

   (A) I only
   (B) III only
   (C) I and II
   (D) II and III
   (E) I, II and III

40. In the second paragraph the author contrasts which of the following?

   (A) the freedom of nature and the confinement of man
   (B) the bountifulness of nature and the greed of man
   (C) the seclusion of nature and the intrusion of man
   (D) the innocence of nature and the corruption of man
   (E) the nobility of nature and the baseness of man

41. The allusion to Don Quixote in lines 32-34 implies that the speaker perceives himself a(n)

   (A) landscape painter
   (B) burgeoning writer
   (C) unstable presence
   (D) chivalrous sentinel
   (E) incurable romantic

42. Lines 40-41, "Out of this rose up trees that preserved their wild attitudes," do which of the following?

   I. Use inversion to demonstrate the trees' majestic ascent.
   II. Personify, somewhat humorously, the unchecked growth of bramble and feeler.
   III. Foreshadow the inherent spirituality of the "foliaged clerestory" (line 54).

   (A) I only
   (B) III only
   (C) I and II
   (D) II and III
   (E) I, II and III

43. The phrase "ordered with an incongruous juxtaposition of birch and oak and elm..." (lines 48-50) is BEST labeled a(n)

   (A) metonymy
   (B) hyperbole
   (C) apostrophe
   (D) irony
   (E) paradox

44. The culminating images in lines 52-58 suggest that the author considers the "Big Wood" to be

   (A) bewitched
   (B) ominous
   (C) impenetrable
   (D) tenebrous
   (E) hallowed

45. Which of the following most directly alludes to the Edenic bliss that the speaker and his sibling enjoyed in the Big Wood in their youth?

   (A) "…and then united boughs in a firmament of leaves…" (lines 14-15)
   (B) "a recollection of them lingers in the heart of the wood" (lines 18-19)
   (C) "…the field where we gathered buttercups before the dignity of knickerbockers…" (lines 24-26)
   (D) "…earth that one might wish to be buried in…" (line 36)
   (E) "…the forest had a real likeness to a temple…." (lines 57-58)

Questions 46-54. Refer to the following passage.

In the following passage the author comments upon the elegiac tributes composed upon the death of President Calvin Coolidge in 1933. Having succeeded President Warren Harding who died while in office, Coolidge was President from 1923-1929.

The editorial writers who had the job of concocting mortuary tributes to the late Calvin Coolidge, LL D, made heavy weather of it, and no wonder. Ordinarily, an American public
(5) man dies by inches, and there is thus plenty of time to think up beautiful nonsense about him. More often than not, indeed, he threatens to die three or four times before he actually does so, and each threat gives the elegists a chance to
(10) mellow and adorn their effusions. But Dr. Coolidge slipped out of life almost as quietly and unexpectedly as he had originally slipped into public notice, and in consequence the brethren were caught napping and had to do
(15) their political embalming under desperate pressure. The common legend is that such pressure inflames and inspires a true journalist, and maketh him to sweat masterpieces, but it is not so in fact. Like any other literary man, he
(20) functions best when he is at leisure, and can turn from his tablets now and then to run down a quotation, to eat a plate of ham and eggs, or to look out of the window.

The general burden of the Coolidge
(25) memoirs was that the right hon. gentleman was a typical American, and some hinted that he was the most typical since Lincoln. As the English say, I find myself quite unable to associate myself with that thesis. He was, in
(30) truth, almost as unlike the average of his countrymen as if he had been born green. The Americano is an expansive fellow, a back-slapper, full of amiability; Coolidge was reserved and even muriatic.[1] The Americano
(35) has a stupendous capacity for believing in what is palpably not true; Coolidge was, in his fundamental metaphysics, an agnostic. The Americano dreams vast dreams, and is hag-ridden by a demon; Coolidge was not mount
(40) but rider, and his steed was a mechanical horse. The Americano, in his normal incarnation, challenges fate at every step and his whole life

is a struggle; Coolidge took things as they came.
(45) Some of the more romantic of the funeral bards tried to convert the farmhouse at Plymouth into a log-cabin, but their attempt was as vain as the effort to make a Lincoln of good Cal. His early days, in fact, were
(50) anything but pinched. His father was a man of substance, and he was well fed and well schooled. He went to a good college, had the clothes to cut a figure there, and made useful friends. There is no record that he was brilliant,
(55) but he took his degree with a respectable mark, proceeded to the law, and entered a prosperous law firm on the day of his admission to the bar. Almost at once he got into politics, and by the time he was twenty-seven he was already on
(60) the public payroll. There he remained without a break for exactly thirty years, always moving up. Not once in all those years did he lose an election. When he retired in the end, it was at his own motion, and with three or four hundred
(65) thousand dollars of tax money in his tight jeans….

….No other President ever slipped into the White House so easily, and none other ever had a softer time of it while there. When, at Rapid
(70) City, S.D., on August 2, 1927, he loosed the occult words, 'I do not choose to run in 1928,' was it prescience or only luck? For one, I am inclined to put it down to luck. Surely there was no prescience in his utterances and
(75) maneuvers otherwise. He showed not the slightest hint that he smelt black clouds ahead; on the contrary, he talked and lived only sunshine. There was a volcano boiling under him, but he did not know it, and was not
(80) singed…

---

[1] of or relation to sea salt; here used figuratively to mean bitter or acerbic

46. The passage is characterized by all of the following contrasts EXCEPT

   (A) Coolidge's nature and the nature of the average American
   (B) Coolidge's roots and persona and Abraham Lincoln's roots and persona
   (C) Coolidge's commemorations by the press and Coolidge's career and life
   (D) Coolidge's entry into political life and Coolidge's departure from it
   (E) Coolidge's death and the more commonplace death of public servants

47. The author likely uses the phrase "the job of concocting mortuary tributes" (lines 1-2) to imply that

   (A) Coolidge did nothing particularly memorable in his term as President
   (B) writing obituaries is an arduous task
   (C) the suddenness of the President's death caught news-writers off-guard
   (D) reporting the deaths of public officials is an official duty
   (E) Coolidge's personality was hard to capture on paper

48. The author suggests all of the following about Coolidge EXCEPT

   (A) that he was restrained and undemonstrative
   (B) that he was stoic and controlled
   (C) that he was privileged and well-connected
   (D) that he was optimistic and oblivious
   (E) that he was self-promoting and avaricious

49. The three infinitive phrases in lines 21-23—"to run down a quotation, to eat a plate of ham and eggs, or to look out of the window"—are intended to

   (A) anticipate the subsequent depiction of Coolidge as an average American
   (B) imply why writers were "caught napping" on the occasion of Coolidge's death
   (C) exemplify pressure-reducing distractions that enhance the ability to write
   (D) poke fun at the idiosyncratic manner in which writers go about their craft
   (E) illustrate how writers place work before pleasure or leisure

50. The English expression that the author cites in lines 28-29—"I find myself quite unable to associate myself with that thesis"—is BEST labeled a(n)

   (A) euphemism
   (B) allusion
   (C) hyperbole
   (D) maxim
   (E) idiom

51. Lines 45-47, "Some of the more romantic of the funeral bards tried to convert the farmhouse at Plymouth into a log-cabin," imply that the writers attempted to do which of the following?

   I. Establish a museum that commemorated the life and career of the former President.
   II. Mythologize the former President's childhood experience.
   III. Explain the President's popular appeal by citing his rural roots.

   (A) II only
   (B) III only
   (C) I and II
   (D) II and III
   (E) I, II and III

52. The third paragraph differs MOST from the other three paragraphs in its

    (A) absence of eulogistic detail
    (B) shift to a more subjective perspective
    (C) catalog of biographical data
    (D) surprisingly pejorative tone
    (E) use of metaphorical language

53. Which of the following most blatantly reveals the author's attitude towards such post-mortem commemorative accounts of public figures?

    (A) "mortuary tributes" (line 2)
    (B) "beautiful nonsense" (line 6)
    (C) "political embalming" (line 15)
    (D) "masterpieces" (line 18)
    (E) "occult words" (line 71)

54. That Calvin Coolidge was a fortunate individual is confirmed LEAST by which of the following?

    (A) "His early days, in fact, were anything but pinched." (lines 49-50)
    (B) "There is no record that he was brilliant, but he took his degree with a respectable mark..." (lines 54-55)
    (C) "Almost at once he got into politics, and by the time he was twenty-seven he was already on the public payroll" (lines 58-60)
    (D) "Not once in all those years did he lose an election" (lines 62-63)
    (E) "There was a volcano boiling under him, but he did not know it, and was not singed...". (lines 78-80)

Section II

Question One

(Suggested time—40 minutes. This question counts as one-third of the total essay section score.)

In this passage a woman looking at photographs of her childhood reflects upon the impact of emigration upon her family. Read the passage carefully. Then, in a well-organized essay, identify the nature of the cultural rifts caused by relocation and show how the author's rich use of language conveys them.

But what about my mother? Like opposite
aspects of the same person: my mother, my
grandmother's shadow. Here, she's smiling,
though not broadly. Her children are gone, but
(5)   her mother's there, telling her *aguántate,*
cálmate,[1] as they sit over *café.*[2] Or maybe
she's relieved. It is, after all, the first time since
their marriage that she and my father are alone,
like newlyweds. But suddenly a kitchen towel,
(10) embroidered with the day of the week, *martes,*[3]
and smeared with another woman's lipstick,
flies from my mother's hand, lands like an
open book by my father's mud-caked boots.

In this photograph, a coffee-dark V shows
(15) through the collar of her dress, evidence of the
enforced labor in the cane fields since the
revolution. Above her head is a wall vase filled
with plastic flowers, hanging under the framed
painting of a saint, who can't be seen above the
(20) melted-chocolate folds of a robe, and above
that, perhaps, two hands are held palms up,
checking the spiritual weather. But the hands
are outside the photograph, just like my hands,
which can't touch my mother at that brief oasis,
(25) or my grandmother, right before she turned and
left with the shadow.

Grandmother left so abruptly, left my mother in
mid-sentence, fingering the legendary length of
fabric her mother had once transformed into
(30) the Miracle of the Three Dresses. Alone, she
collapsed into her mother's absence like a slave
into bed at the end of the day.

Then one afternoon two years later the air of
her kitchen spun like someone whirling toward
(35) her, and she knew something had happened to
her son: locked in a mental ward at sixteen
after chasing his foster mother around the

block with a kitchen knife. He had dropped out
of high school, washed dishes for a living.
(40) Sporting long sideburns, he rewarded himself
first with a round-backed two-toned Chevy,
then a series of garish Mustangs. Married to
his fate, he left a trail of cars, each wrapped
like a wedding ring around a telephone pole.

(45) A vision of her oldest daughter—forever
regretting she hadn't been born into a TV
family—flashed thin against the white walls of
college, her body a blade sharpened to sever
the question from the answer. Her face a glossy
(50) ad of the ideal American living room.

In the newspaper photo above the caption
"Family of Cuban Expatriates Reunited Here,"
I am the only one gazing at the camera, my
face twisted into a complex curiosity. Two
(55) years on my own among strangers had only
taught me how to be one. I stood, my first
tongue ripped out, with my mother's wet, round
cheek pressed to the top of my head. The dark
flag of her mustache. Their sour smell, like
(60) clothes trapped in a hamper. Emblems of the
exile. While bureaucrats toyed with their time
and their fate, my parents had waited,
uncomplaining, afraid.

But I didn't know that back then. I placed
(65) myself instead in the camera lens, looking back
at the spectacle we made in the bus station.
Under my skin, the rice fields of my hometown
were flooding the place of language. Though
my mother pulled me toward her with one arm,
(70) she scooped up only watery absence; my body
had long since drifted downriver. My mother's
face in this photograph, captured by a stranger,
betrays the weight of emptiness in her arms.

---

[1] (Sp) hold on; stay calm
[2] (Sp) coffee
[3] (Sp) Tuesday

Aleida Rodriguez, excerpt from "My Mother in Two Photographs, Among Other Things" from Garden of Exile. Originally from Prairie Scbooner (1994), Copyright (c) 1994, 1999 by Aleida Rodriguez. Meter. Reprinted with the permission of The Permissions Company, Inc., on behalf of Sarabande Books, www .sarabandebooks.org.

Question Two

(Suggested time—40 minutes. This question counts as one-third of the total essay section score.)

In his national best-seller *The Greatest Generation*, Tom Brokaw pays tribute to the enormous sacrifices made by the men and women of the World War II generation who "went from cap and gown directly into uniform [and]….answered the call to help save the world from the two most powerful and ruthless military machines ever assembled…"; who, leaving behind families, friends, home towns, careers and aspirations, fought to preserve the liberties upon which this country was founded; and who upon returning home alive—if they were lucky enough not be one of the nearly three hundred thousand battlefield casualties—"joined in joyous and short-lived celebrations, then immediately began the task of rebuilding their lives and the world they wanted" (ix-xx).

Though Brokaw's poignant portrait of these ordinary yet extraordinary men and women lauds the quiet sense of civic duty that epitomized both these individuals and their actions, it begs the question whether such sacrifice is unique to this generation of Americans or endemic to *all* generations of Americans.

Take a moment to ponder Brokaw's claim. Then, in a well-organized essay, identify what you feel are the contemporary generation's—or some previous generation's—greatest challenges and anticipate how some future chronicler of this age might celebrate or condemn its efforts to overcome them. Use your reading, studies, experience or observation to develop your argument.

Question Three

Reading Time: 15 minutes
Suggested Writing Time: 40 minutes

(This question counts as one-third of the total essay section score.)

Directions:

The following prompt is based on the accompanying six sources.

This question requires you to integrate a variety of sources into a coherent, well-written essay. *Refer to the sources to support your position; avoid paraphrase or summary. Your argument should be central; the sources should support this argument.*

Remember to attribute both direct and indirect citations.

Introduction:

Though the penchant for computer gaming among adolescents is undeniable, the effects of such gaming are hotly debated. While some see this as a deleterious, obsessive fixation that contributes to, even promotes, violent and/or anti-social behavior, others see it as a technological boon that fosters, even enhances, problem-solving skills and imaginative thought.

Assignment:

Read the following sources (including any introductory information) carefully. **Then, in an essay that synthesizes at least three of the sources for support, take a position that defends, challenges or qualifies the claim that Internet and/or computer gaming is indisputably harmful to adolescents' intellectual and social development.**

<u>Document A</u>

Young, Dr. Kimberly S. Young. *Caught in the Net: How to Recognize the Signs of Internet Addiction.*
  New York: John Wiley & Sons, Inc, 1998: 67-69.

Steve never became the quarterback of his high school football team, as his father had hoped. He's not making the dean's list in his sophomore year at a major university in upstate New York, as his mother would like to see. She often reminds Steve that his brother is pulling a solid 3.5 grade point average at Rutgers. Steve also has no friends at school and his girlfriend recently broke up with him.

But in LambdaMOO, all that changes. In LambdaMOO, everyone bows to Steve in recognition of his power, skill, and intelligence. They respect and fear him. In LambdaMOO, Steve has buddies whom he can meet for drinks and small talk at Dred's Tavern. In LambdaMOO, Steve charms every woman he meets. He's recently been dating the beautiful and charming SoftSnow. In LambdaMOO, Steve is regarded as a great wizard—the highest honor anyone can achieve.

LambdaMOO is the land of the Multi-User Dungeon (MUD) where Steve spends most of his time. MUD commonly refers to the Internet's many active games, including the pure adventure type and the more socially oriented games known as MUSHes and MOOs. Traditionally, a MUD is a spinoff of the old Dungeons & Dragons game, where players take on the names of characters who compete through fighting battles, buying weapons, engaging in duels, killing monsters, slaying dragons, storming castles, and saving maidens. There are hundreds of MUDs, each with its own theme….

Because MUDs never end—play is continuous day and night, week to week—the only way to become a wizard is to play often. Steve plays at least 60 to 70 hours every week, following a pattern of jumping on the computer immediately after dinner and staying with it until 2 or 3 a.m. Then he sleeps until noon, skipping his morning classes. He may attend an afternoon class or two before rushing back to his dorm for another night as Chameleon. His grades are slipping to basic passing level, but he hasn't seriously considered cutting down….

Document B

Reeks, Anne. "Teens not just playing games; they're bettering themselves." *Houston Chronicle* 18 Apr 2002:
    4. Online http://proquest.umi.com/pdqweb?index=79&did=114628955&SrchMode
    =1&sid=3&Fmt=... .

EVERYBODY talks about what's wrong with the Internet—raunchy content, unbridled commercialism, rampant misinformation, invasive data-gathering and the list goes on.

I've certainly done my share of journalistic hand-wringing over its dangers to children.

In a refreshing change of pace, someone is talking about what's right with the Internet. Turns out, today's kids aren't only going online to play games, diss classmates and spend money, although they do plenty of that.

"But young people are also using the Internet these days to register to vote, to debate issues of war and peace, even to become social activists," says Kathryn Montgomery, president of the Center for Media Education, based in Washington, D.C. In other words, Web sites are acting as agents of good citizenship....

Examples are Voices of Youth, at www.unicef.org/voy, a worldwide forum for discussions of child labor, the environment, armed conflicts, gender discrimination and other issues; the Diary Project, www.diaryproject.com, where teen-agers can write about day-to-day concerns and respond to others in barebones (and wrenchingly affecting) plain-text posts; YouthNOISE, www.youthnoise.com, which aims to "connect, inform and empower youth" by encouraging them to help themselves and others; and HarlemLive, www.harlemlive.org, an Internet publication whose message boards address meatier fare than concerts and clothes....

Document C

DiConsiglio, John, "Game Over." *Scholastic Choices* 23.4 (Jan 2008): 6-9. Online
http://proquest.umi.com/pdqweb?index=5&did=1403808271&SrchMode=1&sid=3&Fmt=... .

Between 70 percent and 90 percent of teens in the United States play video or online games. Some experts suggest that 5 percent to 10 percent of these teens are gaming addicts. The problem has become serious enough for the American Medical Association to issue a warning about the dangers of gaming addiction.

"The problem is enormous," Dr. Hilarie Cash, co-founder of Internet/Computer Addiction Services tells *Choices*. "But people don't think of gaming addiction as being real. And those who need help with an addiction don't know where to get it"....

"The games are designed to keep you at your computer as long as possible because you can't win," says Liz Woolley of On-Line Gamers Anonymous, a group that helps gamers overcome addiction. "There's a large group of people who just can't stop playing"....

Cash, a therapist, has counseled teens who stop going to school or hanging out with their friends to make more time for their gaming. "Imagine a kid who used to have friends, used to love sports, and used to do things with his family," she says. "Now his grades are falling, he is totally out of shape, and he's withdrawn. He can no longer function in real life. All he wants to do is play the game"....

From "Game Over" by John DiConsiglio. Published in SCHOLASTIC CHOICES, January 2008.
Copyright © 2008 by Scholastic Inc. Reproduced by permission.

Document D

Neiburger, Eli and Matt Gullett. "Out of the Basement: The Social Side of Gaming." *Young Adult Library Services* 5.2 (Winter 2007): 34-37. Online http://proquest.umi.com/pdqweb?index=21&did= 1192061811 &SrchMode=17SID=3&fMT... .

When people play games together, the competition has value in and of itself, but the sharing of knowledge that occurs also increases the social value of the encounter. While both the loser and the winner learn something from every chess match, video games are usually so full of arcane secrets and exploitable glitches that exclamations of "How did you do that?" are central components of any gaming event. Players who can reliably execute difficult maneuvers, but also explain how they were done, have cachet and credibility among their peers that simply can't be obtained in the classroom. These are useful life skills here, unlike trigonometry....

While the social and recreational benefits alone make gaming events a good fit for any public library, games are also learning activities and even, in many cases, literacy activities. On the most basic level, all video games require the development of cognitive skills that are useful in the always "on" modern world, such as pattern recognition, spatial reasoning, and information processing....

Games are widely used as educational tools, not just for pilots, soldiers and surgeons, but also in schools and businesses.... Games require players to construct hypotheses, solve problems, develop strategies, learn the rules of the in-game world through trial and error. Gamers must also be able to juggle several different tasks, evaluate risks and make quick decisions.... Playing games is, thus, an ideal form of preparation for the workplace of the twenty-first century, as some forward-thinking firms are already starting to realize....

Document E

"Hey, it's helped me get this video game generation interested in math..."

Document F

Worthy, Kym. "How Violent Video Games can Cultivate real Youth Violence." *Michigan Chronicle* 69.2 (Sep 28-Oct 4, 2005): A1. Online http://proquest.umi.com/pdqweb?index=43&did=924450061 &SrchMade= 1&sid=3&Fmt=... .

The stark lead in an *Indianapolis Star* news story captures a teenager's glee as he demonstrates proficiency in a video killing game.

The 18-year-old, according to the newspaper, "takes careful aim and shoots, red spray fills the air, and the target falls dead, as (the youth) laughs lightly and says, "There's the blood."

Meanwhile, in Oakland, Calif., a group of teens and young adults were arrested last year in a highly publicized spree of carjackings, robberies, and murders. Some of the alleged assailants acknowledged the role violent video games played in the crimes. A lawyer in a CBSNews.com Q&A reported that older gang members used the Grand Theft Auto III game to "train teens to do carjackings and murders."

According to one arrested youth, "We played the game by day and lived the game by night."

Sample Exam One: Explications and Answers

Précis and Explication of Passage One: From Joseph Addison's and Richard Steele's *The Spectator*, no. 247, Thursday, December 16, 1711

Those familiar with *The Spectator* know that its selections are often satirical and unfailingly droll, and this selection is no exception. Though it opens with a seemingly serious observation about Socrates being "instructed in eloquence by a woman" (lines 2-3) and about public speaking being a "most proper [art] for the female sex…" (line 5), only a sentence later the author makes the observation that it must also "be owned to the honour of the other sex, that there are many among them who can talk whole hours together upon nothing" (lines 8-11). This satirical barb, which indicts women for engaging in meaningless gossip, is quickly followed by the author's observation that he has "known a woman branch out into a long extempore dissertation upon the edging of a petticoat, and chide her servant for breaking a china cup in all the figures of rhetoric" (lines 11-15). The hyperbolic language of "long extempore dissertation" and "all the figures of rhetoric" quickly reveals the mock seriousness of the piece as does the further claim that "Were women admitted to plead in courts of judicature, I am persuaded they would carry the eloquence of the bar to greater heights than it is yet arrived at" (lines 16-19). As if more were needed to persuade, the author then challenges any doubters to present themselves "at those debates which frequently arise among the ladies of the British fishery" (lines 20-22), implying that debate by these lower class fish-mongers over a catch might produce even louder and more boisterous displays of eloquence.

In the four paragraphs that follow, the author employs classification to identify four distinct types of female orators—passionate paramours, hypercritical (and hypocritical) detractors, voluble gossips, and vacuous coquettes—devoting unequal attention to their individual characteristics. The least attention is given to those "who are employed in stirring up the passions" (lines 24-25)—ostensibly wives or lovers—and the author humorously speculates that in this regard Socrates' wife "perhaps made a greater proficiency than his above-mentioned teacher" (lines 26-28). Conversely, the most attention is devoted to those the author labels women "who deal in invectives, and who are commonly known by the name of the censorious" (lines 30-32). These are women who are constantly finding fault and whose "imagination and elocution," the author observes, "is wonderful" (lines 32-33). Using exclamations to affirm his amazement at their inventiveness, the author remarks

> With what a fluency of invention, and copiousness of expression, will they enlarge upon every little slip in the behavior of another! With how many different circumstances, and with what variety of phrases, will they tell over the same story! (lines 33-38).

He follows these effusive exclamations with an anecdote about an old lady who made "an unhappy marriage the subject of a month's conversation" (lines 39-40). The author describes how "She blamed the bride in one place; pitied her in another; laughed at her in a third; wondered at her in a fourth; was angry with her in a fifth; and in short, wore out a pair of coach-horses in expressing her concern for her" (lines 41-45). In these lines the woman's volatile shifts in emotion—and the manner in which they affect her commentary—are conveyed by a series of compound verbs and by a concluding metaphor that compares the fervency of her condolatory efforts to the whipping of horses by a driven coachman or, perhaps, to the scope of her discussions of the unhappy bride with others. However, afterwards the woman does a complete about-face, and the author describes how she made a visit to the newly-married pair, praised the wife for the prudent choice she had made, told her the unreasonable aspersions which some malicious people had cast upon her, and desired that they might be better acquainted…. (lines 45-52). This unflattering depiction makes the satire more vitriolic since the woman comes across as a chameleon-like hypocrite who changes her colors as soon as she runs out of things to say about the newly-wed.

The third and fourth women described are treated less expansively. The first, these "gossips" (line 54) as they are labeled, are epitomized by an allegorical being facetiously named Mrs. Fiddle-Faddle, who immerses herself in an amalgam of trivia, trifles and neighborhood goings-on. As the author reveals,

> she launches out into descriptions of christenings, runs divisions upon an head-dress, knows every dish of meat that is served up in her neighbourhood, and entertains her company a whole afternoon together with the wit of her little boy, before he is able to speak (lines 56-62).

The absurd closing observation about her complimenting her little boy depicts Mrs. Fiddle-Faddle to be so voluble as to invent her boy's witticisms before he is able to conceive them. The coquette, on the other hand, entertains a very different audience. By nature an amorous flirt, she must keep up conversation with a variety of suitors; thus,

> To give herself the larger field for discourse, she hates and loves in the same breath, talks to her lap-dog or parrot, is uneasy in all kinds of weather, and in every part of the room….and indeed seems to speak for no other purpose, but as it gives her an opportunity of stirring a limb, or varying a feature, of glancing her eyes, or playing with her fan…. (lines 64-72).

The description of her discourse runs the gamut from treacly comments to her lap-dog or parrot to vacuous observations about the weather. Her words seem connected to her actions, their sole purpose being to attract attention to herself.

In the concluding paragraph, the author feigns puzzlement over "why women should have this talent of a ready utterance in so much greater perfection than men" (lines 74-76), fancying that they are genetically disposed "to speak everything they think" (lines 79-80), to spew forth whatever is on their minds like an erupting volcano. However, the fact that women "are not altogether strangers to the arts of dissembling, and concealing their thoughts" (lines 81-83) makes him reject that notion. He ends the passage with the suggestion that he will conduct a scientific experiment in an attempt to explain this phenomenon: "In order to it, a friend of mine, who is an excellent anatomist, has promised me by the first opportunity to dissect a woman's tongue, and to examine whether there may not be in it certain juices which render it so wonderfully voluble or flippant…." (lines 85-91). This closing remark subtly implies that the only way of determining why women are so voluble is to cut out their tongues, hence rendering them voiceless.

While undoubtedly written in a tongue-in-cheek tone, the passage from *The Spectator* reinforces the disturbing notion that what most women have to say is not worth listening to and that they are better off not being heard at all. And while more satirical than misogynistic, it reflects the type of pejorative characterization that over the years women have had to fight hard to dispel and overcome.

1. The first indication of the author's satirical intent is evident in **(A) lines 8-11**.

   Though the author's initial observation in lines 6-8, that "It has been said in the praise of some men, that they could talk whole hours together upon anything," suggests that men can hold their own when it comes to trivial conversation, the author's subsequent addendum that "it must be owned to the honour of the other sex, that there are many among them who can talk whole hours together upon nothing" implies that women have the capacity to prate on about nothing of consequence. This renders their oration totally vacuous. This and the sardonic word choice of "honour" deem these lines as the first example of the author's satirical intent.

2. The author cites the "petticoat" (line 13) and the "china cup" (line 14) to exemplify which of the following?

   I.   Chores that dominate a woman's domestic environment.
   II. Trivialities that spawn elaborate orations.
   III. Forums in which women have demonstrated an eloquence that rivals that of the courts.

   (D) II and III.

   Since the author previously suggested that women can prate on about nothing, the "edging of a petticoat" (line 13) and the "breaking of a china cup" (line 14) offer examples of relatively insignificant details that respectively spawn a "long extempore dissertation" (line 12) and "all the figures of rhetoric" (lines 14-15). This offers support for II. These hyperbolic examples of women's ability to talk "whole hours together upon nothing" (lines 10-11) are what prompt the author wryly to observe "Were women admitted to plead in courts of judicature, I am persuaded they would carry the eloquence of the bar to greater heights than it is yet arrived at" (lines 16-19). This provides justification for III. The fact that it is a servant who breaks the china cup and that the comment about the edging of a petticoat seems more about the style than the making of it effectively eliminate I as a possibility.

3. The salient organizing principle of the passage is **(A) classification**.

   Classification is evident in the author's decision to discuss four different types of female orators—passionate paramours, hypercritical (and hypocritical) detractors, voluble gossips, and vacuous coquettes—and to devote a descriptive paragraph to each of them.

4. By "stirring up the passions" (line 25), the author is likely referring to this type of orator's **(D) amorous words**.

   The author suggests that this type of orator is involved in "stirring up the passions" (line 25), labeling it "a part of rhetoric in which Socrates' wife had perhaps made a greater proficiency than his above-mentioned teacher" (lines 25-28). This contrasts the formal eloquence of Aspasia, the woman who allegedly instructed Socrates in public speaking, with the "greater proficiency" (line 27) of Socrates' wife, whose spousal conversation would by nature be much more intimate.

5. The author 'compliments' all of the following traits of the "censorious" female orator (lines 29-52) EXCEPT **(D) her covetous feelings**.

The abilities of the 'censurious' female orators are immediately complimented: "The imagination and elocution of this set of rhetoricians is wonderful" (lines 32-33). This attests to the validity of choice A. Choice B is supported by the author's observation that "With what a fluency of invention and copiousness of expression, will they enlarge upon every slip in the behavior of another!" (lines 33-36). Choice C is validated by lines 36-40, "With how many different circumstances, and with what variety of phrases, will they tell over the same story! I have known an old lady make an unhappy marriage the subject of a month's conversation," while choice E is conveyed by the subsequent anecdote in which the woman shifts from condemning and pitying the bride to visiting the couple and "prais[ing] the wife for the prudent choice she had made" (lines 48-49). There is no basis for choice D in the passage.

6. In light of the context in which it appears, the phrase "wore out a pair of coach horses" (line 44) should likely be considered **(B) metaphorical**.

This phrase conjures the vision of a coachman feverishly whipping his team of horses to make his coach go faster, The intent of the comparison is to show the fervency with which the old lady "express[es] her concern" (line 45) for the unhappy bride, or perhaps to capture the 'whirling dervish' manner in which she visits other women to gossip about the marriage. Choice B represents this best.

7. The author stylistically mirrors the mercurial nature of the typical "censorious" female orator as it is depicted in lines 29-52 via which of the following? **(B) parallel action verbs**.

This is derived from lines 41-52— "She blamed the bride in one place; pitied her in another; laughed at her in a third; wondered at her in a fourth; was angry with her in a fifth; and in short, wore out a pair of coach-horses in expressing her concern for her. At length, after having quite exhausted the subject on this side, she made a visit to the new-married pair, praised the wife for the prudent choice she had made, told her the unreasonable reflections which some malicious people had cast upon her, and desired that they might be better acquainted…."—which capture the fickleness of her thoughts and actions.

8. The most preposterous aspect of Mrs. Fiddle-Faddle's characterization involves her **(E) boasts about the wit of her son**.

Mrs. Fiddle-Faddle is so voluble that the author says she "entertains her company a whole afternoon together with the wit of her little boy, before he is able to speak" (lines 60-62). The mere fact that she celebrates her son's witticisms before he is able to say a word is both absurd and highly sardonic.

9. Which of the following CANNOT be said to be characteristic of the author's style? **(D) misogynistic diction**.

   The use of the first person throughout the piece—"I am persuaded…" (line 17), "I have known an old lady…" (lines 38-39), "I have been often puzzled…" (line 73)—confirms A while observations such as "but it must be owned to the honour of the other sex, that there are many among them who can talk whole hours together upon nothing…" (lines 8-11) and "that they are necessitated to speak everything they think…." (lines 79-80) support B. The author's allegorical character, Mrs. Fiddle-Faddle, validates C while lines such as "With what a fluency of invention, and copiousness of expression, will they enlarge upon every little slip in the behavior of another! With how many different circumstances, and with what variety of phrases, will they tell over the same story!" (lines 33-38) offer support for E. Though the author pokes fun at women, the playful tone is too lighthearted to be labeled misogynistic, making D the exception.

10. The author's comments about the stereotypical coquette (lines 63-72) depict her as **(B) effusive and self-absorbed**.

    Both the diction and choice of details in lines 63-72—"To give herself the larger field for discourse, she hates and loves in the same breath, talks to her lap-dog or parrot, is uneasy in all kinds of weather, and in every part of the room….and indeed seems to speak for no other purpose, but as it gives her an opportunity of stirring a limb, or varying a feature, of glancing her eyes, or playing with her fan…."— suggest that the coquette seems to want to talk about most anything ("larger field for discourse"), no matter how trivial. Moreover, her body language reveals someone who is enormously self-conscious but in a vain manner.

11. The author's remark about the anatomist who has "promised [him] by the first opportunity to dissect a woman's tongue" (lines 87-88) reveals which of the following? **(E) the subtle but wry culmination of the author's satire**.

    The fact that the author can only solve this mystery by performing a dissection of a woman's tongue suggests that it must first be cut out of her mouth. This is the culminating point of the author's droll satire since it further implies the silencing of women's ability to "talk whole hours together upon nothing" (lines 10-11).

12. Upon completion of the passage, the author's allusion to Socrates seems intended to **(C) camouflage his satirical intent by establishing a mock-serious tone**.

    By citing Socrates, noted for the eloquence of his dialogues, and then alluding to Aspasia, the woman who instructed him in oratory, the initial paragraph initially appears to be introducing a serious discussion of women orators. However, by lines 8-11 the careful reader can determine that the piece is headed in a satirical direction; thus, the selection of choice C as the correct answer.

Précis and Explication of Passage Two: From George Howe Colt's *The Big House: A Century in the Life of an American Summer Home*

The passage from George Howe Colt's *The Big House* offers a retrospective and nostalgic look at a century-old summer home on Massachusetts' Cape Cod and the idiosyncrasies and rituals that have grown up with and around it. Opening with a variation of a somewhat trite joke, "How many Boston Brahmins does it take to screw in a light bulb? Ten: one to put in the new bulb, and nine to reminisce about how great the old one was" (lines 1-4), the author symbolically shows the disproportionate balance between future considerations and past recollections. And the subsequent Cape Cod-ian mantra, "If it *used* to be done this way, it *ought* to be done this way, and, by God, it *will* be done this way" (lines 4-6) immediately suggests the unwillingness of the summer inhabitants of the house to brook any change, with italics for additional emphasis. Though readily admitting that none of the summer inhabitants of the vacation home would tolerate its various inconveniences in their normal residences, the author establishes the Orwellian-like dictum "change is heresy" (line 12), arguing that in returning each summer to this seaside abode, he and other members of his family "regress to an innocent, Edenic state by replicating the experiences [they] had as children" (lines 10-12). Employing a tandem of subjunctive "Were we" constructions, the author imagines the consequences of changing traditions such as washing dishes by hand or replacing relics such as the "hypersensitive toilets" (line 21), concluding that doing so would be to forfeit, in the case of the former, "not only the opportunity to watch the boats sail into the harbor, but a precious daily chunk of WASP bonding (which is performed far more adhesively over a mildewed dish towel than over a beer)" (lines 15-20); and, in the case of the latter, to "[take] down the handwritten notes [his] grandmother thumbtacked in each of the seven bathrooms, whose words [they] can recite by heart now, like an affectionate family mantra: NOTHING BUT TOILET PAPER—AND NOT WADS OF THIS—TO GO IN TOILETS. CESSPOOL TROUBLE POSSIBLE, THOUGH NOT PROBABLE, IF WE WATCH" (lines 23-31). Such change, in the author's eyes, is not worth such a weighty surrender.

The author proceeds by comparing the Big House to two, more noteworthy, historical sites: Plimoth Plantation and Colonial Williamsburg. Like the revered colonial artifacts of each of these locations, everything in the Big House "is to be preserved intact, uncontaminated either by throwing anything out or by willingly introducing anything new" (lines 33-36). As the author observes, "Any change is likely the result of serendipity: a book left on a bedside table, a shell on a mantelpiece, a toy car on the kitchen floor" (lines 36-39); in short, by people forgetting items or leaving them accidentally behind. His anecdote about of the copy of Hardy's *Tess of the D'Urbervilles* assuming the role of a lost caster illustrates this adventitious compilation of bric-a-brac. As the author humorously observes about a forsaken guitar pick, "I know that if the house were not being sold, that guitar pick would remain there for decades, as immovable as a barnacle" (lines 50-53), this concluding simile ("as a barnacle") an appropriately obdurate testament to the staying power of these items, and the comparison to "a holy relic" (line 55) a testament to their veneration.

The two long paragraphs that follow explore the rooms of the Big House: more specifically, their anachronistic contents. Comparing an exploration of the rooms to an archaeological dig (lines 57-58), the author catalogs the surviving stockpile of long-expired aspirin vials, antiquated cans of Drano, weed killer and lighter fluid, stacks of sheet music, and photographs of long-dead relatives. The diction he employs—words such as "expired" (line 60), "rusty" (line 63), "predate" (line 66), "turn-of-the-century" (line 78), "yellowed and crinkly" (line 87) and "fading" (line 89)—connotes age, decay, and disuse. Even the globe in the Playroom features pre-Imperialistic countries long since fragmented into tribal sovreignties while the newspaper headline from the *Times* chronicles an event now over forty years past. So daunting are these reminders of the past that the author reveals "Prospective buyers of the Big House are often stunned into silence by its time-warp atmosphere" (lines 93-95). The subsequent mention of one visitor's (an architect's) comparison of the house to the "main hall on Ellis Island after it had been sealed for three decades…." (lines 97-99) suggests that the interior of the Big House has been frozen in time like a scene from Keats' Grecian urn, preserved in its idiosyncratic elegance as a reliquary of another time. Overall, Colt's memoir hints at the universal difficulty people experience in parting with the past, and how strong a claim sentiment may have on the things belonging to it.

13. In the opening paragraph the author reinforces the central theme of the passage—that "change is heresy" (line 12)—by all of the following EXCEPT **(D) citing the novelty of their summer behaviors**.

The opening rhetorical question, "How many Boston Brahmins does it take to screw in a light bulb? Ten: one to put in the new bulb, and nine to reminisce about how great the old one was (lines 1-4), confirms the presence of A while the italicization of "used" (line 4), "ought" (line 5) and "will" (line 6) validates B. The allusion to "washing the dishes by hand" (lines 14-15) and both observing the boats come into the harbor and bonding with WASP brethren (lines 16-20) support the presence of C while lines 12-14, "We bristle when guests expect, well, something a little more *deluxe*," support E. Choice D may be ruled out by lines 8-12, "we change in the winter, but during the summer—a season in which we regress to an innocent, Edenic state by replicating the experiences we had as children—change is heresy."

14. The author's speculations about the consequences of no longer washing dishes by hand or of replacing the antiquated toilets are bolstered MOST by his use of **(A) the subjunctive mode and the loss it prefaces**.

The subjunctive constructions, "Were we to stop…" (line 14) and "Were we to replace…" (line 20), both preface significant losses: the opportunity of watching the boats enter the harbor, the opportunity for WASP bonding, and the loss of the quaint idiosyncratic notes thumbtacked in each of the seven bathrooms by the family's grandmother. Each of these contributes to the special experience of the summer ritual shared by those returning to the Big House.

15. The simile in lines 32-33, "Like Plimoth Plantation or Colonial Williamsburg," implies that the Big House **(C) must be dutifully safeguarded**.

The selection of choice C as the best answer is determined by the remainder of the sentence: "…the Big House is to be preserved intact, uncontaminated either by throwing anything out or by willingly introducing anything new" (lines 33-36). Choice A, while seemingly meritable, is ruled out by the word "national," which would infer that the home has an importance beyond the personal.

16. The BEST equivalent for the word "serendipity" (line 37), as it is used in the passage, would be **(E) accident**.

"Serendipity" is defined as "an aptitude for making discoveries by accident" or as "good fortune." In terms of the passage, the term is applied to "a book left on a bedside table, a shell on a mantelpiece, a toy car on the kitchen floor" (lines 37-39). These appear to be objects left inadvertently behind, objects which have then been assimilated into the other bric-a-brac of the Big House.

17. The anecdotes of the iron bedstead and the guitar pick (lines 40-55) do which of the following?

    I. Exemplify the "serendipity" to which the author refers in line 37.
    II. Illustrate how objects that are not immediately removed are quietly "granted tenure" (line 40).
    III. Establish the "pack rat" mentality of the New England family.

(C) I and II.

Both the copy of Hardy's *Tess of the D'Urbervilles*, used to level the unbalanced bedstead, and the guitar pick placed on the front hall shelf represent items inadvertently left behind that have quietly taken their place among the other items in the house, This confirms the rectitude of I and II. Choice III is eliminated by the fact that, unlike the multiple cans of Drano and lighter fluid and the tubes of sun-screen, there is only a single guitar-pick and a single copy of *Tess*. And while the sunscreen and lighter fluid may evince a "pack rat" mentality, they further illustrate the age and nostalgia of the edifice.

18. The author meticulously details the contents of the bathroom cabinets, front hall closet, and utility room in order to **(E) demonstrate the extent of his emotional ties to the Big House**.

Choice E is primarily determined by the closing lines of paragraph three—"Why have we saved these artifacts? I doubt they will ever be used. And yet when Anne suggests that we throw them out, I cannot bring myself to do it. Not on my watch" (lines 70-74)—which show the reluctance of the author to part with anything related to his summer residence. And though he mentions that the house is to be sold, he still does not want to clean out these items.

19. The allusion to the cans of weed killer and the five half-empty tubes of suntan oil (lines 65-70) have MOST in common with which of the following? **(A) the summertime "regress[ion]" mentioned in lines 9-12**.

Lines 9-12 suggest that during the summer the members of the author's family "regress to an innocent, Edenic state by replicating the experiences [they] had as children…". The allusion to Eden suggests a time of innocence. The relation of this to the weed-killer and sun-screen is apparent in the author's observation that the former "clearly predate Rachel Carson's *Silent Spring*" (lines 66-67), the ground-breaking exposé on the dangers to humans and the environment posed by pesticides and other carcinogens, and that the latter are "from the innocent era, before people worried about skin cancer, when it was not called sunblock but suntan oil" (lines 68-70).

20. Which of the following BEST captures the difference between the objects mentioned in paragraph three (lines 56-74) and those mentioned in paragraph four (lines 75-92)? **(B) The former are primarily products, the latter mostly memorabilia**.

The items in paragraph three—aspirin, life jackets, Drano, weed killer, and sun screen—all have utilitarian uses, either directly for humans or as domestic or gardening applications. On the contrary, the sheet music on the piano comprises all his grandmother's favorite songs and the photograph albums contain a gallery of "long-dead relatives" (lines 84-85); hence, the selection of B as the best answer.

21. Which of the following contributes LEAST towards establishing the "time-warp atmosphere" (lines 94-95) of the Big House in the final three paragraphs? **(B) the personification of the life jackets (lines 61-62)**.

Likening the house to an "archaeological dig" (lines 56-58) associates it with antiquity much as do the age-related participles and adjectives in choice C. The sheet music is comprised of Victorian era operettas, "turn-of-the-century ballads" (line 78) and World War I ditties while the globe features countries that are no longer extant and the newspaper speaks of a moon landing from 1969. Similarly, the allusion to the great hall of Ellis Island recalls the immigration era. Only choice B does not contribute to this ambience.

22. The architect's observation (lines 95-99) is likely made in response to which aspect of the house? **(D) its archival lore**.

The architect's allusion to the re-opening of the great hall at Ellis Island after thirty years implies pretty much the same of the Big House, whose items—pantry contents, music, photos, even the printed notes on the toilets—all hearken back to a bygone time.

23. Which BEST establishes the connection between phrases such as "as immovable as a barnacle" (lines 52-53) and "Not on my watch" (line 74)? **(C) They both exemplify diction that matches the seaside setting**.

This is pretty much determined by the simile "as a barnacle," which connects the guitar pick left on a shelf to marine crustaceans that remain attached to submerged surfaces, and by the word "watch," which alludes to the period of time a shipboard crew is assigned to duty. Although one might associate the adjective "immovable" and the phrase "Not on my watch" with the speaker's reluctance to part with the house, the first refers to the length of time the forgotten guitar pick will remain, and the second to the author's unwillingness to divest himself of something *in* the house, not the house itself.

24. The tone of the passage is BEST labeled **(D) nostalgic**.

Though the first temptation is to choose choice A, "resigned," the Big House has yet to be sold and its atmosphere and artifacts are still in the author's possession. Choice D is preferable because the author is reflecting upon what *will* be lost should he go forth with the sale of the property.

Précis and Explication of Passage Three: From Ralph Waldo Emerson's "The American Scholar"

The selection from Emerson's "The American Scholar" joins the passage midstream, after Emerson has already discussed the nature of the scholar, his books, and his actions. This section of the essay segues into a discussion of the scholar's duties. Emerson describes these as "such as become Man Thinking" (line 4), as if they are the defining characteristics of the intellectual, adding that they may "all be comprised in self-trust" (line 5). To those who have read Emerson's "Self-Reliance," this assertion should be quite familiar since the advocacy of self-reliance and self-trust permeates the essay. As the philosopher passionately avers,

> What I must do is all that concerns me, not what the people think. This rule, equally arduous in actual and in intellectual life, may serve for the whole distinction between greatness and meanness. It is the harder, because you will always find those who think they know what is your duty better than you know it. It is easy in the world to live after the world's opinion; it is easy in solitude to live after our own; but the great man is he who in the midst of the crowd keeps with perfect sweetness the independence of solitude.

In this essay, Emerson first defines the "office of the scholar" (line 6) as being "to cheer, to raise, and to guide men by showing them facts amid appearances" (lines 6-8). According to this definition, the scholar's role is to brighten, edify and direct his fellowman by stripping the veneer off life and exposing its realities. Saying that "He plies the slow, unhonored, and unpaid task of observation" (lines 8-9), Emerson compares this watchman-like figure to Flamsteed and Herschel, two accomplished astronomers who made significant discoveries in the heavens. However, unlike these watchers of the skies, the scholar is in his "private observatory, cataloguing obscure and nebulous stars of the human mind, which as yet no man has thought of as such" (lines 13-16). This meticulous observation of records and facts yields no immediate celebrity or public acclaim, no podium from which he may proclaim the brilliance of his discoveries; rather, "Long must he stammer in his speech; often forego the living for the dead. Worse yet, he must accept—how often!—poverty and solitude" (lines 23-26). According to the author, he who embraces such solitary scholarship forfeits the comfortable conformities of style, learning and belief and "takes the cross of making his own" (lines 28-29), an allusion to the Gospel of Luke, in which the evangelist cites Jesus as saying "If anyone wishes to come after Me, let him deny himself, and take up his cross and follow Me." In this instance the cross becomes a symbol of the hardship brought on by independent thinking, by taking the less traveled road in lieu of the well-worn, predictable thoroughfare.

This forsaking of the conservative and the conformist for the self-reliant and the independent is understandably accompanied by other privations and adversities, "the self-accusation, the faint heart, the frequent uncertainty and loss of time, which are the nettles and tangling vines in the way of the self-relying and self-directed; and the state of virtual hostility in which he seems to stand to society, and especially to educated society" (lines 29-35), making the author rhetorically ask "For all this loss and scorn, what offset?" (lines 35-36). The simple, declarative answer—"He is to find consolation in exercising the highest functions of human nature" (lines 36-38)—is as understated in language as it is in practicality. For all this scorn and isolation, the reward at first glance seems incommensurate and trivial, yet in Emerson's eyes it is singular and sublime. As he ardently declaims to his audience, the scholar breathes and lives on public and illustrious thoughts. He is the world's eye. He is the world's heart. He is to resist the vulgar prosperity that retrogrades ever to barbarism, by preserving and communicating heroic sentiments, noble biographies, melodious verse, and the conclusions of history. Whatsoever oracles the human heart, in all emergencies, in all solemn hours has uttered as its commentary on the world of actions,—these he shall receive and impart. And whatsoever new verdict Reason from her inviolable seat pronounces on the passing men and events of today,—this he shall hear and promulgate (lines 40-53).

The diction here matches the ardor of the sentiment. The scholar's thoughts are "illustrious" (line 40), what he preserves "heroic" (line 44) and "noble" (line 45). Moreover, "He is the world's eye. He is the world's heart" (lines 41-42), synecdoches which endow him with a vision and a passion that are universal in scope. And the wisdom which he imparts takes on an oracular status since, as literally the "voice of Reason," he "shall hear and promulgate" (line 53) with Mosaic certainty.

The scholar's role being so unequivocally defined, Emerson again avers that "it becomes him to feel all confidence in himself, and to defer never to the popular cry" (lines 54-56). Hearkening back to the "self-trust" that he first mentioned in line 5, Emerson again restates the necessary conviction of the scholar that "He and he only knows the world…" (lines 56-57), imperatively urging him to "not quit his belief that a popgun is a popgun, though the ancient and honorable of the earth affirm it to be the crack of doom" (lines 57-60). This absurdly antithetical pairing of toy gun and apocalyptic thunderclap underscores the defiant self-reliance that Emerson so fervently believes is essential to the scholar. The language that follows—"In silence, in steadiness, in severe abstraction, let him hold himself; add observation to observation, patient of neglect, patient of reproach; and bide his own time;—happy enough, if he can satisfy himself alone, that this day he has seen something truly…." (lines 60-66)—mirrors the language of a pledge or oath and suggests the solemnity with which Emerson views the commitment of the scholar. The rich rhythmic syntax of the trinity of prepositional phrases that introduces this sentiment; the admirable parallelism and anaphora of "patient of neglect, patient of reproach" and the clever relocation of the adverb "truly" from its normal position in front of "seen" to its climactic and dramatic affirmation at sentence's end capture Emerson at his *ex cathedra* best, come down from the mountain not only having witnessed a vision but with the tablets to prove it.

The language of the concluding paragraph rivals that of its predecessor, with Emerson declaiming "Free should the scholar be,—free and brave. Free even to the definition of freedom, 'without any hindrance that does not arise out of his own constitution.' Brave; for fear is a thing that a scholar by his very function puts behind him" (lines 68-73). Emerson uses inversion and the loose sentence to front-load his adjectives, emphasizing the two main attributes he believes every scholar must possess. The concluding similes of the ostrich (lines 80-81) and the whistling boy (lines 82-83), along with the image of the scientist feigning to be preoccupied with a microscope, all connote an avoidance of conflict, or a willful ignorance of confrontation. To Emerson, these are the antitheses of the bravery that a scholar must embrace. As Emerson warns, "It is a shame to him if his tranquility, amid dangerous times, arise from the presumption that, like children and women, his is a protected class; or if he seek a temporary peace by the diversion of his thoughts from politics or vexed questions…" (lines 74-79). A scholar must be buoyed by the strength of his convictions "for fear is a thing that the scholar by his very function puts behind him" (lines 72-73).

25. The persuasiveness of the author's rhetoric is abetted MOST by his **(E) certain and didactic tone**.

    Though the four other choices certainly contribute on lesser levels to the success of the essay, it is the author's tone that is the most salient feature of the essay. Declarations such as "The office of the scholar is to cheer, to raise and to guide men by showing them facts and appearances" (lines 5-8), "He is the world's eye. He is the world's heart" (lines 41-42), and "this he shall hear and promulgate" (line 53) establish the duties of the scholar in unequivocal terms while the *ex cathedra* manner in which he delivers them lends the piece the tone of certainty that anyone familiar with Emerson quickly recognizes as singularly his.

26. Among the deprivations that the author claims a scholar must endure are all of the following EXCEPT **(D) restricted liberties**.

    The author points out that in electing to be a scholar, an individual must "accept—how often!—poverty and solitude" (lines 25-26), confirming the presence of A and C. He indicates that the scholar must accept "the state of virtual hostility in which he seems to stand to society…" (lines 33-35) and also avers that the scholar "must relinquish display and immediate fame" (lines 18-19). This information validates choices B and E. There is nothing in the passage to support choice D.

27. Lines 5-8, "The office of the scholar is to cheer, to raise, and to guide men by showing them facts amid appearances," is BEST labeled a(n) **(B) assertion**.

    An "assertion" is an affirmation, a claim, something declared or stated positively. Emerson's taut definition of the office, or primary duty, of the scholar qualifies as such. The other four choices—conjecture (an educated guess), understatement (the deliberate downplaying of something), fallacy (an untruth) and paradox (an apparent contradiction)—are not reflected by this sentence's content.

28. The author likely compares the scholar to an astronomer to highlight the **(B) laborious and meticulous observation his work demands**.

    The author points out that the scholar "plies the slow, unhonored, and unpaid task of observation" (lines 8-9). He contrasts this with the work of two astronomers, Flamsteed and Herschel, whom he says "catalogue the stars with the praise of all men…" (line 11). Unlike these celebrated astronomers, however, the scholar is "in his private observatory, cataloguing obscure and nebulous stars of the human mind…" (lines 13-15). That the work is laborious and meticulous is supported by lines 16-18 which depict him "watching days and months, sometimes, for a few facts; correcting still his old records…". Choice B captures this best.

29. The author describes this "office" in lines 13-19 by using which type of phrase? **(B) participial**.

    Participial phrases function as adjectives. Lines 14-15, "cataloguing obscure and nebulous stars of the human mind," lines 16-17, "watching days and months, sometimes, for a few facts…", and lines 17-18, "correcting still his old records," all describe "he" (line 13), the scholar; thus, the selection of choice B.

30. Which of the following is NOT an object of the verb "takes" (line 28)? **(D) "nettles" (line 32)**.

The author avers in lines 26-35 that "For the ease and pleasure of treading the old road, accepting the fashions, the education, the religion of society, he takes the cross of making his own, and, of course, the self-accusation, the faint heart, the frequent uncertainty and loss of time, which are the nettles and tangling vines in the way of the self-relying and self-directed; and the state of virtual hostility in which he seems to stand to society, and especially to educated society." The "cross" that is alluded to in line 29 and that serves as the direct object of the verb "takes" has several additional objects that are joined to it by the conjunction "and." These include "self-accusation," "faint heart," "frequent uncertainty," "loss of time," and "the state of virtual hostility." The word "nettles" in line 32 is part of a metaphor that functions as the predicate nominative of the relative clause starting with "which."

31. Of the following, which BEST captures the meaning of "the nettles and tangling vines" mentioned in lines 31-32? **(A) personal doubts that the scholar must overcome**.

The phrase "nettles and hanging vines" metaphorically conveys the "the self-accusation, the faint heart, the frequent uncertainty and loss of time" that are cataloged right before it. This is best reflected by choice A.

32. The author effects the major transition in the passage by means of a(n) **(C) rhetorical question**.

Lines 35-36 contain the rhetorical query, "For all this loss and scorn, what offset?," a question that effectively divides the argument into a delineation of all the obstacles and privations the scholar must overcome and/or endure, and the "consolation" (line 37) that he enjoys in carrying out this noble function.

33. The repeated declamations of "He is" in lines 36-46 primarily serve to **(D) celebrate the singular importance of the scholar's contribution to humanity**.

The series of sentences prefaced by "He is" are ushered in by the rhetorical question, "For all this loss and scorn, what offset?" (lines 35-36). Most of the preceding paragraph's content has examined the financial and social deprivations that a scholar must suffer, and these sentences offer an antithesis, a list of the contributions the scholar will make to humanity and a suggestion of the intellectual satisfaction that may accompany these contributions. The author perceives the scholar's duty as "exercising the highest functions of nature" (lines 37-38) and appoints him the viceroy of Reason and the medium of Reason's communication. Choice D captures this most accurately.

34. The subsequent "consolation" that the scholar enjoys (lines 36-53) involves all of the following EXCEPT **(B) receiving public patronage to support his labors**.

The scholar, in pursuing his craft, is said to be "exercising the highest functions of human nature" (lines 37-38). He is seen to be "preserving and communicating heroic sentiments, noble biographies, melodious verse, and the conclusions of history" (lines 44-46). He is said to be "the world's eye…[and] the world's heart" (lines 41-42), someone who "Whatsoever oracles the human heart, in all emergencies, in all solemn hours has uttered as its commentary on the world of actions…he shall receive and impart" (lines 47-50). And as part of his solemn duties "…whatsoever new verdict Reason from her inviolable seat pronounces on the passing men and events of today,—this he shall hear and promulgate" (lines 50-53). This validates choices A, C, D and E. Choice B is eliminated by the author's observation in lines 25-26 that he "must accept—how often!—poverty and solitude."

35. Lines 57-60—"Let him not quit his belief that a popgun is a popgun, though the ancient and honorable of the earth affirm it to be the crack of doom"—do which of the following?

   I. Bolster the author's stalwart belief in "self-trust" (line 5, lines 67-68).
   II. Confirm "the state of virtual hostility" (lines 33-34) that the true scholar encounters.
   III. Exemplify the "vulgar prosperity that retrogrades ever to barbarism…" (lines 42-43).

(C) I and II.

The author states in line 5 that the duties of the scholar "may all be comprised in self-trust," a sentiment he reiterates in lines 67-68, "In self-trust all the virtues are comprehended." His exhortation to the scholar to retain his belief "that a popgun is a popgun" in the face of a more general outcry that it is the sound of apocalyptic thunder exemplifies this well, validating I. Moreover, the reference in the lines to "the ancient and the honorable" who contradict his belief provides support for II. The phrase "vulgar prosperity" in lines 42-43, on the other hand, seems more of a reference to philistinism, to individuals who are guided by materialism and who scoff at and scorn intellectual endeavors. This is the "barbarism" to which he alludes. Thus, III has no relation to the lines cited in the question.

36. The relation of the similes in lines 76-77 and lines 80-81 to the freedom and bravery that are said to be most necessary to the scholar (lines 68-73) is BEST expressed by which of the following?
(C) They advise against a particular misconception and course of action.

The similes in the cited lines caution the scholar against skirting "politics or vexed questions" (line 79) by "hiding his head like an ostrich in the flowering bushes" (lines 80-81) or by pretending not to notice them "as a boy whistles to keep his courage up…." (lines 82-83). The author strongly states that it would be "a shame to him if his tranquility, amid dangerous times, arise from the presumption that, like children and women, his is a protected class…" (lines 74-77). Choice C articulates this best.

Précis and Explication of Passage Four: From Edward Thomas' *Broken Memories*

Any individual who can recall scenes of his childhood, places where youthful imagination ran rampant and yards and cellars and alleyways became imaginary kingdoms, worlds in which time hung suspended and play was elevated to the levels of adventure and quest, can easily relate to the selection from Edward Thomas' *Broken Memories*. Set in two-acres of ploughland, the "Big Wood," as he and his sibling called it, assumes the magical powers and mysteries of Robin Hood's Sherwood or Shakespeare's Arden. So powerful is this enchanted setting of childhood that the author suggests that "when past years bulk into the likeness of a forest, through which the memory takes its pleasure at eventide…it is really this wood that we see, under a halcyon sky" (lines 4-8).

Truly, childhood is a timeless time—when one is experiencing it—and the author notes how he and his sibling wandered through the Big Wood "with weeping like Imogen's, and with laughter like Yorick's laughter…" (lines 3-4). These allusions to Shakespearean characters serve almost as bookends for the range of human emotion: from seemingly inconsolable sorrow to equally inconceivable bliss. Enhanced in size by childhood imagination, the Big Wood becomes an "enormous" (line 10) realm in which they "often lost one another; it had such diversity; it made so genuine a solitude" (lines 11-12). The trees, though undoubtedly tall, grow to Brobdingnagian proportions—"The straight oaks rising branchless for many feet expanded and then united boughs in a firmament of leaves" (lines 13-15)—and the Big Wood, though relatively proximate to the city, seems miles and eons away from civilization. This perception is, however, unreal, and the author notes that though the Big Wood "seemed far enough from London for feelings of security" (lines 15-16), the expansion of the city eventually threatened to encroach upon their personal Eden: "for the houses are fearfully close—a recollection of them lingers in the heart of the wood; and perhaps they will devour it also…." (lines 17-20). The rhetorical question that follows—"Who shall measure the sorrow of him that hath set his heart upon that which the world hath power to destroy, and hath destroyed?" (lines 20-23)—conveys the emotional hurt done by the encroaching development, development that threatened to swallow up their childhood realm forever. As the author sadly (and ironically) notes, "Even to-day the circuit of a cemetery is cutting into the field where we gathered buttercups before the dignity of knickerbockers…" (lines 23-26)—a universal symbol of death supplanting the Edenic garden in which they sported naked. The subsequent simple declaration, "And here was a solitude" (lines 26-27), triggers the subliminal but sorrowful thought, "When comes such another?" As the author himself ruefully admits, "We cannot summon up any thought or reverie which had not in this wood its nativity" (lines 27-28). The subsequent allusion to Cervantes' *Don Quixote* seems to suggest a mixture of romantic (dare I say, quixotic) nostalgia: a longing for the seriousness and folly of his youth, yet a consciousness that those times and that place can never be recovered.

The concluding paragraph of the selection becomes less reflective and more descriptive and imagistic. The author recalls how "The dark earth itself was pleasant to handle—earth one might wish to be buried in—and had the healthy and special quality of wild earth: upon it you could rest deliciously" (lines 35-38), an extremely tactile image which at once connotes the soft accommodation of the ground in life and its welcoming embrace of the human body after it. (He mildly mocks, in the parenthetical comment that follows, the less attractive, "artificial" (line 39), soil of the London common.) Out of this rich loam "rose up trees that preserved their wild attitudes" (lines 40-41), and even trees felled by storm or the toll of years "lay where [they] dropped, or hung balanced in the boughs of others" (lines 42-44). This description of the forest accents the wild, the natural, the symbiotic, and the trees seem to have the personified attributes of Tolkien's Ents, gracefully bridging the pathways and covering them with their pleasant shade. This "incongruous juxtaposition of birch and oak and elm" (lines 49-50) was so magical that to the author it seemed "a fragment of the primeval forest left by a possible good fortune at the city verge" (lines 50-52). However, as he quickly confesses, "…it was more than this" (line 52), and the diction he employs to describe it in the closing sentence—words and phrases such as "lofty roof" (lines 52-53), "foliaged clerestory" (line 54) and "shapely boles in cluster and colonnade" (lines 54-55)—creates an impression of an architectural wonder rising majestically out of nature itself. As the author concludes, with "the glimpses of bright white sky that came and went among the leaves, the forest had a real likeness to a temple…. " (lines 55-58). What the diction in the final sentence ultimately reveals is that for the author and his sibling the Big Wood has become more than just a fond memory of a childhood playground; rather, it has assumed a degree of sacredness and inviolability and become, mentally if not physically, a Wordsworthian retreat from the fevers of their more contemporary existence.

37. All of the following are true about the declarative sentence, "The Big Wood we called it," that opens the passage EXCEPT: **(C) Its vagueness suggests the author's present inability to determine the name of the exact locale**.

The inverted syntax of the opening sentence places the "Big Wood" at the forefront of the sentence, making it assume an immediate prominence (A). The use of the plural pronoun "we" indicates that the experience in the wood was a shared one (B). The simplicity of the sentence—its simple subject-verb-object-appositive construction—seems apropos to the innocent time that the speaker experienced in the Big Wood (D). And the statement in lines 9-10 that "It covered two acres in the midst of ploughland" reveals that it was in actuality not as big as the speaker's childhood memory remembers it (E). On the contrary, the speaker's indication that it was just outside London gives the Big Wood a minimum level of specificity. Moreover, the speaker never indicates any intention of specifying the locale by name, making C the exception.

38. The author's statement, "It seemed far enough from London for feelings of security" (lines 15-16), is likely prompted by his fear of **(B) real-estate development**.

The author's observation, "But even of that our thoughts have changed; for the houses are fearfully close—a recollection of them lingers in the heart of the wood; and perhaps they will devour it also…" (lines 16-20), implies that his original residence was on the outskirts of the city, remote enough to make it feel like country. His present observation about the proximity of the houses and the implication that their encroachment may "devour it also" suggests that urbanity threatens the tranquility of the rural.

39. The rhetorical question, "Who shall measure the sorrow of him that hath set his heart upon that which the world hath power to destroy, and hath destroyed?" (lines 20-23), suggests which of the following?

   I. That the sorrow the author feels is beyond comprehension.
  II. That humans have already displayed a capacity for destruction.
 III. That the author resents being judged by others.

(C) I and II.

The query "Who shall measure" suggests that this task is beyond measurement, that there is no individual capable of doing so. This supports I. The concluding phrase "hath destroyed" alludes to the fact that human beings have already been the agent of ruin. This validates II. Choice III is too broad to be considered seriously.

40. In the second paragraph the author contrasts which of the following? **(C) the seclusion of nature and the intrusion of man**.

Line 12, "it made so genuine a solitude," and lines 26-27, "And here was a solitude," convey the author's conviction that the Big Wood allowed them to play in virtual isolation. This is contrasted with the encroachment of man as manifested by the crowding of houses and his fear that "perhaps they will devour it also" (line 20). He also notes that a cemetery "is cutting into the field where we gathered buttercups before the dignity of knickerbockers…" (lines 24-25). This Edenesque image of naked children playing in a field is antithetical to these images of urban expansion.

41. The allusion to Don Quixote in lines 32-34 implies that the speaker perceives himself a(n) **(D) chivalrous sentinel**.

The selection of D as the best answer is rooted in Don Quixote's vigilance in staying up all night to guard his armor. This implies the author's desire to protect the Big Wood from the incursion of progress. In light of the delusional nature of Cervantes' protagonist, it may also imply the futility of the author's desire to protect the Big Wood.

42. Lines 40-41, "Out of this rose up trees that preserved their wild attitudes," do which of the following?

   I. Use inversion to demonstrate the trees' majestic ascent.
  II. Personify, somewhat humorously, the unchecked growth of bramble and feeler.
 III. Foreshadow the inherent spirituality of the "foliaged clerestory" (line 54).

(C) I and II.

The placement of the verb "rose up" in front of the subject "trees" accents their ascent, confirming I, while the attributing of "wild attitudes"—essentially human qualities—to the trees validates II. Though the imagery of these lines may well relate to that of the "foliaged clerestory," it does nothing to anticipate the spirituality conveyed by the final lines. This leaves C as the best answer.

43. The phrase "ordered with an incongruous juxtaposition of birch and oak and elm" (lines 48-50) is BEST labeled a(n) **(E) paradox**.

The union of the word "ordered" with the phrase "incongruous juxtaposition" merges two antithetical ideas and, as such, appears to be an "apparent contradiction," the very definition of a paradox.

44. The culminating images in lines 52-58 suggest that the author considers the "Big Wood" to be **(E) hallowed**.

The selection of choice E as the correct answer derives primarily from the architectural diction that appears in the final sentence. The forest is said to have a "lofty roof" (lines 52-53) that is supported by "shapely boles in cluster and colonnade" (lines 54-55). Light is seen filtering through the "foliaged clerestory" (line 54), the latter an architectural term for the window-adorned upper part of a church. This and the speaker's closing observation that "the forest had a real likeness to a temple…" (lines 57-58) suggest that for the author the Big Wood is sacred ground.

45. Which of the following most directly alludes to the Edenic bliss that the speaker and his sibling enjoyed in the Big Wood in their youth? **(C) "…the field where we gathered buttercups before the dignity of knickerbockers…" (lines 24-26)**.

The depiction of children gathering flowers in a field "before the dignity of knickerbockers" implies they are at play in a state of innocent bliss. Moreover, the suggestion that it is "before the dignity of knickerbockers" perhaps suggests they are unclothed like Adam and Eve in the Garden.

Précis and Explication of Passage Five: From H. L. Mencken's *The American Mercury*

H. L. Mencken's commentary on editorial writers who eulogized Calvin Coolidge upon the death of this American President examines the difficulties these writers faced in trying to romanticize the life of an otherwise ordinary man. The passage chronicles their frustrated attempts at elevating his status or mythologizing him in the 'common man' type of manner that was afforded Abraham Lincoln.

Mencken's observation that these writers "made heavy weather of [Coolidge's eulogies]" (line 3) figuratively suggests that they labored to come up with something to say about him. Noting how "Ordinarily, an American public man dies by inches, and there is thus plenty of time to think up beautiful nonsense about him" (lines 4-6), Mencken implies that Coolidge's sudden death caught these writers by surprise and ill-prepared to compose their "mortuary tributes" (line 2). As the author observes, "…Dr. Coolidge slipped out of life almost as quietly and unexpectedly as he had originally slipped into public notice, and in consequence the brethren were caught napping and had to do their public embalming under desperate pressure" (lines 10-16). Mencken engages in a minor digression, addressing the "legend" that "pressure inflames and inspires [the] true journalist" (line 17), suggesting to the contrary that the literary man actually "functions best when he is at leisure, and can turn from his tablets now and then to run down a quotation, to eat a plate of ham and eggs, or to look out of the window" (lines 20-23), perhaps implying that the pressure placed on journalists by Coolidge's untimely demise contributed to their less than inspired eulogizing of the late President.

Calling the memorialization of Coolidge a "general burden" (line 24), Mencken notes how most writers tried to paint him as "a typical American…the most typical since Lincoln" (lines 26-27). In an understated British sort of way, Mencken euphemistically notes that he was "quite unable to associate [him]self with that thesis" (lines 28-29). In the next dozen lines, he contrasts Coolidge's characteristics with those of "the Americano," noting that the late President was the antithesis of this conception:

> The Americano is an expansive fellow, a back-slapper, full of amiability; Coolidge was reserved and even muriatic. The Americano has a stupendous capacity for believing in what is palpably not true; Coolidge was, in his fundamental metaphysics, an agnostic. The Americano dreams vast dreams, and is hag-ridden by a demon; Coolidge was not mount but rider, and his steed was a mechanical horse. The Americano, in his normal incarnation, challenges fate at every step and his whole life is a struggle; Coolidge took things as they came (lines 31-44).

Whereas the average American was outgoing, Coolidge was reticent; whereas he was credulous, Coolidge was skeptical; whereas he was a dreamer, Coolidge was practical; and whereas he was defiant and combative, Coolidge was stoical and accepting. In fact, so intent was the press upon posthumously romanticizing Coolidge that "Some of the more romantic of the funeral bards tried to convert the farmhouse at Plymouth into a log-cabin…" (lines 45-47), an allusion to the almost mythical rustic roots of Abraham Lincoln. This comparison is quickly debunked by Mencken who notes that Coolidge's early days were "anything but pinched" (line 50). Born into a wealthy family, given a privileged education, and stepping into a prosperous law firm on the day of his admission to the bar, Coolidge was a far cry from his Illinois counterpart with the sole exception being that both were lawyers. His near-immediate entrance into politics was succeeded by continual ascendance, a thirty-year run of winning elections culminating with his appointment to the highest office of the land. His decision not to seek reelection was one of his own volition, and he departed from office even wealthier than he came into it.

Mencken's summative comments about Coolidge—"….No other President every slipped into the White House so easily, and none other ever had a softer time of it while there" (lines 67-69)— are more matter-of-fact than they are critical. Answering his own rhetorical question, "When, at Rapid City, S.D., on August 2, 1927, he loosed the occult words, 'I do not choose to run in 1928,' was it prescience or only luck?" (lines 69-72), with a stated belief in the latter, Mencken paints Coolidge as a man blithely unaware of approaching problems, ignorant of both "black clouds" (line 76) on the horizon or the "volcano boiling under him" (lines 78-79): namely, the Stock Market crash of 1929 and the Great Depression that followed it. And because he voluntarily abdicated the office, he remarkably "was not singed" (lines 79-80).

46. The passage is characterized by all of the following contrasts EXCEPT **(D) Coolidge's entry into political life and Coolidge's departure from it**.

Lines 31-44 make four contrasting points about Coolidge and the typical American (A). The comparison to Lincoln is first mentioned in line 27 and expanded upon in lines 45-49 with the allusion to the log-cabin (B). Mencken documents the efforts of the press to concoct "mortuary tributes" (line 2) and "political embalming" (line 15), but notes that Coolidge's quiet and unexpected death, his reserved personality, and his privileged and decidedly unromantic roots made him difficult to commemorate (C). In addition, Mencken observes in lines 5-6 that Coolidge"s sudden death was antithetical to the deaths of most public servants who normally "[die] by inches, and there is thus plenty of time to think up beautiful nonsense about [them] (E). Choice D is determined to be the exception by lines 10-13, which state "But Dr. Coolidge slipped out of life almost as quietly and unexpectedly as he had originally slipped into public notice…".

47. The author likely uses the phrase "the job of concocting mortuary tributes" (lines 1-2) to imply that **(A) Coolidge did nothing particularly memorable in his term as President**.

The key words here are "job," which suggests this was difficult to do, and "concocting," which implies that the press has to fabricate positive things to say about President Coolidge. As Mencken observes, "More often than not, indeed, [a public figure] threatens to die three or four times before he actually does so, and each threat gives the elegists a chance to mellow and adorn their effusions" (lines 7-10), implying that writers usually have more time to fabricate a complimentary eulogy. However, "…Dr. Coolidge slipped out of life almost as quietly and unexpectedly as he had originally slipped into public notice, and in consequence the brethren were caught napping and had to do their political embalming under desperate pressure" (lines 10-16). This suggests their efforts were compromised both by the haste with which they were forced to write them and by the less than romantic background and reticent personality of the late President. This is the rationale behind the selection of A.

48. The author suggests all of the following about Coolidge EXCEPT **(E) that he was self-promoting and avaricious**.

Choice A is supported by the author's observation that "Coolidge was reserved and even muriatic" (lines 33-34), choice B by his comment that "Coolidge took things as they came" (lines 43-44). Choice C draws credence from Mencken's comment that Coolidge's "early days were anything but pinched" (lines 49-50) and the fact that he was "well fed and well schooled" (lines 50-51). Choice D is supported by Mencken's observations that Coolidge "talked and lived only sunshine" (lines 77-78) and that "There was a volcano boiling under him, but he did not know it…" (lines 78-80). Though Coolidge left office a wealthy man, this seems to more a product of his astute business sense than any greed, and his reserved nature was certainly not self-promoting. Thus, E becomes the exception.

49. The English expression that the author cites in lines 28-29—"I find myself quite unable to associate myself with that thesis"—is BEST labeled a(n) **(A) euphemism**.

A euphemism is defined as a substitute or a milder way of saying something that might be considered offensive or unpleasant. This understated expression, which Mencken credits the British with coining, is essentially a milder way of saying he thinks writers likening Coolidge to Lincoln to be an absurdity.

50. The three infinitive phrases in lines 21-23—"to run down a quotation, to eat a plate of ham and eggs, or to look out of the window"—are intended to **(C) exemplify pressure-reducing distractions that enhance the ability to write**.

This follows on the heels of the author's observation that Coolidge's unexpected death caught the press "napping" (line 14), forcing them to "do their political embalming under desperate pressure" (lines 14-16). Mencken goes on to note that "The common legend is that such pressure inflames and inspires a true journalist, and maketh him to sweat masterpieces…" (lines 16-18), but quickly debunks this perception as a myth. Rather, his claim is that "Like any other literary man, he functions best when he is at leisure, and can turn from his tablets now and then…" (lines 19-21). The three infinitive phrases cited exemplify ways by which the writer can escape from the pressures of his trade. Choice C captures this most accurately. While choice D certainly deserves consideration, the word "idiosyncratic" suggests that these are peculiarities or oddities when they are just normal leisure activities.

51. Lines 45-47, "Some of the more romantic of the funeral bards tried to convert the farmhouse at Plymouth into a log-cabin," imply that the writers attempted to do which of the following?

   I. Establish a museum that commemorated the life and career of the former President.
   II. Mythologize the former President's childhood experience.
   III. Explain the President's popular appeal by citing his rural roots.

   (A) II only.

The selection of choice A is largely determined by the phrase "more romantic" and the allusion to President Lincoln's rural upbringing in Illinois in the log-cabin. The attempt to connect Coolidge to Lincoln is an attempt to paint him as a "typical American" (line 26), something that his affluent family, privileged education, and comfortable lifestyle refutes. There is no suggestion of making his farmhouse into a museum (I) or suggesting that his New England background increased his popularity with the voters (III).

52. The third paragraph differs MOST from the other three paragraphs in its **(C) catalog of biographical data**.

The biggest difference in the third paragraph is clearly the wealth of biographical information about Coolidge's birthplace, family affluence, schooling, early political endeavors, and ascendance to the Presidency. No other paragraph documents this information with a similar specificity.

53. Which of the following most blatantly reveals the author's attitude towards such post-mortem commemorative accounts of public figures? **(B) "beautiful nonsense" (line 6)**.

This clearly sardonic phrase suggests the author's belief that upon the death of a public figure, the press creates a mythology about him which may far exceed the reality of his public contribution. Though not an oxymoron, this two word construct captures both the exquisite nature of the eulogistic writing and the fatuousness of it as well.

54. That Calvin Coolidge was a fortunate individual is confirmed LEAST by which of the following? **(B) "There is no record that he was brilliant, but he took his degree with a respectable mark..." (lines 54-55)**.

Choice A understatedly suggests that Coolidge was more than financially secure (his father was a "man of substance"), choice C that his rise to political prominence was somewhat meteoric (he was making a living in politics by the age of 27). Choice D notes that he always won his campaigns for public office, choice E that though troubles were brewing under him (metaphorically represented by the "black clouds" and boiling volcano), Coolidge was blissfully unaware of them while in office and exceedingly fortunate to leave the Presidency before the Stock Market Crash of 1929 and the subsequent Great Depression became a bleak reality for him. Though choice B does imply that he may have overcome a less than brilliant intellect to become a lawyer, it nevertheless suggests that his showing was "respectable;" hence, the selection of B as the answer which least conveys his status as a fortunate individual.

Précis and Explication for Free-Response Question One:
From Aleida Rodriguez's "My Mother in Two Photographs"

Free-Response Question One asks students to consider part of an essay called "My Mother in Two Photographs" that is about her childhood memories of emigrating from Cuba to America, and, upon completion, to "identify the nature of the cultural rifts caused by relocation and show how the author's rich use of language conveys them." The essay is not so much a progression of paragraphs as it is a series of short vignettes (in the vein of Sandra Cisneros' *The House on Mango Street*) that provides subtle insights into the problems encountered by immigrants in America. The two photographs—one of the mother she left behind in Cuba, the other of the mother reunited with her children in America—trigger the speaker's flashbacks and reflections on her mother's life as well as the effect of assimilation upon her and her siblings. The passage is replete with interesting language, including expressions in her native language, images of hard work and strong religious faith, cultural allusions (both Cuban and American), and eloquent similes and metaphors.

In the first paragraph the author sees her mother being told to remain calm by the author's grandmother. Perhaps she is worried about the children who have been sent to America, or perhaps by the "kitchen towel, embroidered with the day of the week, *martes*, and smeared with another woman's lipstick" (lines 9-12), the towel that she clutches in her hand until her husband comes home, then flings it "like an open book" at her husband's mud-caked boots (lines 12-13). The simple but effective simile reveals the mother's silent but certain indictment of her husband's betrayal. The second paragraph (the first to include a photograph) and the third paragraph initially focus on two details: the collar of the mother's sweat-soaked dress, and the statue of a saint "who can't be seen above the melted-chocolate folds of a robe, and above that, perhaps, two hands are held palms up, checking the spiritual weather" (lines 19-22). This implies the divorce between the reality of earthly labor and the potential of spiritual reward in that the saint seems oblivious to the suffering below, gazing upwards not down and seemingly more concerned with the weather than with the prayers for his intercession from below. The latter part of the paragraph conveys the speaker's frustration that she cannot touch her mother or see her grandmother before she died. The grandmother's death also impacts the author's mother, who is left alone with an adulterous husband and a family a culture away. The reference to the grandmother's having once transformed a piece of fabric into "The Miracle of the Three Dresses" (lines 29-30) suggests a miraculous engineering of a little into much, similar to the parable of Jesus and the loves and fishes. The simile of her mother's collapsing "like a slave into bed at the end of day" (lines 31-32) shows the physical and emotional toll that the grandmother's death takes upon her.

Occurring two years later, the fourth paragraph again features her mother having to confront tragedy: this time that of her son who has been "locked in a mental ward at sixteen after chasing his foster mother around the block with a kitchen knife" (lines 36-38). Having dropped out of school and taken a menial job, he buys himself a series of fancy cars before leaving them "wrapped like a wedding ring around a telephone pole" (lines 43-44). This implies that the fracture of the family structure by the emigration led to her son's forsaking education for a life of risk and violence, then suffering incarceration for his actions. Similarly, the fifth paragraph provides a brief vignette of her eldest daughter who has gone on to college but forsaken her Cuban heritage, "forever regretting she hadn't been born into a TV family" (lines 45-47), "Her face a glossy ad of the ideal American living room" (lines 49-50). The images and choice of detail in this section—in particular, the hairstyle and cars—suggest the ready assimilation of the children into American teenage culture.

The concluding two paragraphs focus on the second photograph but from very different perspectives. In lines 51-63, the speaker alludes to a newspaper photograph of her family's being reunited in America. She is, however, embarrassed by the reunion, ashamedly admitting that "Two years on my own among strangers had only taught me how to be one" (lines 54-56). A stranger in a strange land, the author now ironically notes the 'foreignness' of her Cuban family: "I stood, my first tongue ripped out, with my mother's wet, round cheek pressed to the top of my head. The dark flag of her mustache. Their sour smell, like clothes trapped in a hamper. Emblems of the exile" (lines 56-61). Her mother's emotional caress is subordinated by the hair on her lip and the funky smell of her clothes, the speaker realizes how much she has assimilated when she remarks "Though my mother pulled me toward her with one arm, she scooped up only watery absence; my body had long drifted downriver" (lines 68-71). Like the archetypal Huck Finn, she has left her home physically and culturally behind her, and her remark "My mother's face in this photograph, captured by a stranger, betrays the weight of emptiness in her arms" (lines 71-73) conveys this severance. Though she may be physically represented in the photo, she has forsaken her Cuban heritage and language for that of a brave new world.

Rodriguez's unique essay allows students to study the cultural rifts that can be caused by emigration, including physical separation, issues with employment and crime, a weakening of the familial bond, and a forfeiture of one's original culture caused by assimilation into a new one. The author does not seem proud of these developments, but in the final scene she does seem resigned to these changes, if a little guilty over succumbing to them.

This question has been reprinted for your convenience.

Section II

Question One

(Suggested time–40 minutes. This question counts as one-third of the total essay section score.)

In this passage a woman looking at photographs of her childhood reflects upon the impact of emigration upon her family. Read the passage carefully. Then, in a well-organized essay, identify the nature of the cultural rifts caused by relocation and show how the author's rich use of language conveys them.

But what about my mother? Like opposite
aspects of the same person: my mother, my
grandmother's shadow. Here, she's smiling,
though not broadly. Her children are gone, but
(5)   her mother's there, telling her *aguántate,*
cálmate,[1] as they sit over *café.*[2] Or maybe
she's relieved. It is, after all, the first time since
their marriage that she and my father are alone,
like newlyweds. But suddenly a kitchen towel,
(10) embroidered with the day of the week, *martes,*[3]
and smeared with another woman's lipstick,
flies from my mother's hand, lands like an
open book by my father's mud-caked boots.

In this photograph, a coffee-dark V shows
(15) through the collar of her dress, evidence of the
enforced labor in the cane fields since the
revolution. Above her head is a wall vase filled
with plastic flowers, hanging under the framed
painting of a saint, who can't be seen above the
(20) melted-chocolate folds of a robe, and above
that, perhaps, two hands are held palms up,
checking the spiritual weather. But the hands
are outside the photograph, just like my hands,
which can't touch my mother at that brief oasis,
(25) or my grandmother, right before she turned and
left with the shadow.

Grandmother left so abruptly, left my mother in
mid-sentence, fingering the legendary length of
fabric her mother had once transformed into
(30) the Miracle of the Three Dresses. Alone, she
collapsed into her mother's absence like a slave
into bed at the end of the day.

Then one afternoon two years later the air of
her kitchen spun like someone whirling toward
(35) her, and she knew something had happened to
her son: locked in a mental ward at sixteen
after chasing his foster mother around the

block with a kitchen knife. He had dropped out
of high school, washed dishes for a living.
(40) Sporting long sideburns, he rewarded himself
first with a round-backed two-toned Chevy,
then a series of garish Mustangs. Married to
his fate, he left a trail of cars, each wrapped
like a wedding ring around a telephone pole.

(45) A vision of her oldest daughter—forever
regretting she hadn't been born into a TV
family—flashed thin against the white walls of
college, her body a blade sharpened to sever
the question from the answer. Her face a glossy
(50) ad of the ideal American living room.

In the newspaper photo above the caption
"Family of Cuban Expatriates Reunited Here,"
I am the only one gazing at the camera, my
face twisted into a complex curiosity. Two
(55) years on my own among strangers had only
taught me how to be one. I stood, my first
tongue ripped out, with my mother's wet, round
cheek pressed to the top of my head. The dark
flag of her mustache. Their sour smell, like
(60) clothes trapped in a hamper. Emblems of the
exile. While bureaucrats toyed with their time
and their fate, my parents had waited,
uncomplaining, afraid.

But I didn't know that back then. I placed
(65) myself instead in the camera lens, looking back
at the spectacle we made in the bus station.
Under my skin, the rice fields of my hometown
were flooding the place of language. Though
my mother pulled me toward her with one arm,
(70) she scooped up only watery absence; my body
had long since drifted downriver. My mother's
face in this photograph, captured by a stranger,
betrays the weight of emptiness in her arms.

---

[1] (Sp) hold on; stay calm
[2] (Sp) coffee
[3] (Sp) Tuesday

Aleida Rodriguez, excerpt from "My Mother in Two Photographs, Among Other Things" from *Garden of Exile.*
Originally from *Prairie Scbooner* (1994), Copyright (c) 1994, 1999 by Aleida Rodriguez. Meter. Reprinted with the permission of
The Permissions Company, Inc., on behalf of Sarabande Books, www .sarabandebooks.org.

Scoring Guide for Free-Response Question One:
From Aleida Rodriguez's "My Mother in Two Photographs"

9   Essays earning a score of 9 meet all the criteria for 8 papers and in addition are especially thorough in their analysis or demonstrate a particularly impressive control of style.

8   Essays earning a score of 8 effectively identify the nature of the cultural rifts caused by relocation and show how the author's rich use of language conveys them. They present a carefully reasoned argument in support of their position and enlist appropriate evidence from the text that supports it. Their prose demonstrates an impressive control of the elements of effective writing, though it is not flawless.

7   Essays earning a score of 7 fit the description of 6 essays but feature either more purposeful arguments or a greater command of prose style.

6   Essays scoring 6 accurately identify the nature of the cultural rifts caused by relocation and show how the author's rich use of language conveys them. Their arguments, while generally sound in nature and adequately supported, are nevertheless not as persuasive as papers earning a score of 7 or better due to their being less developed or less cogent. Though these papers may also feature lapses in diction or syntax, they nevertheless contain the insight and composition skills that characterize a paper in the upper-half.

5   Essays scoring 5 generally understand the task, but are either limited in scope or insufficiently developed. Though they may be marked by errors in syntax or in diction, they nevertheless reflect a certain level of competence.

4   Essays scoring 4 respond inadequately to the question's task, often misunderstanding, misrepresenting, or oversimplifying the cultural rifts caused by relocation and/or failing to show how the author's rich use of language conveys them. Though their prose is often adequate enough to convey their writers' claims, it generally suggests a limited control over organization, diction, or syntax.

3   Essays earning a score of 3 meet the criteria for a score of 4, but are either less persuasive or display a more limited control over the elements of effective composition.

2   Essays scoring 2 achieve little success in identifying the cultural rifts caused by relocation or in showing how the author's rich use of language conveys them. They may on occasion misread the passage, fail to develop their arguments to any substantive level, summarize rather than analyze the passage, or display significant weaknesses in organization, clarity, fluency or mechanics.

1   Essays earning a score of 1 meet the criteria for a score of 2 but are either overly simplistic or marred by severe deficiencies in the elements of composition.

0   Essays scoring 0 offer an off-topic response that receives no credit, or a mere repetition of the prompt.

—   Indicates a blank or completely off-topic response.

Sample Student Essay One

The history of migration is often that of bereavement, cultural conflict, and redefinition of the self. The narrator of this passage traces her Cuban ancestry and contrasts it with her generation's exposure to an alien and synthetic new culture. She reveals the isolation and estrangement caused by relocation. The author's diction, imagery, and juxtaposition generate a nostalgic tone suggestive of loss, confusion, and longing, common accompaniments to emigration. They lament more an exile from an idyllic past condition than a departure from a physical homeland.

The sense of passive endurance and submission to fate emanates throughout the passage through tone, description, and diction. As a child of emigration and cultural duality, the narrator expresses a spectrum of sensations, bearing both resignation and pride towards her lost Cuban heritage. A sense of nostalgia emerges early in the passage through italicized Spanish terminology and romanticized imagery. The foreign terms introduce the reader to certain key characteristics of the narrator's Cuban heritage and linguistically reinforce an intermingling of two cultures. By employing the Spanish words for remaining calm and enduring, she both ascribes these characteristics to her native culture, and accentuates a linguistic divide between herself and her mother and grandmother. The image of the two women sipping "cafe," subdued to fate, visually contextualizes the narrator's background and circumstances. The description of the mother suggests a melancholy powerlessness. Life happens to her: her own mother leaves with the shadow, the towel "flies" from her hand, and "bureaucrats toiled with [her] time and fate," yet she does not have any significant direct action verbs ascribed to her and remains clouded in vague resignation and emotional speculation. Though spoken of as a mother, this woman is removed from all traditional parental roles of authority, left with visions of her children's lives whirling by, out of control in foreign hands. The narrator herself behaves like a passive observer, examining her family's relocation through photographs and mixing ambiguous speculations with bursts of vivid images in a manner typical of fragmented childhood memories. She speaks of her siblings as almost strangers, her mother's "son" and "daughter," rather than her own brother and sister. Emigration brought powerlessness, separation, and a loss of control to this family.

Later portions of the passage juxtapose two cultures and leave the narrator's childhood self on an ambiguous middle ground. The author contrasts organic and synthetic imagery in comparing Cuba with America. The rustic visual of the "coffee-dark V" of her mother's skin, a symbol of struggle, submission, and cultural history, is an antithesis to the polished, glossy-white image of her daughter. Like a sharpened pencil, refined to the thin and controlled perfection of idealized American living. The placement of the photograph beneath a vase of "plastic" flowers further suggests that the author finds American culture synthetic and recalls Cuba with a child's nostalgia for an idyllic and natural homeland. The newspaper photo in line 52 suggests that the estrangement and separation caused by emigration could not be overcome by the family. Despite its caption, the photograph ironically portrays a lack of unity, with only the narrator looking at the camera. "I stood, my first tongue ripped out, with/ my mother's wet round cheek pressed to the top of my head [...] Emblems of the exile." She is a stranger to her old self. The Cuban expatriates are exiles not only from their homeland, but also from their previous condition of family unity.

With the concluding paragraph comes an acknowledgement of the shifting perspective brought by maturity. The insight of future years allows the narrator to combine her childhood sentiments of isolation and psychologically violent separation with her parents' anxiety, oppression, and anticipation under their native government. The eloquent narration bears witness to the narrator's success in finding a new tongue, in overcoming the challenges of relocation. Emigration brought distancing, upheaval, and alienation to the family, yet despite the romanticized childhood images of her homeland, the narrator acknowledges that this journey also provided escape from the realities of slave-like endurance, and subjugation which characterized life under the Cuban regime.

Sample Student Essay Two

Emigrating to a foreign land can tear a family apart, as family members find themselves torn by the desire to integrate culturally and maintain their heritage. In the passage, the narrator reflects on her emigration experience by examining old photographs. This motif creates an image of a bygone era, one whose sentiments and happiness have long since vanished. Cultural rifts caused by poverty, differences in language, and disillusionment with America have ripped her family apart. In using vivid imagery, the narrator creates a sense of melancholic absence and loss. Through her judicious use of metaphor and the photographic motif, the narrator illustrates her family's cultural plight.

Photographs provide windows into the past, freezing moments in time. By reflecting on the differences between her family in the photographs and their present state, the narrator emphasizes the changes that have taken place. The narrator opens the passage describing a scene between her mother and grandmother. The scene appears happy, but masks the difficulties present in their life. As the narrator states, "Here, she's smiling, though not broadly...her mother's there, telling her aguántate, cálmate, as they sit over café" (lines 3-6). The return to the familiar Spanish and the presence of her mother gives the narrator's mother comfort, though the phrase "not broadly," hides the sadness within. In the second photograph, the narrator dwells upon a "coffee-dark V [showing] through the collar of her dress, evidence of the enforced labor in the cane fields since the revolution" (lines 15-18). This detail highlights one of the family's motives for leaving Cuba—seeking a better life. However, the mournful tone of the passage suggests otherwise. The narrator's description of the final photograph emphasizes the transformation of the family. The ironic title—"Family of Cuban Expatriates United Here" (line 53)— suggests a tightening of family ties and kinship, the opposite of what has occurred. As she states, "Two years on my own among strangers had only taught me how to be one. I stood, my first tongue ripped out...While bureaucrats toiled with their time and their fate, my parents had waited, uncompromising, afraid" (lines 55-58, 62-64), the narrator points out the contrast between her American experience and her parents'. In the narrator's case, the unwelcoming nature of American society hardens her, leaving her jaded, a stranger to her own family. The phrase "my first tongue ripped out" suggests the narrator was forced to abandon Spanish in order to survive. On the other hand, her parents, unable to pursue an alternative, wait fearfully for help from the American government, while their daughter mocks the bureaucracy. In the final paragraph, the narrator acknowledges her previous innocence, saying, "But I didn't know that back then" (line 65). In saying this, she emphasizes the key property of photographs, which capture a moment and a mindset in time, preserving it while everything else is torn to pieces.

Throughout the passage, the narrator employs metaphor and simile to emphasize sentiments of disillusionment and loss. In describing the effect of her grandmother's departure, the narrator states, "she collapsed into her mother's absence like a slave into bed at the end of the day" (lines 32-33). This suggests the loss of a familiar person, one who understood her mother and her language, weakened her daily, the grief robbing her of energy. The vision of her oldest daughter, cast as a glossy TV ad, satirizes the stark differences between the ideal American family and her own: "Her face a glossy ad of the ideal American living room" (lines 50-51). In the final paragraph, the narrator uses a water metaphor to describe the rift created in her family, stating, "she scooped up only watery absence; my body had long drifted downriver" (lines 71-72). With this technique, the narrator conveys a sense of futility, suggesting that emigration had rendered her will and ties to her family lifeless, allowing her to drift with the flow of the river. This vivid sense of description, metaphor and simile reinforces the mournful tone of the passage, creating feelings of sadness and loss.

By framing the passage with a photographic motif and enriching it with simile and metaphor, the narrator highlights the cultural rifts caused by poverty and disillusionment with the realities of adjusting to American life. The photographs freeze a moment in time, harkening back to a different mindset, bringing into stark relief in the changes that have occurred. Instead of uniting these Cuban expatriates, the cultural rigors of emigration have torn them apart.

Sample Student Essay Three

Emigration to a new country often stresses a family in a variety of ways and can create unnecessary tension and despair. Families who emigrate must deal with new customs and a new culture, often causing a sense of isolation or even inaccessibility. Looking at old photographs, the woman in this passage specifically recalls the painful and confusing cultural rifts caused by her family's relocation. Although emigrating provided a chance for a new beginning, it also created a language barrier, generated feelings of isolation, and resulted in the loss of individual identity, all of which the author conveys through the use of sensory imagery, hyperbole, similes, and the insertion of Spanish words.

Throughout the author's recollection of her childhood, the language barrier between the Spanish language of her native Cuban country and the language of her new country, presumably America, is strongly evident. Even as the author looks at the first picture of her mother, she remarks that her grandmother whispers encouraging words such as "aguántate, calmate, as they sit over café" (lines 5-6). Although the interaction between the mother and grandmother in their native language seems sweet at first, it actually emphasizes the fact that the two can only understand the Spanish language. The interspersed Spanish words, including another referral to a day of the week as "martes" (line 10), reveal the language barrier as well as the desire to keep this language of their native country alive. The author also remarks about another picture, taken right as her family enters the country, in which she stands with her "first tongue ripped out" (line 55). The author uses hyperbole here as well as metonymy, in which her "first tongue" represents her first language, to reinforce the idea that she can no longer communicate with others. Furthermore, she remarks that "the rice fields of [her] hometown were flooding the place of language" (lines 65-66), an image which reveals that the author has only ever known her childhood in her native country. The knowledge of that time in her life and of that language, therefore, "floods" her mind and prevents her from truly interacting with others in her new country. Unfortunately, the inability to communicate, caused by the language barrier, leads to other complications as well.

Living in their new country, the family also begins to experience feelings of isolation because of the incongruity between their culture and the culture of their new home. In one picture, the author mentions a painting of a saint, "who can't be seen above the melted-chocolate folds of a robe" (lines 19-20). The robe itself serves as a metaphor for the family's customs, which engulf the family and prevent the family from assimilating into the new culture. Moreover, the author draws a connection between the saint's hands, which "are outside the photograph" (line 24), and her own hands, which "can't touch [her] mother at that brief oasis" (line 25-26). This connection stresses the idea that the family not only experiences isolation from others but also experiences isolation from each other. Ironically, the caption of the last photo reads "Family of Cuban Expatriates United Here" (line 53) even though the author is "the only one gazing at the camera" (line 54). This action sadly represents the idea that the family is not really connected and united as one. In addition, the author remarks that "two years on [her] own among strangers had only taught [her] how to be one" (line 55-57), a cold truth which reiterates the family's situation of being lost among strangers. The author even recognizes the family as "emblems of the exile" (line 61) because the cultural rifts which exist are much too strong for her family to ever truly be part of this new country. As a result, the family experiences feelings of isolation for years after their actual emigration.

Finally, the family experiences a loss of identity because of these cultural rifts. As the family grows up in the new country, it begins to appear broken. Within just a few paragraphs, the audience discovers that the father has had some sort of affair when the mother finds a kitchen towel "smeared with another woman's lipstick" (lines 11-12), that the grandmother died and "left [the] mother in mid-sentence" (lines 28-29), that the son is "locked in a mental ward at sixteen" (line 37), and that the daughter forever regretted that "*she hadn't been born into a TV family*" (lines 47-48). In addition, the author mentions that the oldest daughter's face was like "*a glossy ad of the ideal American living room*" (lines 50-51), an association which creates the impression that the daughter has forgotten her Cuban roots and lost her true identity. The author realizes that she herself has lost her identity through the emigration process. Although her mother pulls the author toward her, the mother really "*scooped up only watery absence*" because "*[the author's] body had long drifted downriver*" (lines 71-72). The author's use of sensory imagery and metaphorical language represent the idea that the author has lost her "*body*" or identity because her identity has been left behind in Cuba. The author realizes that she is physically present but feels as though she is filled with "*emptiness*" (lines 74) in this new world of strangers. Unfortunately, emigrants often experience such loss of identity when entering a new country because they find it hard to hold on to their own cultural roots and customs.

Despite the belief that emigrating provides a new beginning for many, the act of relocating actually created a language barrier, generated feelings of isolation, and resulted in the loss of identities for the members of the author's family, all of which the author conveys through the use of sensory imagery, irony, metaphors, and the insertion of some Spanish words. Unfortunately, the family appears to break down almost because of their inability to function in this new country. The reality of emigration proves that strangers will remain strangers for the most part, and outsiders will never truly be welcomed into a new society. The sad truth is that people feel safe within their own communities and often refuse to blend boundaries between cultures.

**Assessment of Student Responses to Free-Response Question One:
From Aleida Rodriguez's "My Mother in Two Photographs"**

Sample Student Essay One:

A. Assessment of Reader One

This essay shines with vocabulary and insight. Taking the tack of dealing with tone and attitude, this writer recreates the images and heartbreak of a family that has been separated through rich vocabulary and metaphor. Sometimes the vocabulary "gets in the way" of what the writer is trying to say, and hence there is some repetition and over-statement at times, but the description of the juxtaposition of the two cultures and the understanding of the tone of the piece makes this a 9.

B. Assessment of Reader Two

This essay has all the trademarks of a 9: deep insight, rich vocabulary, lucid prose, and cogent organization. There is an occasional fragment and instance of questionable word choice, but this merely reinforces the fact that a 9 paper need not be perfect. This paper reflects the work of an AP student at the peak of his/her powers. Impressive.

Sample Student Essay Two:

A. Assessment of Reader One

This paper takes a different stance and spends time on the idea of Emigration and the problems that can be experienced by families who must endure separation because of it. Aware of such techniques as metonymy and hyperbole, this writer explores the idea that the original author puts forth. A different essay, but also a 9.

B. Assessment of Reader Two

This essay is also an excellent one and has much of the same thought as the previous paper. Like its predecessor it explores the contrast between old and new worlds, though its focus on figurative language is different and more precise. Every so often at the Reading one gets a series of papers like this back-to-back, and those moments really make the grueling grading task worthwhile. I would rate this as another 9.

Sample Student Essay Three:

A. Assessment of Reader One

This essay can be described as superior. Encountering an opening that is clear and mature which includes a thesis, the reader settles in for a great read. This writer is a master at understanding the writer's craft. The essay deals with the tone and the cultural rifts caused by emigration, but this writer also clearly understands the techniques used to create the effect. For example, a recognition of the "photo motif and the "framing" of the essay using the photo is masterful and well aware of the irony of such a motif. This essay would receive a 9+ if such a score existed.

B. Assessment of Reader Two

I would like to find fault with this paper that would make it different, but like its predecessors it does a really excellent job. It differs a bit in that it really imbeds citations effortlessly into its argument and looks at other literary devices (hyperbole and metonymy, for example) in novel ways. It has a well-crafted thesis and wonderfully balanced sentences such as "Within just a few paragraphs...tv family" in the fourth paragraph. I would also have to give this a 9.

A short note: users of the book sometimes find essays like this to be implausible if not impossible. However, students in my class averaged 4.71 on the 2011 exam, and this year's group (4.78) did even better. I am humbled daily by what they are capable of doing.

Précis and Explication of Free-Response Question Two:
From Tom Brokaw's *The Greatest Generation*

Tom Brokaw's commemorative book *The Greatest Generation* was admirably responsible for sparking a renewed consciousness and appreciation of the generation of Americans who went to war in two theaters in the four-year period from 1941-1945, all to insure the preservation of our freedoms. These surviving veterans, who sacrificed a portion of their lives or all of it, are now dwindling in number as time stakes yet another, more unavoidable claim on their minds and bodies. Free Response Question Two, however, posed the question "whether such sacrifice is unique to this generation of Americans or endemic to *all* generations of Americans?," asking students to use their reading, studies, experience or observation to "identify what [they] feel are the contemporary generation's—or some other generation's—greatest challenges and anticipate how some future chronicler of the age might celebrate or condemn its efforts to overcome them."

This wide-ranging question could lead students down a number of promising paths. For example, students could examine the issue of nuclear power, from reactor safety to the acquisition by a terrorist group of enough nuclear material to make a "dirty bomb." Students could reference books such as John Hersey's *Hiroshima* and movies such as *The Day After* to place this issue in historical or futuristic contexts and to examine how individuals have worked tirelessly to raise consciousness of this potential danger. Other respondees might look at issues in the environment, things such as global warming, fracking, or the destruction of the rain forest, incorporating books such as Rachel Carson's *Silent Spring*, Al Gore's *An Inconvenient Truth*, and Alan Weisman's *The World Without Us* to buttress their arguments. Still others might explore the issue of race and the impact of individuals such as Martin Luther King, Medgar Evers, Rosa Parks and others who have had on improving the lot of African-Americans in this country, in light of current issues such as employment opportunities and racial profiling. Or they might explore the contributions made by the political voices of Elizabeth Cady Stanton and Susan B. Anthony or the literary voices of Virginia Woolf and Kate Chopin to woman's suffrage. Similar essays could be developed around immigration, the Great Depression and the AIDS epidemic and the literature that derived from them.

Whether students choose a contemporary or historical perspective, they should be able to comment at length on whether the actions of the "greatest generation" are truly unique or just another in a long and hallowed tradition of sacrifice.

This question has been reprinted for your convenience.

<u>Question Two</u>

(Suggested time—40 minutes. This question counts as one-third of the total essay section score.)

In his national best-seller *The Greatest Generation*, Tom Brokaw pays tribute to the enormous sacrifices made by the men and women of the World War II generation who "went from cap and gown directly into uniform [and]....answered the call to help save the world from the two most powerful and ruthless military machines ever assembled..."; who, leaving behind families, friends, home towns, careers and aspirations, fought to preserve the liberties upon which this country was founded; and who upon returning home alive—if they were lucky enough not be one of the nearly three hundred thousand battlefield casualties—"joined in joyous and short-lived celebrations, then immediately began the task of rebuilding their lives and the world they wanted" (ix-xx).

Though Brokaw's poignant portrait of these ordinary yet extraordinary men and women lauds the quiet sense of civic duty that epitomized both these individuals and their actions, it begs the question whether such sacrifice is unique to this generation of Americans or endemic to *all* generations of Americans.

Take a moment to ponder Brokaw's claim. Then, in a well-organized essay, identify what you feel are the contemporary generation's—or some previous generation's—greatest challenges and anticipate how some future chronicler of the age might celebrate or condemn its efforts to overcome them. Use your reading, studies, experience or observation to develop your argument.

Scoring Guide for Free-Response Question Two: From Tom Brokaw's *The Greatest Generation*

9   Essays earning a score of 9 meet all the criteria for 8 papers and in addition are especially thorough in their analysis or demonstrate a particularly impressive control of style.

8   Essays earning a score of 8 effectively identify what their writers feel is the contemporary generation's—or some other generation's—greatest challenge and sensibly anticipate how some future chronicler of the age might celebrate or condemn its efforts to overcome it. They present a carefully reasoned argument in support of their position and enlist appropriate evidence from the sources that supports it. Their prose demonstrates an impressive control of the elements of effective writing, though it is not flawless.

7   Essays earning a score of 7 fit the description of 6 essays but feature either more purposeful arguments or a greater command of prose style.

6   Essays scoring 6 accurately identify the contemporary generation's—or some other generation's — greatest challenge and anticipate how some future chronicler of the age might celebrate or condemn its efforts to overcome it. Their arguments, while generally sound in nature and adequately supported, are nevertheless not as persuasive as papers earning a score of 7 or better due to their being less developed or less cogent. Though these papers may also feature lapses in diction or syntax, they nevertheless contain the insight and composition skills that characterize a paper in the upper-half.

5   Essays scoring 5 generally understand the task, but are either limited in scope or insufficiently developed. Though they may be marked by errors in syntax or in diction, they nevertheless reflect a certain level of competence.

4   Essays scoring 4 respond inadequately to the question's task, often misrepresenting or oversimplifying the contemporary generation's—or some other generation's —greatest challenge or providing little evidence as to how some future chronicler might celebrate or condemn its efforts to overcome it. Though their prose is often adequate enough to convey their writers' claims, it generally suggests a limited control over organization, diction, or syntax.

3   Essays earning a score of 3 meet the criteria for a score of 4, but are either less persuasive or display a more limited control over the elements of effective composition.

2   Essays scoring 2 achieve little success in identifying the contemporary generation's—or some other generation's —greatest challenge or in providing evidence as to how some future chronicler might celebrate or condemn its efforts to overcome it. They may on occasion misunderstand the citation, fail to develop their arguments to any substantive level, or display significant weaknesses in organization, clarity, fluency or mechanics.

1   Essays earning a score of 1 meet the criteria for a score of 2 but are either overly simplistic or marred by severe deficiencies in the elements of composition.

0   Essays scoring 0 offer an off-topic response that receives no credit, or a mere repetition of the prompt.

—   Indicates a blank or completely off-topic response.

Sample Student Essay One

In each generation there are sacrifices made that establishes that generation as a success or a failure. The generation during World War II is no different as they chose to step up and go to battle for the country and help to preserve freedom for the world. Tom Brokaw lauds them as the contemporary generation and talks about their many challenges in his book The Greatest Generation. Their fetes were many and their accomplishments many as well, but at the same time their answers to the challenges they faced were hasty and could possibly put their generation in a negative view in the future. Many of the soldiers went to fight directly after graduating high school and chose not to go onto higher education, and this generation also once they came back from war were very hasty in making up for lost time in family life. These factors would shed a negative light on this otherwise very well balanced generation.

The primary problem that the "great generation" faced was their lower level of education than previous or future generations. This is due to their very active involvement in the military, as they left right from high school to join the army and fight for their country and for the world. While they protected the world very bravely and willingly they also left a big gap in the education system. With so many people choosing war over higher education it left a big gap for the next generation as many people of the older generation were not trained in every day jobs or even as teachers. This meant that the following generation was unable to get the best education possible and it also made things like finding skilled workers for certain jobs difficult. How is a soldier just back from war with no higher training supposed to step into a job that requires skill? The war left many soldiers jobless and added to the rift in the social system. Many of these soldiers although very brave and willing to fight were unable to do the simple jobs held generally by trained individuals. The soldiers also left the educational system depleted as the colleges were no longer getting as many students and they were unable to train them for teaching jobs. Not having teachers for a new generation is very difficult as they limited the opportunities that this new generation had. How were the soldiers' kids supposed to survive in a post-war world when they couldn't even get a proper education? Many soldiers attempted to come back and work in skilled jobs but because of their lack of training they were left working in factories. This led to an increase in manufacturing but a dramatic decrease in small businesses. Thus there was a large strain on the small towns that generally ran on the production of the small stores and not on the large corporations. By leaving early for war the soldiers left the country unprepared for the post-war period.

Along with the gap in the system left by the soldiers, there was a large baby boom directly after the war. Many soldiers came back home and wanted to form a family right away, disregarding the normal practices of spacing out children and planning for the future. What this ended up doing was flooding the United States with children all at a certain age. This in the future will almost certainly bend the Social Security system to the brink of breaking if not a complete and total breakdown. The baby boom puts too much pressure on the generation twice removed from the war veterans as they will have to deal will the enormous pressure of funding the system with money for their parents. The increased rate of children per family was bad as well for the economy as there was a food shortage during the war and after the war it continued as there was a dramatic increase in mouths to feed. The large volumes of food needed to sustain the new generation put a large strain on the farms of America and thus made it more reliant on foreign countries for production. This need for foreign countries could come back and be very bad for the United States as it could make it too reliable on outside goods and make it not reliable at all on itself. That is when nations begin to breakdown, when there is so much influence by other countries and no influence by themselves. They lose their identity and slowly breakdown.

The great generation may have fought proudly for the safety of the world and the country but it also did a lot to strain the world and the country. Their gap in the education system and their overproduction of kids made it very difficult on the American society and the economy for the present and the future. They may well be viewed as brave but their actions may well be overshadowed by the strains they put on America.

Sample Student Essay Two

The parents of this current generation were revolutionaries in the 1960s. They were participants in the greatest social movement that the United States has ever known. It stands to reason that their children are also destined to change the world especially with the multitude of global problems that await them. Today's generation faces the challenge of creating a sustainable earth for future generations as well as solving the crises of hunger and poverty in developing third world nations. The largest goal awaiting this generation is reuniting the United States into one nation instead of two partisan parties and later the world.

Past generations have put off the issue of conserving the earth and its resources in hopes that someone else will deal with it. The current generation has bravely stepped up to the plate partly because they have to face it now or there might not be a future tomorrow. With the price of gasoline in the United States jumping to over four dollars a gallon, Americans have finally reached their price limit as stated in Op-Ed pieces from the <u>New York Times</u>. Celebrities, musicians and even some politicians teamed up to produce Live Earth, a day filled with music which united the world under one simple message: Save Planet Earth. This willingness to attack the environmental problems facing the world is only the beginning of the epic battle that lies ahead. Future historians might view this commitment cynically, saying that the world was forced into a live or die position, but they must accept that in the end, something was done. Hopefully, this movement was not too little, too late.

If the world is saved from the lifestyles of its inhabitants, the same people must then face the destitution that one third of the world lives in. The majority of these people live in developing nations in Asia and Africa which makes it easy for the five percent richest people in the world (who are all located in the United States) to ignore the plight of their fellow man. Children are forced to grow up never knowing a full meal or even a nutritious meal. There are always those in each generation who are willing reach out to help, but the rest are all waiting for a push to motivate them into helping. Historians may look back on these times and condemn the lack of compassion that the current generation showed to those in need of their help, donation of food or even an opportunity to save themselves.

The final step to saving the predicament that the world is in is to unite the countries behind one common purpose. The same can be said on a smaller scale for the United States which is currently divided into what seems like two separate nations because the two political parties have torn the people to two sides of an invisible line they've drawn. Until society stops fighting each other, can they join together to do any good in the world. This has been proven in the politics between the two candidates for the Democrats who will have let Republicans use their pettiness against them. Future historians will hopefully or praise these efforts to rejoin the two parties from their extremes, especially if this movement is successful.

The current generation comes from the same generation of the 1960s who in turn come from the same men and women who defeated the Nazis while simultaneously pulling the nation out of the horrible depression. If this is true than they can conserve the planet's environment, its people while also uniting everyone under a common goal.

Sample Student Essay Three

Every generation can attest to its share of obstacles along with its crowning achievements. Tom Brokaw lauds the World War II generation as having handled an obstacle as disorienting and invasive as a war with unwavering selflessness and determination, deeming them "The Greatest Generation". While the challenges faced by the modern generation may not present themselves in the shape of a worldwide military outbreak, they do exist in other forms. In the future, the contemporary generation will be defined by its efforts to preserve states of environmental, economic, and military stability on both the national and global scale.

The environment's condition has been slowly deteriorating since humans first appeared on the Earth, a process that has only been accelerated over the last century. Only recently, however, have people started taking action to prevent further harm and to sustain the Earth's natural resources for future generations. Al Gore's documentary, "An Inconvenient Truth," made many Americans aware of the effects of global warming and how their daily activities could be contributing to the massive carbon emissions that our country produces. From companies creating more eco-friendly products to families taking steps to make their lives a bit "greener", improving the condition of the environment has been a major goal and obstacle of the modern generation. Both individuals and large corporations are starting to realize that repairing the dilapidated state of the environment is vital to all other aspects of life since without a clean, functional Earth to live on, all other aspects of society will collapse.

With recent stock market crashes paired with the failure of many once-powerful corporations, there is no doubt that one of the modern generation's biggest obstacles has been the effect of a devastating economy. The 2007 stock market crash wreaked havoc on America and its foreign associates, causing widespread unemployment and a major change in commerce patterns both domestically and abroad. Americans have had to make great alterations to their lifestyle, taking on multiple jobs and changing their spending habits in order to provide for themselves and their families and to ensure a reasonable quality of life. Rather than allowing the recession to depress the population's spirits, Americans have held their heads high and used it as a chance to show their true, hard working nature that has endured since the Revolution.

The current War on Terror may not be on the same global scale as World War II had been since it lacks the presence of the "ruthless military machines". The United States' involvement in the Middle East, however, has made a significant impact on the national sentiment and on the lives of its inhabitants. The war has been the subject of countless political debates and has appeared on various party platforms over the past few elections. American men and women have sacrificed their lives and time to defend our country and to send aid to countries that need help. While the War's validity and necessity is a topic of constant debate that cannot be easily tried, the fact that Americans remain overseas is a testament to the contemporary generation's willingness to show national support. Though many may argue against the war, no one can deny the bravery and selflessness possessed by the soldiers and commanders that fight and have fought in the War on Terror.

The contemporary generation is one of the first to take action today for the people of tomorrow. Society is making provisions to make life a bit easier in the future, rather than opting for quick fixes that only deal with the current issue. People of the modern generation have made considerable changes in their lifestyles, from eliminating plastic shopping bags and driving more fuel-efficient cars to buying domestic products to stimulate the economy and sending supplies to the troops abroad. Though they may not have made such immense physical sacrifices for their country as the men and women of the World War II generation, they are among the few generations to realize the endangered state of the Earth and what that means for its inhabitants, and to make an effort to repair the damage. Retrospectively, they surely will be commended for these contributions.

Assessment of Student Responses to Free-Response Question Two:
Citation from Tom Brokaw's *The Greatest Generation*

Sample Student Essay One:

A. Assessment of Reader One

As sometimes happens, this writer misunderstands the prompt and focuses on the World War II generation of the quote. That said, he/she does try to deal with some of the negative results of the challenges of that generation as left to future generations which edges on the prompt but doesn't ever get there. In addition, the essay has some troubling composition problems such as redundant language, faulty punctuation, and awkward sentence structure. Overall the essay form is retained, and the writing can be considered competent. Unfortunately this writer "responds inadequately to the question's task, often misrepresenting, etc," limiting this essay to a 4.

B. Assessment of Reader Two

The first student sample offers a very difficult case. In its favor are its lengthy development and its reasonably competent compositional skills. Against it is a very large failure to comprehend any part of the question. It focuses on critiquing the greatest generation rather than upon considering the problems of another generation and its response to those problems. Thus, though the content seems to demand a 2 on the rubric, the mechanics deserve a 6. I split the difference and award it a 4. It simply cannot be upper half if it does not answer the question.

Sample Student Essay Two:

A. Assessment of Reader One

This writer clearly understands the prompt. The challenges facing the current generation as ecological, political and economic are clearly illustrated, but none are examined in great depth. Not without errors, this essay sustains a clear focus and pulls together three generations and their relationship to each other in its conclusion earning it a 7.

B. Assessment of Reader Two

The second student sample offers substantially better fare. The writer's paper is well-developed, but unlike that of its predecessor, on task, focusing on environmental and humanitarian concerns. It has good unity and good organization, linking the "greatest generation" with the socially conscious movement of the '60s generation before finally progressing to the present day generation. It is detailed but not overly so; it is fluent but not without some patches of rough syntax. This is an upper-half essay that rides the border between a 6 and a 7.

Sample Student Essay Three:

A. Assessment of Reader One

This essay also deals with the current generation and masterfully illustrates and supports the three challenges of economics, world domination and failing environment which face it. Well-developed and well-written, this essay includes appropriate support and sources which further examine its points— clearly a 9.

B. Assessment of Reader Two

I felt this was the best of the three responses. It had a wonderful organization, built around three central hubs—the environment, the economy, and national security—that were clearly laid out in its thesis and addressed in admirable detail in the body of the essay. Though it gave lip service to the second half of the question, addressing it only in the essay's final line, this is an excusable oversight in light of the paper's overall excellence. It is hard for me to imagine a much more coherent and fluent paper could be written under the constraints of time. I would score this a 9.

Précis and Explication of Free-Response Question Three:
Synthesis Question on the Effects of Internet and Computer Gaming On Adolescents

Free-Response Question Three asked students to consider five articles and one cartoon on whether Internet or computing gaming has a beneficial or detrimental impact upon the adolescents who play them. The prompt asked students to "take a position that defends, challenges or qualifies the claim that Internet and/or computer gaming is indisputably harmful to adolescents' intellectual and social development."

The six sources provided offered students a diversity of perspectives on this topic. Document A, from a book on Internet addiction by Dr. Kimberly Young, offers a peek into the life of a college age sophomore who is not making the Dean's List at his school, has no friends, and who recently broke up with his girlfriend. However, in the LambdaMOO, an interactive Internet game, he has achieved cult status as a dragon-slaying, castle-storming, maiden-saving hero who can socialize easily with anonymous players in this fantasy realm. So compulsive is his addiction that he spends up to sixty to seventy hours a week playing the game, at the expense of slipping grades and serious sleep deprivation. Document B, an article from the *Houston Chronicle*, takes the opposite tack: that young people's involvement on the Internet is not merely about games but an avenue to voter registration and a forum to discuss important social issues. The author cites several websites that promote what she calls "meatier fare than concerts and clothes" and that promote dialogue among young people about everything from global concerns to personal issues. Document C, entitled "Game Over," returns to the negative aspect of computer gaming, stressing again the social withdrawal that such solitary involvement abets while also providing statistics on the percentage of teens who have become "gaming addicts."

Document D, an article in *Young Adult Library Services* magazine, again offers a contrary take, stressing the social gains provided by online gaming. Not only do the authors compliment the skills that such players exhibit, but they claim that such success achieves "a cachet and credibility among their peers that simply can't be obtained in the classroom." They credit these games with improving skills in "pattern recognition, spatial reasoning, and information processing" and argue that such games are regularly used to develop the skills of pilots, soldiers and surgeons, claiming they are an ideal "preparation for the workplace." Document E, a droll cartoon, shows a teacher using terminology of a popular video game, "Space Invaders," to get his students interested in learning mathematics while Document F, the most unique of the six, attributes an increase in real-life murders and carjacking to kids playing the "Grand Theft Auto" video game, implying that criminal behavior can be spawned by violent video games.

These six sources provide a rich variety of perspectives on the relative merits or demerits of Internet and computer gaming that should allow students plenty of latitude in developing their responses to the prompt.

This question has been reprinted for your convenience.

<u>Question Three</u>

Reading Time: 15 minutes
Suggested Writing Time: 40 minutes

(This question counts as one-third of the total essay section score.)

Directions:

The following prompt is based on the accompanying six sources.

This question requires you to integrate a variety of sources into a coherent, well-written essay. *Refer to the sources to support your position; avoid paraphrase or summary. Your argument should be central; the sources should support this argument.*

Remember to attribute both direct and indirect citations.

Introduction:

Though the penchant for computer gaming among adolescents is undeniable, the effects of such gaming are hotly debated. While some see this as a deleterious, obsessive fixation that contributes to, even promotes, violent and/or anti-social behavior, others see it as a technological boon that fosters, even enhances, problem-solving skills and imaginative thought.

Assignment:

Read the following sources (including any introductory information) carefully. **Then, in an essay that synthesizes at least three of the sources for support, take a position that defends, challenges or qualifies the claim that Internet and/or computer gaming is indisputably harmful to adolescents' intellectual and social development**.

Scoring Guide for Free-Response Question Three:
Synthesis Question on the Effects of Internet and Computer Gaming On Adolescents

9   Essays earning a score of 9 meet all the criteria for 8 papers and in addition are especially thorough in their analysis or demonstrate a particularly impressive control of style.

8   Essays earning a score of 8 effectively take a position that defends, challenges or qualifies the claim that Internet and/or computer gaming is indisputably harmful to adolescents' intellectual and social development. They present a carefully reasoned argument in support of their position and enlist appropriate evidence from the sources that supports it. Their prose demonstrates an impressive control of the elements of effective writing, though it is not flawless.

7   Essays earning a score of 7 fit the description of 6 essays but feature either more purposeful arguments or a greater command of prose style.

6   Essays scoring 6 also take a position that defends, challenges or qualifies the claim that Internet and/or computer gaming is indisputably harmful to adolescents' intellectual and social development. Their arguments, while generally sound in nature and adequately supported, are nevertheless not as persuasive as papers earning a score of 7 or better due to their being less developed or less cogent. Though these papers may also feature lapses in diction or syntax, they nevertheless contain the insight and composition skills that characterize a paper in the upper-half.

5   Essays scoring 5 generally understand the task, but are either limited in scope or insufficiently developed. Though they may be marked by errors in syntax or in diction, they nevertheless reflect a certain level of competence.

4   Essays scoring 4 respond inadequately to the question's task, often misunderstanding, misrepresenting, or oversimplifying the claim that Internet and/or computer gaming is indisputably harmful to adolescents' intellectual and social development, or by providing insufficient evidence to support their claims. Though their prose is often adequate enough to convey their writers' claims, it generally suggests a limited control over organization, diction, or syntax.

3   Essays earning a score of 3 meet the criteria for a score of 4, but are either less persuasive or display a more limited control over the elements of effective composition.

2   Essays scoring 2 achieve little success in defending, challenging, or qualifying the claim that Internet and/or computer gaming is indisputably harmful to adolescents' intellectual and social development. They may on occasion misread a passage, fail to develop their arguments to any substantive level, summarize rather than analyze the sources, or display significant weaknesses in organization, clarity, fluency or mechanics.

1   Essays earning a score of 1 meet the criteria for a score of 2 but are either overly simplistic or marred by severe deficiencies in the elements of composition.

0   Essays scoring 0 offer an off-topic response that receives no credit, or a mere repetition of the prompt.

—   Indicates a blank or completely off-topic response.

Sample Student Essay One

There is no denying that, over the last few decades, video games have earned a pivotal role in the lives of modern students. Whereas video games may have previously been used as a harmless pastime that allowed students to relax and get their minds off of schoolwork, they have more recently become a dangerous obsession in which students are no longer developing vital social skills.

In the past, when one thought of video games, images of Mario Kart racing and Super Smash Brothers came to mind: games with fictional cartoon characters that allowed friends to compete against each other in short matches. The gaming world, however, has evolved immensely since those times of simplicity and friendly competition. Now, there exist worlds such as LambdaMOO (Document A), a Multi-User Dungeon site where success means a never-ending game. One website aimed at helping victims of gaming addiction remarked that "the games are designed to keep you at your computer as long as possible because you can't win" (Document C). Students who spend up to 10 hours a day on such games are losing valuable sleeping, studying, and socializing opportunities, and are jeopardizing their mental and physical health. Students are replacing their human friends with digital ones; their only form of exercise is the furious clicking of the mouse or game controller as they spend hours in front of a bright screen. Among other dangerous effects, gaming can impair cardiovascular health due to lack of exercise, damage eyesight, and induce carpal tunnel syndrome in a player's hands and arms. The health hazards which video games present are irrefutable.

As they have developed and become more popular, video games have become increasingly violent in nature. Some may argue that the games are harmless and that students should be able to differentiate between using violence in a fictional world and using it in the real world. Current events, however, have proved that teenagers are unable to make this distinction. Arrested gangs in Indianapolis have admitted to using violent video games to "train teens to do carjackings and murders" (Document F). Video games teach young adults to kill and steal mercilessly and to take pride in such actions. While it is a shame that students are unable to distinguish fiction from reality and what is appropriate in each world, there is no doubt that the pervading violence in video games is negatively influencing the actions of teens across the globe.

Some may argue that video games foster social and intellectual development, as players can teach each other "difficult maneuvers" and learn from their mistakes. One game analyst Eli Neiburger defends video games due to their role as an "educational tool", claiming that video games promote "useful life skills...unlike trigonometry" (Document D). While this argument holds some merit, teaching and interacting with one's peers is not confined to the gaming world; tutoring, participating in sports, and holding a job are all activities which require constant exchange of knowledge and human interaction. So, while educational games do exist and may play an important role in preparing young adults for the workplace, there are other, previously stated activities that accomplish the same thing with fewer health hazards.

Video games have evolved immensely from the Nintendo 64 console that older teenagers remember from their childhood. There are now games on the market which allow players to "interact" with and have real life conversations with a simulated human, who is able to give intelligent, lucid responses. While this is an impressive development for technology, what does it say about our nation's youth that parents are essentially buying their children cyber-companions instead of promoting real friendships? Perhaps modern society needs to focus its technological efforts on other, more pressing matters and allow teenagers to put down the controllers and reconnect with their peers, face to face.

Sample Student Essay Two

Every day, over nine million people log onto "World of Warcraft"; an online computer game. For some, it is just a game. For others, it is an addiction. There are thousands of people around the world who spend more than 40 hours a week playing games like "World of Warcraft". These games can become addicting because they have no "end". Someone could play for a hypothetically infinite amount of time and still have things to do. The game developers incorporate this feature into the games because to play many of them, a monthly subscription fee must be paid. They want the players to become addicted so they continue to pay the fee.

This addiction to gaming is harmful to the development of adolescents everywhere. The players become socially inept, they lose interest in school and they can become a danger to themselves and society. Video games are an inherent threat to adolescents.

Before computers, most young adults would go outside for entertainment. Pick up games of basketball and baseball would bring groups of adolescents together socially. However, with the dawn of the new age of technology, the personal computer has become readily available for almost anyone who wants it. Now, instead of going outside and interacting with other people in person, a player in an online game can make "friends" and socially interact online. This is going to have a negative affect on the adolescents who play these games. Because they are spending less time with other people their age, they are liable to have less friends and/or serious relationships in their lives. In some cases of severe addiction, these adolescents can lose all their friends because they are sitting in front of a computer screen for over 60 hours a week (Young).

The adolescents who play these games are not (for the most part) talking to their online "friends". Instead they message them quickly with impersonal questions or requests. This form of communication does not hone their interpersonal skills. They have no need for tone or inflection; they simply use the keys under their fingers for all their communication. This lack of communication will render them useless in the "real world". Most jobs require some personal interaction. If someone is unable to effectively communicate with other people there is little chance that they will be able to become successful with anything. In addition, someone who has little or no interpersonal skills is probably not going to enter into marriage. A relationship that involved empathy would be nigh impossible for someone who plays video games "full time". These addicts would be too immersed in the game to care about anything but their character in the gaming world.

In some schools many students go to the computer lab at school during their lunch or study halls. However, most of these students are not going to work on the big project due in their near future. They are going to play online games, check gaming forums and overall avoid schoolwork. There are countless examples of adolescents who could be succeeding in school, but do not because of their video game addiction. If a student is strongly addicted to video games, they can lose total interest in school. They will cut classes to play these games and they will avoid doing homework to play these games. Because of these things, their grades will slip (Young). Without a strong focus in school, these students intellectual development will be strongly hampered. There are skeptics who say that many skills in school are totally useless. However, the point of taking a trigonometry class is not only to learn the math, but how to be responsible and how to manage your time. If an adolescent loses interest in school, their future intellectual progress will be mired by their failure to learn basic academic skills in middle and high school.

On top of social and intellectual problems, video games can be a danger to the player and those around him/her. Gamers spend most of their time being sedentary. They get little to no exercise every day (DiConsiglio). This is bad in the short and long term health of this adolescent. It is unhealthy in the short term because it can lead to obesity and high blood pressure. In the long term, these gamers will have little desire to live healthy lifestyles as adults. This can become a danger later in life. The lack of exercise can increase their risk of heart attack and stroke. Being out of shape and unhealthy will make gamers a danger to themselves in the future. In addition, these gamers can become a threat to others. Many adolescents see the violence portrayed in games like "Grand Theft Auto" and think it is acceptable in real life. However, training young minds that killing and stealing are acceptable creates people who are a danger to society (Worthy). In some cases, it can lead them to committing felonies as horrible as murder.

Video games are an inherent threat to adolescents everywhere. The addiction to video games can cause young adults to become socially inept, running their prospective for jobs and friends in the future. The addiction can also compromise these peoples' interest in school, which can stunt their intellectual development. Finally, the messages of violence and debauchery shown in these games can negatively influence some adolescents to commit crimes in the real world. Video games are unequivocally dangerous to the youth of the world.

Sample Student Essay Three

In recent decades a new form of interactive media has entered the global market: video games. These games have grown into an immensely popular form of entertainment and an incredibly profitable industry. However, critics claim that playing these games, and in fact using the internet in general, is having a negative effect on modern youth. What these critics fail to recognize is the social good which the internet does, the ways in which games assist youth in developing life skills, and the relatively small number of gamers who in fact face troubles in life as a result of playing video games.

Critics of internet use have posited that youth use the web simply to goof off and play games. This is patently untrue. According to Kathryn Montgomery, president of the Center for Media Education, youth use the internet, "to register to vote, to debate issues of war and peace, even to become social activists" (Document B). The internet is also home to sites such as "freerice.com", which allows it's users to play a vocabulary game online. For each correct answer a sponsor donates ten grains of rice to the United Nation's World Food Program. So while many social critics attack the internet it ought to be celebrated. By providing youth with a medium through which they may voice their opinions and help others the internet has potential to insure that a generation of young people is not apathetic to the problems of the world.

A sense of social responsibility, however, is not the only positive which the internet and video games are instilling in youth. Games in particular assist in the development of, "cognitive skills...such as pattern recognition, spatial reasoning, and information processing" (Document D). They also force users to learn to adapt and communicate better, since in many games, particularly those which require online interaction with other people, adaptability and good communication skills are vital to victory. These social skills are vital, although often lacking in people in the modern world, and in teaching them to youth games are clearly a force for social good.

An argument often leveled against games and the internet is that they train youth to be murderers and that youth come to solely rely on them for social interaction (Documents F and A, respectively). What critics rarely acknowledge is the miniscule number of gamers and internet users who in fact end up in such extreme situations or who take violent action. While stories of reclusive college students (Document A) and violent teens (Document F) are tragic they are few and far between. Such stories are generally trumped up by advocates of anti-video game groups and by sensationalist reporters. By focusing on such rare cases and ignoring the large numbers of people who benefit from such games critics do society a disservice.

Ultimately the internet and video games are tools by which a young generation and those which follow in its wake may better themselves. To deny them such tools would be reckless and irresponsible. Therefore the only reasonable course of action is to allow, perhaps monitor but still allow these tools to be used.

Assessment of Student Responses to Free-Response Question Three:
The Effects of Computer Gaming Upon Adolescents

Sample Student Essay One:

A. Assessment of Reader One

This essay is a well-constructed argument which supports the statement that video gaming is harming adolescents. Although not perfect, the thesis statement is clear and four of the six sources are cited and documented. The student uses descriptive language to illustrate what he/she believes to be the frenzied and obsessive student and the literal pull of the games: "furious clicking mouse." The concession is clear in paragraph four, "Some may argue….". The opposing argument is dealt with quickly and dismissed. The essay concludes with a nod to technology, but encourages human interaction as opposed to the fascination with a digital universe. This essay would score a 9.

B. Assessment of Reader Two

I felt this essay had a good deal of merit. Its strengths were the fluid manner with which it incorporated citations from the documents into the core of its argument and the way in which it connected information gleaned from the sources to prior personal experiences and knowledge (e.g., the references to Super Mario brothers and to such things as cardiovascular impairment and carpal tunnel syndrome). Two other big selling points for me were the students' challenging of the perspective taken by the author of Document D and the eloquence of the essay's conclusion. There are some minor lapses in diction here and there, but I would rate this paper a 9.

Sample Student Essay Two:

A. Assessment of Reader One

This essay is also a well-constructed argument against video gaming. The writer includes some personal knowledge about the world of video games and its effect on friends in paragraph three: "Pick up games of basketball and baseball….a player in an online game can make friends and interact online." Documentation is sparse with the first instance coming after paragraph three. Only two sources are actually documented, but the reading of the essay indicates more than two are used. Although this essay is not as concise as the previous essay, it certainly is full of evidence to support the point of view. A bit more workmanlike, this essay will earn a score of 7.

B. Assessment of Reader Two

This was also a decent paper though not of the same caliber as Sample Student Essay One. The author cites several of the sources, directly or implicitly, and takes a strong stand in defense of the claim that such gaming is harmful. The student elaborates a bit upon the deleterious impact of too much gaming upon health and social well-being though his generalizations on its impact upon marriage may be a tad extreme. The author also introduces some novel commentary on instant messaging, and though the essay lacks some of the "spark" of the previous paper, it does a good job overall. I would score this a 7.

Sample Student Essay Three:

A. Assessment of Reader One

This is a competent essay which takes the "other side" or the positive aspects of the video-gaming question. The thesis is clear and uses a "pro-gaming" argument: "What these critics fail to recognize is the social good….". The sources are clearly documented, and the writer uses four of the sources to support his argument, even those which tend to be against it. The concession is clear in paragraph four—"…games…train youth to be murderers…"—yet by using the most inflammatory sources, the writer is able to defuse the opposition by stating that these instances are "few and far between." The essay is not as full as it might be, and the counter-arguments to the opposition to video gaming are large and generalized: "…to deny such tools would be reckless and irresponsible." This leads to "an argument that is generally sound but not persuasive…" (Scoring Guide, point 6).

B. Assessment of Reader Two

This final paper both challenged and qualified the claim that Internet and computer gaming is harmful to adolescents' intellectual and social development. It stressed the positive aspects of the Internet cited by Source B and added a socially conscious website of its own in freerice.com, a website that addresses world hunger. Though it qualifies the claims of the documents that connect video games to violence, suggesting that these are more the exception than the norm, this response seemed a bit too glib and dismissive of what is a significant downside to Internet and computer gaming. Though an upper-half essay, it doesn't do enough in my eyes to counter the opposing argument. I would score this a 6.

Sample Examination II

Questions 1-12. Refer to the following passage.

In the following passage a young immigrant girl tries to come to grips with a disturbing family secret.

….Chinese-Americans, when you try to understand what things in you are Chinese, how do you separate what is peculiar to childhood, to poverty, insanities, one family,
(5)   your mother who marked your growing with stories, from what is Chinese? What is Chinese tradition and what is in the movies?

If I want to learn what clothes my aunt wore, whether flashy or ordinary, I would have
(10) to begin, "Remember Father's drowned-in-the-well sister?" I cannot ask that. My mother has told me once and for all the useful parts. She will add nothing unless powered by Necessity, a riverbank that guides her life. She plants
(15) vegetable gardens rather than lawns ….

Adultery is extravagance. Could people who hatch their own chicks and eat the embryos and the heads for delicacies and boil the feet in vinegar for party food, leaving only
(20) the gravel, eating even the gizzard lining—could such people engender a prodigal aunt? To be a woman, to have a daughter in starvation time was a waste enough. My aunt could not have been the lone romantic who
(25) gave up everything for sex. Women in the old China did not choose. Some man had commanded her to lie with him and be his secret evil. I wonder whether he masked himself when he joined the raid on her family.
(30) Perhaps she had encountered him in the fields or on the mountain where the daughters-in-law collected fuel. Or perhaps he first noticed her in the marketplace. He was not a stranger because the village housed no
(35) strangers. She had to have dealings with him other than sex. Perhaps he worked an adjoining field, or he sold her the cloth for the dress she sewed and wore. His demand must have surprised, then terrified her. She obeyed him;
(40) she always did as she was told.

When the family found a young man in the next village to be her husband, she had stood tractably beside the best rooster, his proxy, and promised before they met that she would be his
(45) forever. She was lucky that she was his age and that she would be the first wife, an advantage secure now.

The other man was not, after all, much different from her husband. They both gave
(50) orders: she followed. "If you tell your family, I'll beat you. I'll kill you. Be here again next week." No one talked sex, ever. And she might have separated the rapes from the rest of living if only she did not have to buy her oil from
(55) him or gather wood in the same forest. I want her fear to have lasted just as long as the rape lasted so that the fear could have been contained. No drawn-out fear. But women at sex hazarded birth and hence lifetimes. The
(60) fear did not stop but permeated everywhere. She told the man, "I think I'm pregnant." He organized the raid against her.

On nights when my mother and father talked about their life back home, sometimes
(65) they mentioned an "outcast table" whose business they still seemed to be settling, their voices tight. In a commensal[1] tradition, where food is precious, the powerful older people made wrongdoers eat alone. Instead of letting
(70) them start separate new lives like the Japanese, who could become samurais and geishas, the Chinese family, faces averted but eyes glowering sideways, hung on to the offenders and fed them leftovers. My aunt must have
(75) lived in the same house as my parents and eaten at an outcast table. My mother spoke about the raid as if she had seen it, when she and my aunt, a daughter-in-law to a different household, should not have been living
(80) together at all. Daughters-in-law lived with their husbands' parents, not their own; a synonym for marriage in Chinese is "taking a daughter-in-law." Her husband's parents could have sold her, mortgaged her, stoned her. But
(85) they had sent her back to her own mother and father, a mysterious act hinting at disgraces not told me….

---

[1] a symbiotic relationship in which one organism benefits and the other is unaffected; in this instance, the righteous and powerful enjoy a true meal and the outcast is fed only leftovers.

From THE WOMAN WARRIOR by Maxine Hong Kingston, copyright © 1975, 1976 by Maxine Hong Kingston. Used by permission of Alfred A. Knopf, a division of Random House, Inc.

1. Which of the following BEST reflects the author's feelings about her aunt's adultery and its consequences?

   (A) abhorrence of her physical weakness and disdain for her failure to defend herself
   (B) disbelief at her naiveté and surprise at her failure to terminate the pregnancy
   (C) pity for her vulnerability and empathy for her ostracism
   (D) disgust at her promiscuity and approval of her punishment
   (E) regret at her silence and revulsion at her suicide

2. The author's primary interest in examining the events that befell her aunt has to do with

   (A) righting an injustice
   (B) restoring a reputation
   (C) exploring an identity
   (D) understanding a motive
   (E) erasing a memory

3. All of the following seem to be Old World Chinese traditions EXCEPT

   (A) prearranging a daughter's marriage
   (B) eating non-traditional animal parts as delicacies
   (C) carrying out punitive actions on a adulteress and her family
   (D) keeping women subservient and submissive
   (E) moving in with the bride's family after marriage

4. The syntax of the opening sentence is complicated by which of the following?

   (A) an introductory apostrophe
   (B) the omission of expected prepositions
   (C) the use of a rhetorical question
   (D) second-person perspective
   (E) the elliptical nature of the word "things"

5. The phrase "once and for all" (line 12) implies which of the following?

   I. That the author has pestered her mother with questions about her deceased aunt.
   II. That the stigma of the aunt's suicide has made it a topic never to be broached.
   III. That the author's mother is unwilling to provide additional details about the suicide.

   (A) II only
   (B) III only
   (C) I and II
   (D) I and III
   (E) I, II and III

6. It may be inferred by the reader that what the author's mother considers the "useful parts" (line 12) of the aunt's story would most likely exclude which of the following?

   (A) the salacious details of the assault
   (B) the punitive actions of the villagers
   (C) the discovery of her unfortunate pregnancy
   (D) the ignominious banishment by her husband's family
   (E) the stigmatizing tradition of the "outcast table"

7. Lines 14-15, "She plants vegetable gardens rather than lawns…," convey the mother's

   (A) orthodoxy
   (B) provinciality
   (C) impracticality
   (D) serenity
   (E) agrarianism

8. The shift in tone from the disbelief expressed in paragraph three (lines 16-29) to the speculation manifested in paragraph four (lines 30-40) is primarily achieved by the

   (A) use of local color: the settings of field, marketplace and village
   (B) repetition of the adverb "perhaps"
   (C) shift in focus from victim to attacker
   (D) diction that alludes to confrontation
   (E) antithetical verbs that convey threat and submission

9. The BEST interpretation of the word "tractably" (line 43) would be

   (A) indifferently
   (B) obediently
   (C) sullenly
   (D) proudly
   (E) resentfully

10. Which of the following BEST paraphrases the point the author wishes to make about her aunt's "fear" in lines 55-58?

   (A) She wishes that her aunt had been unafraid to resist her attacker.
   (B) She wishes her aunt had not been so terrified during the assault.
   (C) She wishes that her aunt had not been so afraid of his attempts at verbal intimidation.
   (D) She wishes that her aunt had found the courage to identify her assailant or to tell her family.
   (E) She wishes that her aunt could have avoided additional post-rape consequences.

11. Of the following, which BEST exemplifies the author's adept use of climactic order?

   (A) "...to childhood, to poverty, insanities, one family, your mother..." (lines 3-5)
   (B) "...hatch their own chicks and eat the embryos and heads for delicacies..." (lines 17-18)
   (C) "His demand must have surprised, then terrified her" (lines 38-39)
   (D) "'If you tell your family, I'll beat you. I'll kill you.'" (lines 50-51)
   (E) "...sold her, mortgaged her, stoned her" (line 84)

12. A feminist reading of the passage might find which of the following words ironic?

   (A) "peculiar" (line 3)
   (B) "romantic" (line 24)
   (C) "obeyed" (line 39)
   (D) "lucky" (line 45)
   (E) "glowering" (line 73)

Questions 13-27. Refer to the following passage.

To-day we rather intended to write an essay on Laziness, but were too indolent to do so.

(5) The sort of thing we had in mind to write would have been exceedingly persuasive. We intended to discourse a little in favour of a greater appreciation of Indolence as a benign factor in human affairs.

It is our observation that every time we get
(10) into trouble it is due to not having been lazy enough. Unhappily, we were born with a certain fund of energy. We have been hustling about for a number of years now, and it doesn't seem to get us anything but tribulation.
(15) Henceforward we are going to make a determined effort to be more languid and demure. It is the bustling man who always gets put on committees, who is asked to solve the problems of other people and neglect his own.
(20) The man who is really, thoroughly, and philosophically slothful is the only thoroughly happy man. It is the happy man who benefits the world. The conclusion is inescapable.

We remember a saying about the meek
(25) inheriting the earth. The truly meek man is the lazy man. He is too modest to believe that any ferment and hubbub of his can ameliorate the earth or assuage the perplexities of humanity.

O. Henry said once that one should be
(30) careful to distinguish laziness from dignified repose. Alas, that was a mere quibble. Laziness is always dignified, it is always reposeful. Philosophical laziness, we mean. The kind of laziness that is based upon a carefully reasoned
(35) analysis of experience. Acquired laziness. We have no respect for those who were born lazy; it is like being born a millionaire: they cannot appreciate their bliss. It is the man who has hammered his laziness out of the stubborn
(40) material of life whom we chant praise and alleluia.

The laziest man we know—we do not like to mention his name, as the brutal world does not yet recognize sloth at its community

(45) value—is one of the greatest poets in this country; one of the keenest satirists; one of the most rectilinear thinkers. He began life in the customary hustling way. He was always too busy to enjoy himself. He became surrounded
(50) by eager people who came to him to solve their problems. "It's a queer thing," he said sadly; "no one ever comes to me asking for help in solving my problems." Finally the light broke upon him. He stopped answering letters,
(55) buying lunches for casual friends and visitors from out of town, he stopped lending money to old college pals and frittering his time away on all the useless minor matters that pester the good-natured. He sat down in a secluded café
(60) with his cheek against a seidel of dark beer and began to caress the universe with his intellect.

The most damning argument against the Germans is that they were not lazy enough. In the middle of Europe, a thoroughly
(65) disillusioned, indolent and delightful old continent, the Germans were a dangerous mass of energy and bumptious push. If the Germans had been as lazy as indifferent, and as righteously-laissez-fairish as their neighbours,
(70) the world would have been spared a great deal.

People respect laziness. If once you get a reputation for complete, immovable, and reckless indolence the world will leave you to your own thoughts, which are generally rather
(75) interesting....

Mind your business is a good counsel; but mind your idleness also. It's a tragic thing to make a business of your mind. Save your mind to amuse yourself with.

(80) The lazy man does not stand in the way of progress. When he sees progress roaring down upon him he steps nimbly out of the way. The lazy man doesn't (in the vulgar phrase) pass the buck. He lets the buck pass him. We have
(85) always secretly envied our lazy friends. Now we are going to join them. We have burned our boats or our bridges or whatever it is that one burns on the eve of a momentous decision.

Writing on this congenial topic has roused
(90) us up to quite a pitch of enthusiasm and energy.

13. Which of the following BEST articulates the author's thesis?

    (A) "It is our observation that every time we get into trouble it is due to not having been lazy enough." (lines 9-11)
    (B) "The man who is really, thoroughly, and philosophically slothful is the only thoroughly happy man." (lines 20-22)
    (C) "Laziness is always dignified, it is always reposeful." (lines 31-32)
    (D) "People respect laziness." (line 71)
    (E) "The lazy man does not stand in the way of progress." (lines 80-81)

14. The author's use of the collective "we" is likely intended to do which of the following?

    I. Establish himself as a proponent of and advocate for lethargy.
    II. Echo the characteristic indolence of royalty or the aristocracy.
    III. Fit the conventional style of an editorial.

    (A) I only
    (B) III only
    (C) I and II
    (D) II and III
    (E) I, II and III

15. The diction of the passage establishes which of the following contrasts?

    (A) pride and humility
    (B) activity and idleness
    (C) reason and irrationality
    (D) progress and regression
    (E) serenity and discord

16. In lines 1-19 the author reinforces his natural inclination to avoid action through all of the following EXCEPT

    (A) verbs that imply intent rather than action
    (B) a humorous vow to be even more lethargic
    (C) the equation of industry with troubles and unwanted involvements
    (D) a chronological record of postponements
    (E) the use of passive constructions to reinforce indolence

17. Lines 20-23—"The man who is really, thoroughly, and philosophically slothful…. The conclusion is inescapable"—exemplify which of the following rhetorical techniques?

    (A) *ad hominem* argument
    (B) syllogism
    (C) ironical understatement
    (D) anaphora
    (E) causal analysis

18. The conclusion that to the author seems "inescapable" (line 23) is that

    (A) happiness is illusory
    (B) initiative insures success
    (C) sloth is beneficial
    (D) accomplishment breeds arrogance
    (E) meekness leads to peace

19. Line 33, "Philosophical laziness, we mean," offers an example of a(n)

    (A) qualification
    (B) conjecture
    (C) assertion
    (D) maxim
    (E) generalization

20. The most persuasive example of "Philosophical laziness" as it is defined in lines 33-35 would be epitomized by which of the following individuals?

    (A) the "bustling man" mentioned in lines 17-19
    (B) the "truly meek man" in lines 25-28
    (C) "those who were born lazy" in line 36
    (D) "one of the greatest poets" in lines 45-61
    (E) the "Germans" in lines 62-70

21. The syntax of lines 54-59—"He stopped answering letters… and frittering his time away on all the useless minor matters that pester the good-natured"—is characterized by a series of

    (A) gerundive phrases
    (B) participial phrases
    (C) prepositional phrases
    (D) infinitive phrases
    (E) appositive phrases

22. In lines 81-82—"When he sees progress roaring down upon him he steps nimbly out of the way" —the author depicts progress as

    (A) practical and necessary
    (B) methodical and steady
    (C) innovative and beneficial
    (D) noble and edifying
    (E) inexorable and threatening

23. Lines 82-84—"The lazy man doesn't (in the vulgar phrase) pass the buck. He lets the buck pass him"—exemplify which of the following figures of speech?

    (A) personification
    (B) hyperbole
    (C) chiasmus
    (D) allusion
    (E) irony

24. Lines 86-88—"We have burned our boats or our bridges or whatever it is that one burns on the eve of a momentous decision"—are primarily intended to demonstrate the author's

    (A) resolve to be languid
    (B) ignorance of popular idiom
    (C) self-destructive spontaneity
    (D) flair for the metaphorical
    (E) tendency to be melodramatic

25. In light of the context in which it appears, which of the following should NOT be viewed as ironic?

    (A) that the indolence of the author prevented him from writing an essay on laziness
    (B) that the author's troubles arise from not being lazy enough
    (C) that the type of man whom the author admires most has actually labored to be lazy
    (D) that writing on the topic of laziness seems to have invigorated the author
    (E) that the lazy man does not impede progress

26. In the course of his essay, the author alludes to all of the following EXCEPT

    (A) the First World War
    (B) other prominent writers
    (C) the New Testament
    (D) the Industrial Revolution
    (E) a well-known adage

27. The tone of the passage is BEST labeled

    (A) disapproving and derisive
    (B) abashed and resigned
    (C) tongue-in-cheek and droll
    (D) rueful and apologetic
    (E) embittered and envious

Questions 28-40. Refer to the following passage.

In the following article, published in Time magazine in 1945, the author, James Agee, reflects upon the consequences of America's using the atomic bomb to end the Second World War.

The greatest and most terrible of wars was ending, this week, in the echoes of an enormous event—an event so much more enormous that, relative to it, the war itself

(5) shrank to minor significance. The knowledge of victory was as charged with sorrow and doubt as with joy and gratitude. More fearful responsibilities, more crucial liabilities rested on the victors even than on the vanquished.

(10) In what they said and did, men were still, as in the aftershock of a great wound, bemused and only semi-articulate, whether they were soldiers or scientists, or great statesmen, or the simplest of men. But in the dark depths of their

(15) minds and hearts, huge forms moved and silently arrayed themselves: Titans,[1] arranging out of the chaos an age in which victory was already only the shout of a child in the street.

With the controlled splitting of the atom,

(20) humanity, already profoundly perplexed and disunified, was brought inescapably into a new age in which all thoughts and things were split—and far from controlled. As most men realized, the first atomic bomb was a merely

(25) pregnant threat, a merely infinitesimal promise.

All thoughts and things were split. The sudden achievement of victory was a mercy, to the Japanese no less than to the United Nations; but mercy born of a ruthless force

(30) beyond anything in human chronicle. The race had been won, the weapon had been used by those on whom civilization could best hope to depend; but the demonstration of power against living creatures instead of dead matter created

(35) a bottomless wound in the living conscience of the race. The rational mind had won the most Promethean[2] of its conquests over nature, and had put into the hands of common man the fire and force of the sun itself.

(40) Was man equal to the challenge? In an instant, without warning, the present had become the unthinkable future. Was there hope in that future, and if so, where did hope lie?

Even as men saluted the greatest and most

(45) grimly Pyrrhic[3] of victories in all the gratitude and good spirit they could muster, they recognized that the discovery which had done most to end the worst of wars might also, quite conceivably, end all wars—if only man could

(50) learn its control and use.

The promise of good and evil bordered alike on the infinite—with this further, terrible split in the fact: that upon a people already so nearly drowned in materialism even in peace-

(55) time, the good uses of this power might easily bring disaster as prodigious as the evil. The bomb rendered all decisions made so far, at Yalta and at Potsdam,[4] mere trivial dams across tributary rivulets. When the bomb split

(60) open the universe and revealed the prospect of the infinitely extraordinary, it also revealed the oldest, simplest, commonest, most neglected and most important of facts: that each man is eternally and above all else responsible for his

(65) own soul, and, in the terrible words of the Psalmist, that no man may deliver his brother, nor make agreement unto God for him.[5]

Man's fate has forever been shaped between the hands of reason and spirit, now in

(70) collaboration, again in conflict. Now reason and spirit meet on final ground. If either or anything is to survive, they must find a way to create an indissoluble partnership.

---

[1] pre-Olympian deities whose existence dates back almost to the creation of the world out of nothingness

[2] the Titan who steals fire from Olympus and gives it to humans, an act for which he is severely punished

[3] Greek general whose victory at Asculum in 279 B.C. against the Romans cost him such a heavy loss of life that he bemoaned it

[4] meetings of the victorious heads-of-state to discuss the reestablishment of post-war Europe

[5] Psalms 49:7

28. The primary unifying device of the author's argument is his use of

    (A) the extended metaphor of fission
    (B) classical and Biblical allusions
    (C) horrifying images of destruction
    (D) dashes and rhetorical questions
    (E) foreboding diction

29. In the opening paragraph the author primarily dramatizes his fears about the future consequence of nuclear weaponry through

    (A) onomatopoeia
    (B) comparative adjectives
    (C) antitheses
    (D) action verbs
    (E) hyperbole

30. In light of the context in which it appears, the BEST equivalent for "bemused" (line 11) would be

    (A) entertained
    (B) injured
    (C) shocked
    (D) muted
    (E) amazed

31. The metaphor in lines 17-18—"…in which victory was already only the shout of a child in the street"—implies that

    (A) children could not comprehend the ghastliness of the new weapon
    (B) children were relieved that they would not have to fight in the war
    (C) only adults honored the somber nature of the occasion
    (D) most believed the defeat of Japan would not end with the dropping of the atomic bomb
    (E) for many the elation of victory was tempered by a bleak nuclear reality

32. The phrases "pregnant threat" (line 25) and "merely infinitesimal promise" (line 25) are intended to imply which of the following about the bomb dropped upon Hiroshima?

    (A) that it was rudimentary in design and not fully developed when it was deployed
    (B) that it killed many innocent civilians, including mothers
    (C) that reports of its destructive effect were grossly exaggerated
    (D) that it would likely not end the conflict but spawn additional hostilities
    (E) that it would engender a potential for an as yet unimaginable destruction

33. The author likely labels the development of the atomic bomb as "the most Promethean of [man's] conquests over nature" (lines 36-37) on account of which of the following?

    I. The enormous collaborative efforts of the scientific community in creating it.
    II. The brazen, even illicit, tampering by scientists with the most elemental source of power.
    III. The fact that the bomb had been created by the country most morally suited to police it.

    (A) I only
    (B) II only
    (C) I and III
    (D) II and III
    (E) I, II and III

34. The author suggests in lines 44-67 that, upon the initial use of an atomic weapon, humans experienced all of the following epiphanies EXCEPT

    (A) that this terrifying new weapon might, ironically, deter war as well as end it
    (B) that the potential peacetime uses of atomic fission might pose dangers as disastrous as its wartime application did
    (C) that in creating the atomic bomb humans had committed a damnable transgression
    (D) that atomic fission created grave new moral responsibilities for humans
    (E) that discussions about the division of post-war power had been rendered moot by this powerful new weapon

35. The effectiveness of the metaphor "mere trivial dams across tributary rivulets" (lines 58-59) —used to describe the Yalta and Potsdam conferences— lies in its

    (A) alliterative nature
    (B) water imagery
    (C) understated diction
    (D) sprung rhythm
    (E) internal rhyme

36. The phrase "split open the universe" (lines 59-60) is most accurately labeled a(n)

    (A) ironical understatement
    (B) caesura
    (C) paradox
    (D) hyperbole
    (E) personification

37. The diction and figurative language of the concluding paragraph portray man's fate as

    (A) unknown
    (B) malleable
    (C) disintegrating
    (D) predetermined
    (E) ambiguous

38. The author describes the moral after-effects of the bomb-dropping upon the United States' citizenry in words usually associated with

    (A) trauma and injury
    (B) salvation and deliverance
    (C) conscience and remorse
    (D) justice and righteousness
    (E) sadness and compassion

39. Of the following, which BEST conveys the sense of helplessness and lack of control that humans experienced with the splitting of the atom?

    (A) "In what they said and did, men were still, as in the aftershock of a great wound…" (lines 10-11)
    (B) "…humanity, already profoundly perplexed and disunified, was brought inescapably into a new age…" (lines 20-22)
    (C) "…had put into the hands of common man the fire and force of the sun itself" (lines 38-39)
    (D) "…the discovery…might also, quite conceivably, end all wars—if only man could learn its control and use" (lines 47-50)
    (E) "…no man may deliver his brother, nor make agreement unto God for him" (lines 66-67)

40. The author's attitude towards man's ability to harness and control nuclear energy is BEST characterized as

    (A) skeptical
    (B) certain
    (C) sanguine
    (D) contemptuous
    (E) ambivalent

Questions 41-54. Refer to the following passage.

....There is a popular superstition that "realism" asserts itself in the cataloguing of a great number of material objects, in explaining mechanical processes, the methods of
(5) operating manufactures and trades, and in minutely and unsparingly describing physical sensation. But is not realism, more than it is anything else, an attitude of mind on the part of the writer toward his material, a vague
(10) definition of the sympathy and candor with which he accepts, rather than chooses his theme? Is the story of a banker who is unfaithful to his wife and who ruins himself by speculation in trying to gratify the caprices of
(15) his mistresses, at all reinforced by a masterly exposition of the banking system, our whole system of credits, the methods of the Stock Exchange?

The automatic reply to this question is the
(20) name of Balzac[1]. Yes, certainly, Balzac tried out the value of literalness in the novel, tried it out to the uttermost, as Wagner did the value of scenic literalness in the music drama. He tried it, too, with the passion of discovery, with the
(25) inflamed zest of an unexampled curiosity. If the heat of that furnace could not give hardness and sharpness to material accessories, no other brain will ever do it. To reproduce on paper the actual city of Paris; the houses, the upholstery,
(30) the food, the wines, the game of pleasure, the game of business, the game of finance: a stupendous ambition—but, after all, unworthy of an artist. In exactly so far as he succeeded in pouring out on his pages that mass of brick and
(35) mortar and furniture and proceedings in bankruptcy, in exactly so far he defeated his end. The things by which he still lives, the types of greed and avarice and ambition and vanity and lost innocence of heart which he
(40) created—are as vital to-day as they were then. But their material surroundings, upon which he expended such labor and pains...the eye glides over them. We have had too much of the interior decorator and the "romance of
(45) business" since his day. The city he built on paper is already crumbling. Stevenson said he wanted to blue-pencil a great deal of Balzac's "presentation"—and he loved him beyond all modern novelists....
(50) In this discussion another great name

automatically occurs. Tolstoi[2] was almost as great a lover of material things as Balzac, almost as much interested in the way dishes were cooked, and people were dressed, and
(55) houses were furnished. But there is this determining difference; the clothes, the dishes, the moving, haunting interiors of those old Moscow houses, are always so much a part of the emotions of the people that they are
(60) perfectly synthesized; they seem to exist, not so much in the author's mind, as in the emotional penumbra of the characters themselves. When it is fused like this, literalness ceases to be literalness—it is merely
(65) part of the experience.

If the novel is a form of imaginative art, it cannot be at the same time a brilliant form of journalism. Out of the teeming, gleaming stream of the present, it must select the eternal
(70) material of art. There are hopeful signs that some of the younger writers are trying to break away from mere verisimilitude, and, following the development of modern painting, to interpret imaginatively the material and social
(75) investiture of their characters; to present their scene by suggestion rather than by enumeration. The higher processes of art are all processes of simplification. The novelist must learn to write, and then he must unlearn it; just
(80) as the modern painter learns to draw, and then learns when utterly to disregard his accomplishment, when to subordinate it to a higher and truer effect. In this direction only, it seems to me, can the novel develop into
(85) anything more varied and perfect than all of the many novels that have gone before.

One of the very earliest American novels might well serve as a suggestion to later writers. In *The Scarlet Letter* how truly in the
(90) spirit of art is the *mise-en-scène*[3] presented. That drudge, the theme-writing high school student, could scarcely be sent there for information regarding the manners and dress and interiors of the Puritans. The material
(95) investiture of the story is presented as if unconsciously; by the reserved, fastidious hand of an artist, not by the gaudy fingers of a showman or the mechanical industry of a department store window-dresser. As I
(100) remember it, in the twilight melancholy of that book, in its consistent mood, one can scarcely ever see the actual surroundings of the people; one feels them, rather, in the dusk....

---

[1] French novelist and playwright, 1799-1850

[2] Russian novelist/short story writer, 1828-1910

[3] here, the physical setting of Hawthorne's novel

41. The first indication of the author's distaste for realism that is not "perfectly synthesized" with the emotions of a novel's characters is revealed by which of the following phrases?

    (A) "popular superstition" (line 1)
    (B) "vague definition" (lines 9-10)
    (C) "unexampled curiosity" (line 25)
    (D) "stupendous ambition" (line 32)
    (E) "mere verisimilitude" (line 72)

42. In questioning the appropriateness of realism in imaginative art in the opening paragraph, the author relies on all of the following EXCEPT

    (A) quotation marks around a word that suggest skepticism
    (B) an opening sentence that pokes fun at realism by simultaneously listing and imitating its traits
    (C) an initial assertion followed by a mild disclaimer
    (D) a rhetorical question that anecdotally illustrates an extraneous use of realistic detail
    (E) the presentation of an antithetical perspective

43. Lines 23-28 compare Balzac's imagination to a(n)

    (A) opera
    (B) kiln
    (C) romance
    (D) explorer
    (E) obsession

44. In recounting the "realism" of Balzac's Paris (lines 28-33), the author relies upon

    (A) participles
    (B) appositives
    (C) prepositional phrases
    (D) descriptive adjectives
    (E) onomatopoeic diction

45. The phrase, "the eye glides over them" (lines 42-43) BEST exemplifies the author's use of

    (A) imagery
    (B) understatement
    (C) synecdoche
    (D) paradox
    (E) allusion

46. The phrase "blue-pencil" (line 47) likely means

    (A) annotate
    (B) strike
    (C) highlight
    (D) footnote
    (E) question

47. The author's preference for Tolstoi's "realism" over that of Balzac is founded upon

    (A) Tolstoi's use of domestic detail rather than detail from the world of business and finance
    (B) her own preference for the city of Moscow over the city of Paris
    (C) the manner in which Tolstoi integrates setting as part of the characters' experience
    (D) her own dislike for the corrupting vices of Balzac's characters
    (E) her own distaste for the zest and zeal with which Balzac promoted his realism

48. Lines 68-70, "Out of the teeming, gleaming stream of the present, it must select the eternal material of art," compare the manner in which a novelist chooses detail to the work of a(n)

    (A) prospector
    (B) blacksmith
    (C) shopper
    (D) fisherman
    (E) recruiter

49. In noting the trend of more contemporary writers to eschew "mere verisimilitude" (line 72), the author makes use of a parallel series of

    (A) noun clauses
    (B) infinitive phrases
    (C) adjectival clauses
    (D) participial phrases
    (E) appositives

50. The primary difference between paragraph four (lines 66-86) and the paragraphs that precede it lies in its

    (A) shift in focus from writing to painting
    (B) movement from ancient writers to more contemporary practitioners
    (C) resignation to the fact that "literalness" cannot be unlearned
    (D) expression of sentiment in a more didactic tone
    (E) reversal of its earlier assessment of the place of realism in imaginative writing

51. Which of the following BEST captures the author's point about the artist and realism as it is expressed in lines 70-83?

    (A) Realism is permissible in moderation.
    (B) Realism is more apropos in painting than it is in the novel.
    (C) Realism is a bad habit that all artists, regardless of genre, must unlearn.
    (D) Realism, as a technique, must not interfere with the artist's greater vision.
    (E) Realism is a journalistic technique that has no business in the novel.

52. Lines 94-99—"The material investiture of the story…a department store window-dresser"— are intended to do which of the following?

    I. Compliment Hawthorne as a writer whose economy of detail allows him to achieve a "truer effect."
    II. Sardonically deride writers who clutter their work with superfluous scenic detail.
    III. Contrast the imagination of a celebrated American novel with the prosaic writing assigned in schools.

    (A) I only
    (B) III only
    (C) I and II
    (D) II and III
    (E) I, II and III

53. The author likely uses the words "twilight" (line 100) and "dusk" (line 103) to illustrate the

    (A) somber and ascetic garb of the Puritans
    (B) ambiguity of detail that makes Hawthorne's novel successful
    (C) difficulty she has in recalling the plot-line of the novel
    (D) time of day at which pivotal scenes of the novel take place
    (E) obscurity into which this early American novel has faded

54. Which of the following adverbs may be perceived as having a double meaning?

    (A) "unsparingly" (line 6)
    (B) "masterly" (line 15)
    (C) "automatically" (line 51)
    (D) "unconsciously" (line 96)
    (E) "scarcely" (line 101)

Section II

Question One

(Suggested time–40 minutes. This question counts as one-third of the total essay section score.)

The following passage follows a paragraph in which the author has recounted the exploits of a boyhood friend whose life-path had been starkly different from his own. Read the passage carefully. Then, in a well-organized essay, discuss what the passage reveals about the way(s) in which aging has modified the author's youthful attitude towards life and analyze how his rhetorical strategies convey this.

    For there were times, full many a year ago, when my brains were full of bison and grizzly bear, mustang and big-horn, Blackfoot and Pawnee, and hopes of wild adventure in the Far West, which I shall never see; for ere I was three-and-twenty, I discovered, plainly enough, that my lot was to stay at home and earn my bread in a very quiet way; that England was to be henceforth my prison or my palace as I
(5)   should choose to make it; and I have made it, by Heaven's help, the latter.
    I will confess to you, though, that in those first heats of youth, this little England—or rather this little patch of moor in which I have struck roots as firm as the wild fir-trees do—looked at moments rather like a prison than a palace; that my foolish young heart would sigh, "Oh, that I had wings" not as a dove, to fly home to its nest and croodle,[1] but as an eagle, to swoop away over land and sea, in a rampant and
(10)   self-glorifying fashion, on which I now look back as altogether unwholesome and undesirable. But the thirst for adventure and excitement was strong in me, as perhaps it ought to be in all at twenty-one. Others went out to see the glorious new worlds of the West, the glorious old worlds of the East—why should not I? Others rambled over Alps and Apennines, Italian picture-galleries and palaces, filling their minds with fair memories—why should not I?....It is not learned in a day, the golden lesson of the old
(15)   Collect,[2] to "love the thing which is commanded, and desire that which is promised." Not in a day, but in fifteen years one can spell out a little of its worth; and when one finds oneself on the wrong side of forty, and the first grey hairs begin to show on the temples, and one can no longer jump as high as one's third button—scarcely, alas! to any button at all; and what with innumerable sprains, bruises, soakings, and chillings, one's lower limbs feel in a cold thaw, much like an old post-horse's, why, one makes a virtue of
(20)   necessity: and if one still lusts after sights, takes the nearest, and looks for wonders, not in the Himalayas or Lake Ngami, but in the turf on the lawn and the brook in the park....
    For there it is, friend, the whole infinite miracle of nature in every tuft of grass, if we have only eyes to see it, and can disabuse our minds of that tyrannous phantom of size. Only recollect that great and small are but relative terms; that, in truth, nothing is great or small save in proportion to the quantity of
(25)   creative thought which has been exercised in making it; that the fly who basks upon one of the trilithons[3] of Stonehenge is, in truth, infinitely greater than all Stonehenge together, though he may measure a tenth of an inch, and the stone of which he sits five-and-twenty feet....

---

[1] To huddle and shiver
[2] In Christian liturgy, a short general prayer
[3] A prehistoric structure consisting of two standing stones supporting a third lying across them.

<u>Question Two</u>

(Suggested time—40 minutes. This question counts as one-third of the total essay section score.)

Hannah Arendt, in her essay "Ideology and Terror: A Novel Form of Government," makes the following observation: "…the greatness, but also the great perplexity, of laws in free society is that they only tell what one should not, but never what one should do."

Take a moment to reflect on the preceding observation. Then, in a well-organized essay, examine both the contradiction and the moral dilemma inherent in Arendt's claim. Use your reading, studies, experience or observation to develop your argument.

Question Three

Reading Time: 15 minutes
Suggested Writing Time: 40 minutes

(This question counts as one-third of the total essay section score.)

Directions:

The following prompt is based on the accompanying six sources.

This question requires you to integrate a variety of sources into a coherent, well-written essay. *Refer to the sources to support your position; avoid paraphrase or summary. Your argument should be central; the sources should support this argument.*

Remember to attribute both direct and indirect citations.

Introduction:

Over the last decade schools across America have been forced to confront an increasing incidence of violence, ranging from bullying to bias-motivated crimes to tragic shootings on school campuses. The resultant clamor for greater school security has included calls for everything from increases in security personnel to the installation of surveillance cameras and metal detectors, from training in conflict resolution to the psychological profiling of students. However, is ensuring a safe educational environment for America's students a technological issue or a social one? Is vigilance best served by screening for weapons or screening for potentially unstable students?

Assignment:

Read the following sources (including any introductory information) carefully. **Then, in an essay that synthesizes at least three of the sources for support, take a position that defends, challenges or qualifies the claim that insuring students the right to a secure learning environment is less an issue of technological deterrence than it is of social deterrence, and that true security can only be assured by identifying and monitoring students who pose a potential threat to the greater school community.**

<u>Document A</u>

Schier, Helga. *The Causes of School Violence*. Edina, MN: Abdo, 2008: 86-87.

It seems evident that weapons should be banned from schools. Some school districts have imposed strict gun and weapon control policies. It is much more likely that a conflict among students will escalate into physical violence and result in injury if weapons are involved. But the increased security necessary to enforce such a ban may involve undesirable procedures and side effects. Stationing uniformed security officers around a school and installing security cameras or metal detectors to insure that the ban is not broken may increase the atmosphere of fear and distrust. In turn, this environment might spur more violence. Critics of such measures note that a lockdown mentality better suits a prison than an educational institution meant to foster creativity and curiosity. Enforcing a weapons ban by a zero-tolerance philosophy brings with it an entire set of problematic issues of its own….

Reprinted with the permission from ABDO Publishing.

Document B

Newman, Katherine S. "Before the Rampage: What Can be Done." *The Chronicle of Higher Education* 53.35 (May 4, 2007): B.20. Online http://proquest.umi.com/pdqweb?index=44&did=1283159801&SrchMode=1&sid=1&Fmt=... .

....The desire to protect a student's privacy or to avoid influencing next year's teachers with news of this year's infractions generally means that disciplinary records and other vital information are simply discarded when students move across institutional boundaries or from middle school to high school—and particularly from high school to college....What do any of us know of the students in our high schools?

There are good reasons for us to be in the dark. In high school contexts, we want to avoid what sociologists call "labeling." We do not want one bad year to predispose teachers to expect the next one to be equally troubled. The Americans with Disabilities Act teaches us that people with mental problems can lead productive lives and should be shielded from discrimination. But we pay a high price for clearing the slate, and an even higher price for the civil liberties that prevent us from locking up someone who is simply writing scary stories or sending bizarre e-mail messages.. We strip information from the system that might yield clues to an unraveling mind when we destroy disciplinary records. We run the risk of a catastrophe when we hit the limits of what we can do to push someone into therapy.....

RAMPAGE: THE SOCIAL ROOTS OF SCHOOL SHOOTINGS. Reprinted with permission from Katherine S. Newman.

Document C

Document D

Thomas, R. Murray. *Violence in America's Schools: Understanding, Prevention, and Responses*. Westport, CT: Praeger, 2006: 45.

Security concerns have become high-priority considerations in architects' school designs. For example, when Supai Middle School in Scottsdale (Arizona) was razed and rebuilt in 2002, it was constructed in a courtyard style that required visitors to enter through the office. Previously, visitors could wander around the campus without reporting to the office. Under a similar plan, the aging elementary school in Tualatin (Oregon) was replaced in 2004. The new school consisted of a single building, with the office by the main door so the staff could control who came and went. In contrast, the old campus had several buildings, allowing people to go directly to classrooms and avoid the office. To cope with the problem of having multiple buildings to monitor, officials at Sandy High School in the Oregon Trail School District installed a thirty-two camera surveillance system. And the new high school in Clackamas (Oregon) was built to optimize clear lines of sight through corridors, avoiding small alcoves and places with blocked views; a door-locking system enabled the staff to put the entire 2,000-student body on lockdown within seconds (Lopez, 2005).

Officials also make schools safer when they:

Enclose the campus with a robust fence that forces people to consciously trespass, rather than allowing uninhibited, casual entry.

Install classroom doors that teachers can lock from either the inside or the outside.

Ensure that the school building and classroom areas can be locked off from the gym and other facilities that are used during off hours.

Provide a drop off/pick up lane for buses only.

Add secure skylights that allow light in but are less vulnerable to entry than typical windows.

Minimize the number of flat roofs from which an assailant could fire a gun.

Locate buildings and other student gathering areas back from streets, driveways, or parking areas by at least 50 feet.

Install security alarms in administrative offices and rooms containing high-value property, such as computers, VCRs, shop equipment, laboratory supplies, and musical instruments (Green, 1999).

Document E

Larkin, Ralph W. *Comprehending Columbine*. Philadelphia: Temple UP, 2007: 214-215.

The following selection summarizes the principal of Columbine High School's response—Columbine was the site of a tragic campus massacre in 1999—to suggestions he should have foreseen the tragedy.

DeAngelis is correct when he avers that there is no way he could have anticipated the assault on Columbine High School. He pointed out that he had no information about Dylan Klebold's and Eric Harris's arrest and remand to a diversion program, although his ignorance has been disputed by others. Until after the shootings, he was unaware of the existence of Eric's Trenchcoat Mafia web site that contained threats directed at the school....Over the past twenty years there have been approximately thirty rampage shootings in American middle and high schools, an average of about 1½ per year. They are extremely rare occurrences. Yet for every rampage shooting, there are literally thousands of verbalized threats and millions of discussions among students in which they fantasize about trashing their schools....

DeAngelis stated that he was in touch with FBI profilers. The problems associated with profiling of school assaults are manifold: first, it individualizes what is essentially an issue of social relationships. Of the twenty-seven rampage shooters documented by Newman (1999), nineteen were socially marginalized among their peers compared to fifteen who evinced severe psychological disorders and fourteen who were abused or neglected or had other home-related problems....Second, and worse, is that profiling ignores the etiology of rampage shootings....That is, the shooters perceived themselves as punishing peers or teachers that had done them wrong. Third is the problem of labeling. The major problem with profiling is the false positive. Certainly the Columbine shootings were retaliatory violence. For every rampage shooter, however, there are tens of thousands, perhaps hundreds of thousands, of students who fit the profile. It further victimizes students who, for whatever reason, dislike or are alienated from the school and are otherwise socially marginalized....

Document F

Fraser, Don. "Proactive Prevention." *American School and University* 79.6 (Feb 2007): 49.
Online http:proquest.umt.com.pdqweb/index=67&sid=1&srchmode=1&vinst=PROD&fmt=3&st.... .

....About 70 percent of the nation's schools do not use security cameras. These devices can be an integral component for protecting public safety; they can deter illicit activities, create a visual record of incidents and provide an early warning of potential hazards....The best approach is to install cameras in areas that are common violence "hot spots"—gyms, cafeterias, hallways, and outside school buildings.

Video surveillance technology can alert security personnel of potential safety concerns. Cameras can be programmed to identify suspicious activity and alert authorities immediately. For example, if a system detects someone loitering on school grounds, a signal can be sent to a security officer, who can take control of the surveillance camera to investigate further. The security system can also be used to establish a perimeter around the campus so that authorities are notified instantly if someone enters the premises during the school day. Instead of relying on security personnel to catch suspicious activity, video systems provide a constant means to identify and thwart threat.

Technology alone will not stem the threat of violence in schools. The more parents are involved in their children's lives and their school communities, the less likely their children are to behave violently in school. Schools should encourage parents to watch whom their children are spending time with in and out of school. Foster an environment where parents can communicate regularly with one another to share concerns,

Parents and teachers should pay attention to changes in a child's behavior. Warning signs may include a child's developing an obsession with violence or weapons, experiencing a significant drop in grades, or avoiding school and other activities....

Sample Exam Two: Explications and Answers

Précis and Explication of Passage One:
From Maxine Hong-Kingston's *The Woman Warrior*

From the opening query, in which the narrator musingly poses the question "….Chinese-Americans, when you try to understand what things in you are Chinese, how do you separate what is peculiar to childhood, to poverty, insanities, one family, your mother who marked your growing with stories, from what is Chinese?" (lines 1-6), the narrator establishes her interest in exploring her identity, in separating the elements of her New World immigrant existence from those belonging to her Old World heritage. In this particular episode, the author focuses upon a story, told to her by her mother, of an unwed aunt who became pregnant, was shunned and humiliated by the villagers, and who then took her life by throwing herself down a well. However, in light of the ignominious nature of the episode, the mother clearly tells her only the parts that might serve as a moral exemplum, what the author wryly labels the "useful parts" (line 12). The amusing observation in lines 14-15—"She plants vegetable gardens rather than lawns…"—metaphorically conveys the cultural and generational differences between mother and daughter.

The terse observation, "Adultery is extravagance" (line 16), that opens the third paragraph prefaces the author's bewildered query, "Could people who hatch their own chicks and eat the embryos and the heads for delicacies and boil the feet in vinegar for party food, leaving only the gravel, eating even the gizzard lining—could such people engender a prodigal aunt?" (lines 16-22). Clearly, the adultery committed by her aunt is antithetical to the economy shown in their eating habits, forcing the author incredulously to wonder whether her aunt could have possibly been "the lone romantic who gave up everything for sex" (lines 24-25). Aware of the traditional subservience of women in Chinese culture, she elects to imagine that "Some man had commanded her to lie with him and be his secret evil" (lines 26-28), a man who then hypocritically concealed his identity and took part in the punitive raid carried out by the villagers against her family.

With the fourth paragraph, the author begins speculating about the circumstances that might have preceded, even accounted for, the assault. Through a series of clauses that begin with or contain the adverb "perhaps," the author posits scenarios in which the victim and her seducer might have first encountered each other:

> Perhaps she had encountered him in the fields or on the mountain where the daughters-in-law collected fuel. Or perhaps he first noticed her in the marketplace. He was not a stranger because the village housed no strangers. She had to have dealings with him other than sex. Perhaps he worked an adjoining field, or he sold her the cloth for the dress she sewed and wore (lines 30-38).

Regardless of the circumstance, in the author's eyes the sexual relationship was not consensual but a submission to tradition and power. When the family, following the long-held tradition of arranged marriages, secures her aunt a husband in the form of a man from a neighboring village, she stands "tractably beside the best rooster, his proxy, and promises[s]…that she [will] be his forever" (lines 43-45). Though she has never met the man, she is considered "lucky" (line 45) in that they are of similar age and he is still unmarried. Unfortunately, despite her marital vow, she continues to be victimized by her attacker, whose threats of personal violence and public exposure keep her submissive. When she becomes pregnant with the abuser's child, he righteously, if hypocritically, organizes the raid against her. The author's empathy for her aunt comes across in lines 55-58, "I want her fear to have lasted just as long as the rape lasted so that the fear could have been contained," but, given her aunt's suicide, it is a futile empathy. Her use of the present tense shows how strongly she would like to rectify this injustice, to spare her aunt this pain, but the finality of the rape and her aunt's suicide make this a fantasy.

In the concluding paragraph of the passage, the author discusses the "outcast table" to which her aunt, having been rejected by her husband's parents, was relegated; the table at which "the powerful older people made wrongdoers eat alone " (lines 68-69); the table at which her own family, their "faces averted but eyes glowering sideways, hung on to the [offender] and fed [her] leftovers" (lines 72-74). This ostracism, she concludes, hints at another mystery since "Her husband's parents could have sold her, mortgaged her, stoned her. But they had sent her back to her own mother and father..." (lines 83-86), a decision, she suggests "[hints] at disgraces not told [her]..." (lines 85-86).

Hong-Kingston's memoir of her aunt conjures thoughts of fictional counterparts such as Hester Prynne and Tess Durbeyfield, women who too bear the burden of an unwanted rape or an unlooked for pregnancy. Whether truth or fiction, they serve as sober reminders of the intolerance often directed at such women by society and even family; reminders that the stigmatization of scarlet letter or outcast table can be ignominious, painful and unfair.

1. Which of the following BEST reflects the author's feelings about her aunt's adultery and its consequences? **(C) pity for her vulnerability and empathy for her ostracism**.

The author's comments about her aunt's adultery suggest that her aunt was victimized both by the lust of an individual and by a society that compels women to be submissive. She remarks wryly in lines 23-25, "My aunt could not have been the lone romantic who gave up everything for sex," adding that "Women in the old China did not choose. Some man had commanded her to lie with him and be his secret evil" (lines 25-28). In the subsequent paragraph, she ponders how this unfortunate incident befell her aunt, speculating how "Perhaps she had encountered him in the fields or on the mountain where the daughters-in-law collected fuel. Or perhaps he first noticed her in the marketplace….Perhaps he worked an adjoining field, or he sold her the cloth for the dress she sewed and wore" (lines 30-38). Her subsequent remark, that "His demand must have surprised, then terrified her. She obeyed him; she always did as she was told" (lines 38-40), shows her empathy for her aunt's terror and her sense of the submissive upbringing which prohibited her from resisting his commands and advances. Later, she observes how her aunt had to relive the trauma of the event every time she encountered him, noting how "The fear did not stop but permeated everywhere" (lines 59-60). Finally, in discussing the "outcast table" to which her aunt was condemned, she notes the injustice of Chinese culture which did not let such offenders start new lives but instead encouraged the Chinese family to humiliate them further by sitting at table with their "faces averted but eyes glowering sideways…[feeding] them leftovers" (lines 72-74).

2. The author's primary interest in examining the events that befell her aunt has to do with **(C) exploring an identity**.

The choice of C derives from the long rhetorical question that opens the passage—"….Chinese-Americans, when you try to understand what things in you are Chinese, how do you separate what is peculiar to childhood, to poverty, insanities, one family, your mother who marked your growing with stories, from what is Chinese?" (lines 1-6)—from her interest in the second paragraph about what her aunt wore, and from her somewhat incredulous query as to how such a frugal family could conceivably "engender a prodigal aunt" (lines 21-22). In each case the author seems interested in learning more about her aunt and the situation that prompted her suicide.

3. All of the following seem to be Old World Chinese traditions EXCEPT **(E) moving in with the bride's family after marriage**.

Lines 41-47 describe the aunt's parents finding a suitable mate for her in a neighboring village (A). Lines 17-21 describe how these people "hatch their own chicks and eat the embryos and the heads for delicacies and boil the feet in vinegar for party food, leaving only the gravel, eating even the gizzard lining….". Lines 28-29, 61-62 and 76-77 reference the raid that was carried out against her aunt and her aunt's family on account of her adulterous action. Lines 25-26, "Women in the old China did not choose," confirm the forced subservience of women. Choice E is contradicted by the information provided in lines 80-83, "Daughters-in-law lived with their husbands' parents, not their own; a synonym for marriage in Chinese is 'taking a daughter-in-law,'" making E the exception.

4. The syntax of the opening sentence is complicated by which of the following? **(B) the omission of expected prepositions**.

The question, "…how do you separate what is peculiar to childhood, to poverty, insanities, one family, your mother who marked your growing with stories, from what is Chinese?" (lines 3-6), starts out with a series of prepositional phrases ("to childhood," "to poverty"), then inexplicably drops the preposition. This initially makes the syntax of the latter part of the clause difficult to follow. Neither the use of second person (D), which is part of the author's direct address of fellow Chinese-Americans, nor the rhetorical question (C) complicates the syntax. The word "things" (E) is readily identified as "elements" or "parts" while the opening address of the author's audience does not really exemplify apostrophe (A).

5. The phrase "once and for all" (line 12) implies which of the following?

   I. That the author has pestered her mother with questions about her deceased aunt.
   II. That the stigma of the aunt's suicide has made it a topic never to be broached.
  III. That the author's mother is unwilling to provide additional details about the suicide.

(E) I, II and III.

The author confesses in lines 11-14, "My mother has told me once and for all the useful parts. She will add nothing unless powered by Necessity, a riverbank that guides her life," an admission that validates I and III. This and her earlier remark, "If I want to learn what clothes my aunt wore, whether flashy or ordinary, I would have to begin, 'Remember Father's drowned-in-the-well sister?' I cannot ask that" (lines 8-11), confirm II. This accounts for her speculation about the exact circumstances that prompted her aunt's suicide.

6. It may be inferred by the reader that what the author's mother considers the "useful parts" (line 12) of the aunt's story would most likely exclude which of the following? **(A) the salacious details of the assault**.

The details mentioned in choice B (lines 26-28; 61-62), C (line 61), D (lines 84-86) and E (lines 65-74) are all familiar to the author, which suggests her mother shared these specifics with her. It is the more shameful details of her aunt's situation about which the author is forced to speculate.

7. Lines 14-15, "She plants vegetable gardens rather than lawns…," convey the mother's **(A) orthodoxy**.

The vegetable gardens and lawns are metonymies that respectively reflect Old World (Chinese) and New World (American) gardening traditions. That her mother sticks to the former reflects her maintenance of tradition and cultural values.

8. The shift in tone from the disbelief expressed in paragraph three (lines 16-29) to the speculation manifested in paragraph four (lines 30-40) is primarily achieved by the **(B) repetition of the adverb "perhaps."**

Unable to persuade her mother to provide more specific details about what happened to her aunt—"My mother has told me once and for all the useful parts. She will add nothing unless powered by Necessity, a riverbank that guides her life…" (lines 11-14)—the author is reduced to speculating about the circumstances that prompted her aunt's suicide. This is primarily achieved through a series of clauses, initiated by the adverb "Perhaps," in which the author imagines various scenarios in which her aunt might have encountered her attacker: "Perhaps she had encountered him in the fields or on the mountain where the daughters-in-law collected fuel. Or perhaps he first noticed her in the marketplace. He was not a stranger because the village housed no strangers. She had to have dealings with him other than sex. Perhaps he worked an adjoining field, or he sold her the cloth for the dress she sewed and wore" (lines 30-38). Though the author uses images of local color (A) in paragraph four, these do not add to the "speculation."

9. The BEST interpretation of the word "tractably" (line 43) would be **(B) obediently**.

The word "tractably" comes from a Latin verb meaning "to pull or draw." This suggests that she allows herself to be drawn into the arranged marriage and stands by obediently while her parents carry out the marriage ritual "by proxy" since the man to whom she will be wed is likely already in America.

10. Which of the following BEST paraphrases the point the author wishes to make about her aunt's "fear" in lines 55-58? **(E) She wishes that her aunt could have avoided additional post-rape consequences**.

The author states in lines 55-58, "I want her fear to have lasted just as long as the rape lasted so that the fear could have been contained." This suggests a desire to limit her suffering to a short duration, to have it end with the attack and not be extended into such shame and nightmare that it would force her to throw herself down a well. Choice E captures this best.

11. Of the following, which BEST exemplifies the author's adept use of climactic order? **(E) "…sold her, mortgaged her, stoned her" (line 84)**.

In climactic order the details increase in importance or intensity from first to last. Here the details rise in severity from dispensing with her for money to putting her to death by a brutal and primitive ritual.

12. A feminist reading of the passage might find which of the following words ironic?
(D) "lucky" (line 45).

Though the family likely perceives marrying their daughter off as beneficial, the woman herself is being forced by tradition to marry a total stranger and to agree to a life of subservience and submission. A feminist reading of the passage would hardly see this as a fortunate development.

Précis and Explication of Passage Two: From Christopher Morley's "On Laziness"

From the opening of Christopher Morley's essay "On Laziness"—"To-day we rather intended to write an essay on Laziness, but were too indolent to do so" (lines 1-3)—to its ironic conclusion—"Writing on this congenial topic has roused us up to quite a pitch of enthusiasm and energy" (lines 89-91)—the reader is treated to a droll examination of procrastination as well as to an active example of such dilly-dallying in action. The opening two paragraphs are replete with diction that suggests a desire to do something— "we rather intended to write…" (line 1); "The sort of thing we had in mind to write…" (line 4); "We intended to discourse a little…" (lines 5-6)—aided by a dash of the subjunctive, to establish a playful tone that characterizes the author as the embodiment of indolence. Moreover, the author's repeated use of the plural pronoun "we" when referring to himself lends the piece an air of royal or aristocratic privilege that abets his characteristic inertia. The declarative statement that opens paragraph three—"It is our observation that every time we get into trouble it is due to not having been lazy enough" (lines 9-11)—blithely implies that initiative spawns difficulties and that "hustling about" (lines 12-13) only seems to lead to "tribulation" (line 14). Though clearly tongue-in-cheek, the author's argument actually mirrors a Romantic sentiment manifest in the poetry of Wordsworth that such hustle and bustle has vitiated our ability to appreciate nature. Morley's essay, however, quickly returns the reader to its more droll agenda via the author's dramatic declaration that "Henceforward we are going to make a determined effort to be more languid and demure. It is the bustling man who always gets put on committees, who is asked to solve the problems of other people and neglect his own" (lines 15-19).

Indeed, it is this pervasively droll tone that effectively checks the essay from ever becoming truly serious. For example, the author's claim that "The man who is really, thoroughly, and philosophically slothful is the only thoroughly happy man" (lines 20-22) seems almost brazenly blasphemous, especially when he follows this with a mock allusion to the Beatitudes, "We remember a saying about the meek inheriting the earth" (lines 24-25). In the lines which follow the author parodies a solemn promise made by Jesus to the disenfranchised multitude that their sufferings would someday be rewarded with the irreverent observation that "The truly meek man is the lazy man. He is too modest to believe that any ferment and hubbub of his can ameliorate the earth or assuage the perplexities of humanity" (lines 25-28). Like his earlier observation that industriousness just brings the individual still more work and tribulation, these lines suggest that there is no human action that can ease the travails of humanity; therefore, laziness is best.

In the middle section of his essay, the author shifts to literary and historical allusions to justify his thoughts on laziness. He first cites acclaimed short story writer O. Henry's admonition that "one should be careful to distinguish laziness from dignified repose" (lines 29-31). Calling this a "mere quibble" (line 31), or a petty distinction, the author shamelessly declares that "Laziness is always dignified…" (lines 31-32). To be fair, however, he does draw a line between what he calls "Philosophical laziness" (line 33) and "Acquired laziness" (line 35). The former he says is "based upon a carefully reasoned analysis of experience" (lines 34-35), an indolence born from careful reflection. This is unlike the latter which he summarily dismisses as having required no work to attain: "We have no respect for those who were born lazy; it is like being born a millionaire: they cannot appreciate their bliss" (lines 35-38). As the author unabashedly concludes in a droll irony, "It is the man who has hammered his laziness out of the stubborn material of life whom we chant praise and alleluia" (lines 38-41). Eager to provide an example of successful philosophical laziness, the author alludes to a poet whom he declares to be the laziest person he knows. He relates how "He began life in the customary hustling way. He was always too busy to enjoy himself. He became surrounded by eager people who came to him to solve their problems" (lines 47-51). This industry and openness, however, soon made his life miserable—until he experienced a life-changing epiphany:

> He stopped answering letters, buying lunches for casual friends and visitors from out of town, he stopped lending money to old college pals and frittering his time away on all the useless minor matters that pester the good-natured. He sat down in a secluded café with his cheek against a seidel of dark beer and began to caress the universe with his intellect" (lines 54-61).

This closing comic image, which almost seems a parody of Mersault's epiphany in *The Stranger*, when he "lay[s] himself open to the benign indifference of the universe," returns the poet to an indolent—and blissful—harmony. The subsequent allusion to the German military aggression that spawned the First World War provides a more macrocosmic historical parallel to the poet. Claiming the Germans were a "dangerous mass of energy and bumptious push" (lines 66-67) that was out of synch with the "thoroughly disillusioned, indolent and delightful old continent…" (lines 64-66), the author humorously blames the subsequent hostilities on the Germans' innate lack of indolence: "If the Germans had been as lazy as indifferent, and as righteously-laissez-fairish as their neighbours, the world would have been spared a great deal" (lines 67-70).

In the final twenty lines, the author succinctly and declaratively hammers home his points about indolence: "People respect laziness," he says. "If once you get a reputation for complete, immovable, and reckless indolence the world will leave you to your own thoughts, which are generally rather interesting…." (lines 71-75). In the following paragraph, he reiterates this advice in the form of two Ben Franklin-like aphorisms, saying "Mind your business is a good counsel; but mind your idleness also" (lines 76-77) and "It's a tragic thing to make a business of your mind. Save your mind to amuse yourself with" (lines 77-79). He depicts the indolent man as self-serving and accommodating, saying "The lazy man does not stand in the way of progress. When he sees progress roaring down upon him he steps nimbly out of the way" (lines 80-82). Using chiasmus, a verbal pattern in which the second half of a phrase mirrors the first but in reverse order, he remarks that "The lazy man doesn't (in the vulgar phrase) pass the buck. He lets the buck pass him" (lines 82-84). And finally, in a culminating irony, the author confesses "We have always secretly envied our lazy friends. Now we are going to join them" (lines 84-86), the irony lying in the implication that laziness requires choice and action.

Morley's witty and entertaining essay reminds the reader of the best moments of Oscar Wilde, and though clearly light-hearted and tongue-in-cheek, it raises legitimate questions about the need for respite and inactivity in a world that is too often "too much with us." It also shows the versatility of the essay and reinforces the fact that it need not always be heavy-handed, argumentative or reflective.

13. Which of the following BEST articulates the author's thesis? **(B) "The man who is really, thoroughly, and philosophically slothful is the only thoroughly happy man." (lines 20-22)**.

Morley's essay advocates, albeit somewhat humorously, indolence as a lifestyle. Industry, he suggests, only creates problems: "It is our observation that every time we get into trouble it is due to not having been lazy enough" (lines 9-11), and "We have been hustling about for a number of years now, and it doesn't seem to get us anything but tribulation" (lines 12-14). On the contrary, the lazy man is "too modest to believe that any ferment and hubbub of his can ameliorate the earth or assuage the perplexities of humanity" (lines 26-28); thus, he does not trouble himself with issues that regularly torment others. As the author observes in lines 17-19, "It is the bustling man who always gets put on committees, who is asked to solve the problems of other people and neglect his own." A perfect example of this is the notable poet to whom he anonymously refers in lines 42-61. The author observes how he "began life in the customary hustling way [and] was always too busy to enjoy himself" (lines 47-49). However, after "seeing the light" and cutting himself off from others who were monopolizing his attention, he "sat [himself] down in a secluded café with his cheek against a seidel of dark beer and began to caress the universe with his intellect" (lines 59-61), a thoroughly happy man. Choice B reflects this best.

14. The author's use of the collective "we" is likely intended to do which of the following?

    I. Establish himself as a proponent of and advocate for lethargy.
    II. Echo the characteristic indolence of royalty or the aristocracy.
    III. Fit the conventional style of an editorial.

(C) I and II.

Clearly the author celebrates indolence as if it were an admirable virtue (I), and though there are many different rationales for individuals referring to themselves in the second person plural—the collective "we," the editorial "we," and the royal "we"—the latter seems most appropriate here since the tone of the piece seems terribly self-centered and self-indulgent and calls to mind the sense of privilege that such pompous individuals expect, even demand (II). III does not make sense given the nature of this piece of nonfiction.

15. The diction of the passage establishes which of the following contrasts? **(B) activity and idleness**.

From the opening sentence, "To-day we rather intended to write an essay on Laziness, but were too indolent to do so" (lines 1-3), the author establishes his preferences for idleness over action. As was established in the explanation of question #13, the author believes that industry breeds trouble and tribulation, things he clearly eschews. His example of the poet serves to illustrate the problems an industrious spirit can cause. The poet, he observes, "began life in the customary hustling way [and] was always too busy to enjoy himself" (lines 47-49). Soon, however, he reveals, "He became surrounded by eager people who came to him to solve their problems. 'It's a queer thing,' he said sadly; 'no one ever comes to me asking for help in solving my problems'" (lines 49-53). Only after he ceases "answering letters, buying lunches for casual friends and visitors from out of town …[stops] lending money to old college pals and frittering his time away on all the useless minor matters that pester the good-natured" (lines 54-59) can he free himself from these annoyances. The author even goes so far as to blame Germany's aggression in the First World War upon a "dangerous mass of energy and bumptious push" (lines 66-67) that spurred their desire for conquest. This contrast culminates metaphorically in lines 80-82 when the author observes, "The lazy man does not stand in the way of progress. When he sees progress roaring down upon him he steps nimbly out of the way."

16. In lines 1-19 the author reinforces his natural inclination to avoid action through all of the following EXCEPT **(D) a chronological record of postponements**.

Choice A is reflected by verbs such as "intended" (lines 1 and 6) and "had in mind" (line 4), choice B by lines 15-17, "Henceforward we are going to make a determined effort to be more languid and demure." Choice C is validated by lines 9-11, "It is our observation that every time we get into trouble it is due to not having been lazy enough" and lines 12-14, "We have been hustling about for a number of years now, and it doesn't seem to get us anything but tribulation." Choice E gains support from lines 9-11, "It is our observation that every time we get into trouble it is due to not having been lazy enough" and lines 17-19, "It is the bustling man who always gets put on committees, who is asked to solve the problems of other people and neglect his own," which both exemplify the use of the impersonal passive, passive constructions that begin with "it is." Nowhere does the passage support choice D.

17. Lines 20-23—"The man who is really, thoroughly, and philosophically slothful ….The conclusion is inescapable"—exemplify which of the following rhetorical techniques? **(B) syllogism**.

A syllogism is defined as a form of deductive reasoning consisting of a major premise, a minor premise, and a conclusion. Here the major premise is that only a man who is totally indolent is happy. The minor premise is that only happy men benefit the world. The logical conclusion, which the author labels "inescapable" and hence leaves unsaid, is that indolence is beneficial to humanity.

18. The conclusion that to the author seems "inescapable" (line 23) is that **(C) sloth is beneficial**.

This may be directly inferred from what precedes the word "inescapable"—namely, the author's observation that "The man who is really, thoroughly, and philosophically slothful is the only thoroughly happy man. It is the happy man who benefits the world" (lines 20-23). The "conclusion" to be drawn from this is that indolence is beneficial.

19. Line 33, "Philosophical laziness, we mean," offers an example of a(n) **(A) qualification**.

A qualification, in this usage, may be defined as a "modification" or "clarification." The author does not want "philosophical laziness" to be confused with "acquired laziness," for which he displays nothing but unadulterated scorn: "We have no respect for those who were born lazy; it is like being born a millionaire: they cannot appreciate their bliss" (lines 35-38). Rather, the author believes that "It is the man who has hammered his laziness out of the stubborn material of life whom we chant praise and alleluia" (lines 38-41).

20. The most persuasive example of "Philosophical laziness" as it is defined in lines 33-35 would be epitomized by which of the following individuals? **(D) "one of the greatest poets" in lines 45-61**.

Once the poet decides to stop answering letters and squandering his time helping others, he is able to "[sit] down in a secluded café with his cheek against a seidel of dark beer and [begin] to caress the universe with his intellect" (lines 59-61). This is the epitome of philosophical laziness.

21. The syntax of lines 54-59—"He stopped answering letters… and frittering his time away on all the useless minor matters that pester the good-natured"—is characterized by a series of **(A) gerundive phrases**.

The words "answering," "buying," "lending," and "frittering" are all objects of the verb "stopped." This makes them gerunds.

22. In lines 81-82—"When he sees progress roaring down upon him he steps nimbly out of the way"—the author depicts progress as **(E) inexorable and threatening**.

In lines 81-82 progress is seemingly compared to a steam engine barreling inexorably down the track. In the eyes of the author, the lazy man sagely "…does not stand in the way of progress." Rather, "When he sees progress roaring down upon him he steps nimbly out of the way" (lines 81-82). This paints progress as a minatory presence and suggests that the lazy man's actions are pragmatic and self-preservational.

23. Lines 82-84—"The lazy man doesn't (in the vulgar phrase) pass the buck. He lets the buck pass him"—exemplify which of the following figures of speech? **(C) chiasmus**.

Chiasmus is defined as a verbal pattern in which the second half of a phrase mirrors the first but in reverse order. This line demonstrates this perfectly.

24. Lines 86-88—"We have burned our boats or our bridges or whatever it is that one burns on the eve of a momentous decision"— are primarily intended to demonstrate the author's **(A) resolve to be languid**.

The fact that the author does not know whether the idiom involves boats or bridges—and does not care enough to look it up—suggests that he is well on his way toward fulfilling the vow he makes in lines 15-17 "to make a determined effort to be more languid and demure." Choice A is the answer choice that reflects this.

25. In light of the context in which it appears, which of the following should NOT be viewed as ironic? **(E) that the lazy man does not impede progress**.

Choices A, B, C and D all contain examples in which the opposite of what is expected occurs, qualifying them as ironies. That the lazy man would not impede progress is logical.

26. In the course of his essay, the author alludes to all of the following EXCEPT **(D) the Industrial Revolution**.

    The author's allusion to First World War (A) is apparent in his reference to the Germans in lines 62-70 while his allusion to other writers (B) may be seen in his referencing of O. Henry (lines 29-31) and the "great poet" (lines 42-61). His allusion to the New Testament (C) appears in lines 24-25, in his parody of a line from the Beatitudes while his allusion to a well-known adage (E) is evident in line 76, "Mind your business is good counsel." The Industrial Revolution is never alluded to directly.

27. The tone of the passage is BEST labeled as **(C) tongue-in-cheek and droll**.

    This is immediately apparent in the author's mock-serious approach to a clearly humorous topic and in the satire of his own characteristic laziness.

Précis and Explication of Passage Three:
From James Agee's "Victory: The Peace." *Time* 20 Aug 1945.

The dropping of the atomic bomb in 1945 and the subsequently quick surrender of Japan in the wake of its awesome destructive power could not possibly have been fully appreciated by an American public still being fed dribbles of information in censored newspaper stories, grainy newsreels, and crackling radio broadcasts. America had not yet entered the world of a television in every home (even a black and white one), and a live video broadcast of this destructive new weapon was still a remote technical dream. Thus, the American consciousness of nuclear power lay somewhere between imagination and nightmare, in a no man's land between dreams of peace and the safe return of their loved ones, and specters of the brave new atomic world into which they had just embarked.

James Agee's short article in *Time* magazine, published a scant two weeks after the Hiroshima bombing, endeavors to capture this troubling dichotomy. Indeed, his remark in the opening sentence that "The greatest and most terrible of wars was ending, this week, in the echoes of an enormous event—an event so much more enormous that, relative to it, the war itself shrank to minor significance" (lines 1-5) almost captures the deafening detonation of "Little Boy" (the first nuclear weapon) over Japan as well as its resonance in the human psyche. The remainder of his opening paragraph conveys the duality of a victory that was "charged with sorrow and doubt" as much as it was greeted with "joy and gratitude" (lines 6-7). Lines 7-9, "More fearful responsibilities, more crucial liabilities rested on the victors even than on the vanquished," relate the wry irony that by dropping the bomb America assumed a moral responsibility both for the almost unfathomable human carnage wreaked on the citizens of Hiroshima and for the security and safety of the population of the post-war world. So stunning was this blow to end all hostilities that Agee compares it to "the aftershock of a great wound" (line 11) and to "a bottomless wound in the living conscience of the race" (lines 35-36). Men of all callings were left "bemused and only semi-articulate, whether they were soldiers or scientists, or great statesmen, or the simplest of men" (lines 11-14), and Agee compares their attempts at restoring some psychological order to "Titans, arranging out of chaos an age in which victory was already only the shout of a child in the street" (lines 16-18). The closing metaphor seems to imply the transient nature of victory, the impetus with which the survivors of the Second World War were flung, ignorant and unprepared, into the atomic age and subsequent Cold War. As Agee remarks, "With the controlled splitting of the atom, humanity, already profoundly perplexed and disunified, was brought inescapably into a new age in which all thoughts and things were split—and far from controlled" (lines 19-23). In addition, his observation in lines 24-25 that this first atomic bomb was "a merely pregnant threat, a merely infinitesimal promise" both acknowledges its place as the rudimentary mother of much more sophisticated weaponry while foreshadowing the as yet inconceivable nuclear stockpile that the U.S. and Soviet Union would eventually compile.

Using this "split," or nuclear fission, as a conceit, Agee goes on to examine the further ramifications of our use of this new weapon. Calling the dropping of the bomb a "mercy born of a ruthless force beyond anything in human chronicle" (lines 29-30), he at once compliments the American scientists—"those on whom civilization could best hope to depend" (lines 32-33)—and aligns them with the audacious Prometheus for "put[ting] into the hands of common man the fire and force of the sun itself" (lines 38-39). The series of rhetorical questions that follows—"Was man equal to the challenge? In an instant, without warning, the present had become the unthinkable future. Was there hope in that future, and if so, where did hope lie?" (lines 40-43)—speculates whether humanity could be a responsible custodian of such a prodigious power.

Still, the potential for great good was also evident in that the force that annihilated Hiroshima and then Nagasaki might perhaps prove an equally strong deterrent to future aggression. Agee pondered this in lines 44-50, noting how "Even as men saluted the greatest and most grimly Pyrrhic of victories in all the gratitude and good spirit they could muster, they recognized that the discovery which had done most to end the worst of wars might also, quite conceivably, end all wars—if only man could learn its control and use." Ultimately the Thinking Man who had created the bomb would be compelled to become the Moral Man who governed its use. This great responsibility was worrisome in that, as Agee recognized, "the good uses of this power might easily bring disaster as prodigious as the evil" (lines 55-56). In fact, by employing an implied metaphor, Agee suggests that the splitting of the atom "rendered all decisions made so far, at Yalta and at Potsdam, mere trivial dams across tributary rivulets" (lines 57-59), rupturing the tenuous bonds of political compromise.

When one considers the proximity of the date of Agee's article to the actual bombing of the cities of Hiroshima and Nagasaki, it seems eerily prescient, especially in light of the meltdown fears in Japan's nuclear facilities caused by the recent devastating earthquake and subsequent tsunami. Nuclear power, whether employed in war or in industry, demands great moral responsibility of its users. As Agee observes,

> When the bomb split open the universe and revealed the prospect of the infinitely extraordinary, it also revealed the oldest, simplest, commonest, most neglected and most important of facts: that each man is eternally and above all else responsible for his own soul, and, in the terrible words of the Psalmist, that no man may deliver his brother, nor make agreement unto God for him (lines 59-67).

With the escalation of the Cold War and the nuclear empowerment of smaller countries, this responsibility shifted from one nation to many nations. Agee's concluding comments acknowledge this dichotomy of mind and spirit, the brain that imagined this peace-making weapon and the soul that must now responsibly control it. He leaves the reader with the sage admonition that "If either or anything is to survive, they must find a way to create an indissoluble partnership" (lines 71-73).

28. The primary unifying device of the author's argument is his use of **(A) the extended metaphor of fission**.

   Throughout the passage the author returns to the idea of fission, or the splitting of the atom. Line 19, "With the controlled splitting of the atom;" line 26, "All thoughts and things were split;" lines 51-53, "The promise of good and evil bordered alike on the infinite—with this further, terrible split in the fact;" and lines 59-61, "When the bomb split open the universe and revealed the prospect of the infinitely extraordinary…" function collaboratively as an extended metaphor which unifies the passage's argument.

29. In the opening paragraph the author primarily dramatizes his fears about the future consequence of nuclear weaponry through **(C) antitheses**.

   Lines 5-7, "The knowledge of victory was as charged with sorrow and doubt as with joy and gratitude" and lines 7-9, "More fearful responsibilities, more crucial liabilities rested on the victors even than on the vanquished," both contain antitheses that suggest the ambiguity created by this new weapon. Though the atomic bomb brought about the cessation of World War Two hostilities, it simultaneously ushered in a new and more dangerous age in which the careful monitoring of this new weapon would become an urgent charge.

30. In light of the context in which it appears, the BEST equivalent for "bemused" (line 11) would be **(C) shocked**.

   The selection of C is largely determined by the words which precede this, "as in the aftershock of a great wound," which suggest that humanity is shell-shocked, rendered inarticulate by the awesome destructive power of this new weapon.

31. The metaphor in lines 17-18—"…in which victory was already only the shout of a child in the street"—implies that **(E) for many the elation of victory was tempered by a bleak nuclear reality**.

   This metaphor suggests the evanescent nature of joy and relief created by the dropping of the bomb. The child's cry is transient and commonplace, fading into the other sounds of the street, much as the initial euphoria of the end of the war was quickly replaced by the daunting reality of this powerful weapon. The child's cry parallels the "echoes of an enormous event" (lines 2-3) in that both quickly fade and are replaced by an alternate consciousness.

32. The phrases "pregnant threat" (line 25) and "merely infinitesimal promise" (line 25) are intended to imply which of the following about the bomb dropped upon Hiroshima? **(E) that it would engender a potential for an as yet unimaginable destruction**.

This derives directly from the diction. The word "pregnant" implies that something new is to be born; the word "infinitesimal," in this context, means "barely measurable," an allusion both to the microscopic size of the atom and to the fact that in creating a mere two atomic bombs, America had barely cracked the door on the nuclear age. Taken together, these phrases suggest that the bombs that have been created are just the precursors of still more destructive weaponry. Choice E reflects this best.

33. The author likely labels the development of the atomic bomb as "the most Promethean of [man's] conquests over nature" (lines 36-37) on account of which of the following?

  I. The enormous collaborative efforts of the scientific community in creating it.
 II. The brazen, even illicit, tampering by scientists with the most elemental source of power.
III. The fact that the bomb had been created by the country most morally suited to police it.

(B) II only.

In classical mythology, Prometheus, one of the Titans, steals fire from Olympus and gives it to humans, a transgression for which he is severely punished. The allusion to Prometheus suggests that in splitting the atom scientists did something comparably illicit. II is the only choice that reflects this.

34. The author suggests in lines 44-67 that, upon the initial use of an atomic weapon, humans experienced all of the following epiphanies EXCEPT **(C) that in creating the atomic bomb humans had committed a damnable transgression**.

Lines 46-50, "they recognized that the discovery which had done most to end the worst of wars might also, quite conceivably, end all wars—if only man could learn its control and use," and lines 55-56, "the good uses of this power might easily bring disaster as prodigious as the evil," confirm both A and B respectively. Lines 59-67, "When the bomb split open the universe and revealed the prospect of the infinitely extraordinary, it also revealed the oldest, simplest, commonest, most neglected and most important of facts: that each man is eternally and above all else responsible for his own soul, and, in the terrible words of the Psalmist, that no man may deliver his brother, nor make agreement unto God for him," support choice D while lines 56-59, "The bomb rendered all decisions made so far, at Yalta and at Potsdam, mere trivial dams across tributary rivulets," validate E. Choice C is not supported by anything mentioned in these lines.

35. The effectiveness of the metaphor "mere trivial dams across tributary rivulets" (lines 58-59)—used to describe the Yalta and Potsdam conferences— lies in its **(C) understated diction**.

The words "mere" and "trivial" both imply the miniscule impact of the agreements reached at the Yalta and Potsdam conferences in light of this powerful new weapon. The words "tributary" and "rivulets" both are moving bodies of water that are smaller than a river.

36. The phrase "split open the universe" (lines 59-60) is most accurately labeled a(n) **(D) hyperbole**.

   That the scientists split the atom is incontrovertible; that it "split open the universe" is a dramatic overstatement designed to emphasize the long-term significance of the discovery.

37. The diction and figurative language of the concluding paragraph portray man's fate as **(B) malleable**.

   Lines 68-70, "Man's fate has forever been shaped between the hands of reason and spirit, now in collaboration, again in conflict," portray man's fate as capable of being molded. Choice B reflects this best.

38. The author describes the moral after-effects of the bomb-dropping upon the United States' citizenry in words usually associated with **(A) trauma and injury**.

   Twice in the passage, in line 11 ("as in the aftershock of a great wound") and in lines 35-36 ("…created a bottomless wound in the living conscience of the race"), the author describes the moral after-effects of the use of the atomic weapon in terms associated with trauma and injury.

39. Of the following, which BEST conveys the sense of helplessness and lack of control that humans experienced with the splitting of the atom? **(B) "…humanity, already profoundly perplexed and disunified, was brought inescapably into a new age…" (lines 20-22)**.

   This is largely derived from the passive voice verb "was brought" and the adverb "inescapably" which suggest that humans lack control of their future; hence, the selection of B as the answer.

40. The author's attitude towards man's ability to harness and control nuclear energy is BEST characterized as **(A) skeptical**.

   The author pejoratively labels humans as being "nearly drowned in materialism" (line 54) and states in the concluding lines that "Man's fate has forever been shaped between the hands of reason and spirit, now in collaboration, again in conflict. Now reason and spirit meet on final ground. If either or anything is to survive, they must find a way to create an indissoluble partnership" (lines 68-73). This, and the ironic observation in 55-56 that "the good uses of this power might easily bring disaster as prodigious as the evil," at best suggest skepticism about human's ability to control this power.

Précis and Explication of Passage Four: From Willa Cather's "The Novel Demeuble"

There are numerous examples of writers reflecting upon the craft of writing, and Cather's essay falls squarely into this tradition. In her essay Cather explores the tradition of realism, the movement dedicated to the depiction of things as they appear in everyday life. Her essay contrasts the realism of the French author Balzac with that of the great Russian writer Tolstoi before closing with some brief commentary on Hawthorne's *The Scarlet Letter*. The title, which translated from the French means "the unfurnished novel," figuratively anticipates Cather's claim that realism is "more than it is anything else, an attitude of mind on the part of the writer toward his material…" (lines 7-9), not an exercise "in the cataloguing of a great number of material objects, in explaining mechanical processes, the methods of operating manufactures and trades, and in minutely and unsparingly describing physical sensation" (lines 2-7). The rhetorical question that climaxes the opening paragraph—"Is the story of a banker who is unfaithful to his wife and who ruins himself by speculation in trying to gratify the caprices of his mistresses, at all reinforced by a masterly exposition of the banking system, our whole system of credits, the methods of the Stock Exchange?…." (lines 12-18)—whimsically but sardonically censures what Cather perceives is a misuse of realism.

Cather's negative perspective on excessive and extraneous realism is decisively and declaratively conveyed by the transition sentence "The automatic reply to this question is the name of Balzac" (lines 19-20). Though Cather readily acknowledges "Yes, certainly, Balzac tried out the value of literalness in the novel, tried it out to the uttermost, as Wagner did the value of scenic literalness in the music drama" and that "He tried it, too, with the passion of discovery, with the inflamed zest of an unexampled curiosity" (lines 20-25), the implication is that this is not, in Cather's eyes, the height of Balzac's realism. Though acknowledging his attempt "To reproduce on paper the actual city of Paris; the houses, the upholstery, the food, the wines, the game of pleasure, the game of business, the game of finance…" (lines 28-31), Cather dismisses this as "unworthy of an artist" (lines 32-33), saying that in attempting to reproduce "that mass of brick and mortar and furniture and proceedings in bankruptcy…[he] defeated his end" (lines 34-37) and that the "eye glides over [these realistic details]" (lines 42-43). Speaking authoritatively, she wryly remarks "We have had too much of the interior decorator and the 'romance of business' since his day" (lines 43-45), noting that even Robert Louis Stevenson, a great fan of Balzac, had wanted to "blue-pencil," or cross out, "a great deal of [his] 'presentation'" (lines 47-48).

Cather's discussion of Balzac's realism leads her into a subsequent discussion of Tolstoi, whom she labels "almost as great a lover of material things" (lines 51-52), a man who was "almost as much interested in the way dishes were cooked, and people were dressed, and houses were furnished [as Balzac was]" (lines 53-55). However, Cather is quick to point out a significant difference: namely, that "the clothes, the dishes, the moving, haunting interiors of those old Moscow houses, are always so much a part of the emotions of the people that they are perfectly synthesized; they seem to exist, not so much in the author's mind, as in the emotional penumbra of the characters themselves" (lines 56-63). To Cather, when character and setting are so masterfully integrated, "literalness ceases to be literalness—it is merely part of the experience" (lines 64-65).

Clearly, Cather believes in a limited, or selected, realism, not merely an inclusion of detail for detail's sake. She avers that "If the novel is a form of imaginative art, it cannot be at the same time a brilliant form of journalism" (lines 66-68) and that "Out of the teeming, gleaming stream of the present, it must select the eternal material of art" (lines 68-70), claims that suggest some details are mere flotsam and jetsam that should be eschewed by the artist. In a sentence characterized by parallel infinitive phrases,

Cather celebrates the fact that some younger artists are "trying to break away from mere verisimilitude, and, following the development of modern painting, to interpret imaginatively the material and social investiture of their characters; to present their scene by suggestion rather than by enumeration" (lines 71-77). These two latter words, "suggestion" and "enumeration," are virtual metonymies for what she advocates and what she rejects in the attempt to establish a "realistic" setting. She believes that rather than clutter a scene with superfluous detail, the writer must instead engage in a process of simplification in order to elevate his writing to a "higher and truer effect" (line 83).

In the closing paragraph of the passage, Cather alludes to Nathaniel Hawthorne's *The Scarlet Letter* as a representative example of the effective use of realism in a novel, wryly suggesting that "That drudge, the theme-writing high school student, could scarcely be sent there for information regarding the manners and dress and interiors of the Puritans" (lines 91-94). Rather, Cather claims that the realism of Hawthorne's novel is so subdued, so well-integrated into the fabric of his novel that it is "presented as if unconsciously; by the reserved, fastidious hand of an artist, not by the gaudy fingers of a showman or the mechanical industry of a department store window-dresser" (lines 95-99). For Cather, the enduring impression of Hester's tale is a "twilight melancholy" (line 100), an ambience in which "one can scarcely ever see the actual surroundings of the people…" but one in which "one feels them, rather, in the dusk…." (lines 101-103).

Though literary criticism can often be esoteric and remote to a reader who is unfamiliar with the text(s) being discussed, Cather's discussion of realism is pleasantly accessible and permits even the reader who has never read Balzac or Tolstoi to appreciate the artistry of each. Her discourse on realism clearly conveys what she admires about the tradition and what she sees as its flaws, and the passage provides an effective testing ground to determine whether young writers can engage and comprehend literary criticism effectively.

41. The first indication of the author's distaste for realism that is not "perfectly synthesized" with the emotions of a novel's characters is revealed by which of the following phrases? **(A) "popular superstition" (line 1)**.

The word "superstition" has an immediately pejorative connotation that suggests that one should not take the assertion about realism seriously. Thus, her comment about realism asserting itself in the "cataloguing of a great number of material objects, in explaining mechanical processes, the methods of operating manufactures and trades, and in minutely and unsparingly describing physical sensation" (lines 2-7) is the first sign of her distaste for unadulterated realism.

42. In questioning the appropriateness of realism in imaginative art in the opening paragraph, the author relies on all of the following EXCEPT **(E) the presentation of an antithetical perspective**.

The quotation marks around "realism" immediately indicate sarcasm while the initial sentence not only lists what realism does but mimics it via its long-winded listing of dull activities. The author begins by asserting the "popular superstition" (line 1) that realism consists of the "cataloguing of a great number of material objects..." (lines 2-3), but quickly challenges that assertion by asking "But is not realism, more than anything else, an attitude of mind on the part of the writer toward his material, a vague definition of the sympathy and candor with which he accepts, rather than chooses his theme?" (lines 7-12). Lines 12-18, on the other hand, consist of a rhetorical question that uses an anecdote about an unfaithful banker to demonstrate the inappropriateness of specific banking details. This information confirms the presence of choices A, B, C and D. Choice E draws no support from the passage.

43. Lines 23-28 compare Balzac's imagination to a(n) **(B) kiln**.

The selection of B is derived directly from lines 23-28, "He tried it, too, with the passion of discovery, with the inflamed zest of an unexampled curiosity. If the heat of that furnace could not give hardness and sharpness to material accessories, no other brain will ever do it," which contain diction ("inflamed;" "heat;" "furnace") that creates the implied metaphor.

44. In recounting the "realism" of Balzac's Paris (lines 28-33), the author relies upon **(B) appositives**.

Lines 29-31, "the houses, the upholstery, the food, the wines, the game of pleasure, the game of business, the game of finance," all are appositives, nouns that qualify in greater specificity "the actual city of Paris" (line 27).

45. The phrase, "the eye glides over them" (lines 42-43) BEST exemplifies the author's use of **(C) synecdoche**.

Synecdoche, or the substitution of the part for the whole, is evidenced by the word "eye," which in this case substitutes for the reader.

46. The phrase "blue-pencil" (line 47) likely means **(B) strike**.

This phrase is preceded by Cather's observation that "We have had too much of the interior decorator...," a phrase which crystallizes her criticism of Balzac's excess of detail. The author notes that Stevenson loved Balzac more than anyone, but that he still wished to do this to "a great deal of Balzac's 'presentation'..." (lines 47-48). The context implies that the phrase "blue pencil" means to edit out since one of the meanings of "strike" is to "cancel" or "remove".

47. The author's preference for Tolstoi's "realism" over that of Balzac is founded upon **(C) the manner in which Tolstoi integrates setting as part of the characters' experience**.

Choice C is largely determined by lines 56-65: "...the clothes, the dishes, the moving, haunting interiors of those old Moscow houses, are always so much a part of the emotions of the people that they are perfectly synthesized; they seem to exist, not so much in the author's mind, as in the emotional penumbra of the characters themselves. When it is fused like this, literalness ceases to be literalness—it is merely part of the experience."

48. Lines 68-70, "Out of the teeming, gleaming stream of the present, it must select the eternal material of art," compare the manner in which a novelist chooses detail to the work of a(n) **(A) prospector**.

The selection of A as the correct answer comes directly out of the diction and metaphor, "the teeming, gleaming stream of the present." The word "teeming" suggests that the stream is laden; the word "gleaming" connotes something that shines. The fact that the artist must "select" things out of the stream makes him similar to a prospector who pans for this precious metal.

49. In noting the trend of more contemporary writers to eschew "mere verisimilitude" (line 72), the author makes use of a parallel series of **(B) infinitive phrases**.

This is evidenced by the underlined phrases, "to break away from mere verisimilitude, and, following the development of modern painting, to interpret imaginatively the material and social investiture of their characters; to present their scene by suggestion rather than by enumeration.

50. The primary difference between paragraph four (lines 66-86) and the paragraphs that precede it lies in its **(D) expression of sentiment in a more didactic tone**.

Whereas the earlier paragraphs are devoted to a demonstration of Balzac's and Tolstoi's realism, the fourth paragraph gives instructions as to what young writers must do to avoid mere verisimilitude. The author assumes a didactic tone, suggesting that "The higher processes of art are all processes of simplification. The novelist must learn to write, and then he must unlearn it; just as the modern painter learns to draw, and then learns when utterly to disregard his accomplishment, when to subordinate it to a higher and truer effect. In this direction only, it seems to me, can the novel develop into anything more varied and perfect than all of the many novels that have gone before" (lines 77-86); thus, the selection of D as the best answer.

51. Which of the following BEST captures the author's point about the artist and realism as it is expressed in lines 70-83? **(D) Realism, as a technique, must not interfere with the artist's greater vision**.

Cather suggests in lines 78-83 that "The novelist must learn to write, and then he must unlearn it; just as the modern painter learns to draw, and then learns when utterly to disregard his accomplishment, when to subordinate it to a higher and truer effect." This suggests that detail should be subservient to the greater artistic purpose. This is the point of her subsequent allusion to *The Scarlet Letter*.

52. Lines 94-99—"The material investiture of the story...a department store window-dresser"—are intended to do which of the following?

   I. Compliment Hawthorne as a writer whose economy of detail allows him to achieve a "truer effect."
   II. Sardonically deride writers who clutter their work with superfluous scenic detail.
   III. Contrast the imagination of a celebrated American novel with the prosaic writing assigned in schools.

(C) I and II.

The suggestion that the "material investiture of the story"—in this case, its specific setting—is presented "unconsciously," or unnoticeably, and that Hawthorne has a "reserved, fastidious hand" support I. The comparisons to the "gaudy fingers of a showman or the mechanical industry of a department store window-dresser" are pejorative and intended to deride writers who are overly realistic. This validates II. There is no support offered for III in these lines.

53. The author likely uses the words "twilight" (line 100) and "dusk" (line 103) to illustrate the **(B) ambiguity of detail that makes Hawthorne's novel successful**.

The selection of choice B is based upon the vagueness that words such as "twilight" and "dusk" connote. This, according to Cather, makes the reader "feel" the surroundings rather than see them.

54. Which of the following adverbs may be perceived as having a double meaning? **(A) "unsparingly" (line 6)**.

The adverb "unsparingly" not only implies the amplitude of this detail but also suggests the merciless tedium that including it creates; hence, the selection of A as the correct answer.

Précis and Explanation of Free-Response Question One:
From Charles Kingsley's "My Winter Gardens"

In this passage from Charles Kingsley's essay "My Winter Gardens," the author reflects upon a change in perspective partially brought about by changes in circumstance and age. Though his early years, by his own admission, were marked by a *wanderlust* for the adventurous landscape of the American West, he quickly discovered that such an escape was not to be his and that his native England was to become his prison or palace "as [he] should choose to make it" (lines 4-5). This realization leads him to a heightened consciousness of the natural world and the understanding that the temptation of the larger world is purely one of size and not necessarily one of quality.

The author confesses in the passage's opening sentence how in the early days of his life his "brains were full of bison and grizzly bear, mustang and big-horn, Blackfoot and Pawnee, and hopes of wild adventure in the Far West…" (lines 1-2). These examples of local color, indigenous animals and Native American tribes serve almost as metonymies for the foreignness and excitement of a land far different from his own. This dream, however, was to be dissipated when he "discovered before he was twenty-three that "[his] lot was to stay at home and earn [his] bread in a very quiet way; that England was to be henceforth [his] prison or [his] palace as [he] should choose to make it…" (lines 3-5). For many this realization is a painful one since it establishes firm limitations to their futures. And though the author does not go into specifics as to why his own boundary was established, one gets the sense that his opportunity is checked by social standing or by economics. He readily admits that in "those first heats of youth" (line 6), the "little patch of moor" (lines 6-7) to which he was confined looked more "like a prison than a palace" (lines 7-8), his description capturing both the smallness and the bleakness of his environment, a sharp contrast to the color and expansiveness of the West of which he had dreamed. He reinforces this contrast through the similes of a dove and an eagle, the former condemned "to fly home to its nest and croodle" (lincs 8-9), the latter free "to swoop away over land and sea, in a rampant and self-glorifying fashion…" (lines 9-10). The contrast between the mundane "fly" and the more majestic "swoop" is buttressed by the antithesis of the domestic "nest" and the more unfettered "land and sea." Moreover, the archaic verb "croodle," meaning "to huddle and shiver," paints a grim picture of impoverished deprivation and discomfort.

At first the author's confinement to this sparse life chafes him, and he expresses this bitterness using anaphora, rhetorical questions, and images of exotic locales: "Others went out to see the glorious new worlds of the West, the glorious old worlds of the East—why should not I? Others rambled over Alps and Apennines, Italian picture-galleries and palaces, filling their minds with fair memories—why should not I?.… (lines 12-14). As he readily acknowledges, the thirst for adventure and excitement in youth is not easily quenched, and "It is not learned in a day, the golden lesson of the old Collect, to 'love the thing which is commanded, and desire that which is promised'" (lines 14-15). Paraphrased, this allusion to a common prayer implies that one must accept one's earthly lot and desire only the salvation to come. Only fifteen years later can the author begin to understand the wisdom of this prayer, when "the first grey hairs begin to show on the temples, and [he] can no longer jump as high as [his] third button—scarcely, alas! to any button at all…" (lines 17-18). These foreshadowings of physical decline, combined with the "innumerable sprains, bruises, soakings, and chillings, one's lower limbs feel in a cold thaw…" (lines 18-19), allow him to attain a modium of mature wisdom—that "if one still lusts after sights, [take] the nearest, and [look] for wonders, not in the Himalayas or Lake Ngami, but in the turf on the lawn and the brook in the park.…" (lines 20-21).

The opening sentence of the closing paragraph, "For there it is, friend, the whole infinite miracle of nature in every tuft of grass, if we have only eyes to see it, and can disabuse our minds of that tyrannous phantom of size…" (lines 22-23), provides a concise summary of the overall passage, suggesting that wonder is right in front of us if we learn to look for it there and not yearn for it elsewhere. His concluding analogy, about the "fly who basks upon one of the trilithons of Stonehenge…" (lines 25-26), reinforces this once more through the gross disparity between the physical size of the pillars and the tiny complexity of the insect, proving that there was as much beauty in his "little patch of moor" as there was in the prairies of the American West: he only needed to be older to see that.

This question has been reprinted for your convenience.

<u>Question One</u>

(Suggested time–40 minutes. This question counts as one-third of the total essay section score.)

The following passage follows a paragraph in which the author has recounted the exploits of a boyhood friend whose life-path had been starkly different from his own. Read the passage carefully. Then, in a well-organized essay, discuss what the passage reveals about the way(s) in which aging has modified the author's youthful attitude towards life and analyze how his rhetorical strategies convey this.

     For there were times, full many a year ago, when my brains were full of bison and grizzly bear, mustang and big-horn, Blackfoot and Pawnee, and hopes of wild adventure in the Far West, which I shall never see; for ere I was three-and-twenty, I discovered, plainly enough, that my lot was to stay at home and earn my bread in a very quiet way; that England was to be henceforth my prison or my palace as I

(5) should choose to make it; and I have made it, by Heaven's help, the latter.

     I will confess to you, though, that in those first heats of youth, this little England—or rather this little patch of moor in which I have struck roots as firm as the wild fir-trees do—looked at moments rather like a prison than a palace; that my foolish young heart would sigh, "Oh, that I had wings" not as a dove, to fly home to its nest and croodle,[1] but as an eagle, to swoop away over land and sea, in a rampant and

(10) self-glorifying fashion, on which I now look back as altogether unwholesome and undesirable. But the thirst for adventure and excitement was strong in me, as perhaps it ought to be in all at twenty-one. Others went out to see the glorious new worlds of the West, the glorious old worlds of the East—why should not I? Others rambled over Alps and Apennines, Italian picture-galleries and palaces, filling their minds with fair memories—why should not I?....It is not learned in a day, the golden lesson of the old

(15) Collect, to "love the thing which is commanded, and desire that which is promised." Not in a day, but in fifteen years one can spell out a little of its worth; and when one finds oneself on the wrong side of forty, and the first grey hairs begin to show on the temples, and one can no longer jump as high as one's third button—scarcely, alas! to any button at all; and what with innumerable sprains, bruises, soakings, and chillings, one's lower limbs feel in a cold thaw, much like an old post-horse's, why, one makes a virtue of

(20) necessity: and if one still lusts after sights, takes the nearest, and looks for wonders, not in the Himalayas or Lake Ngami, but in the turf on the lawn and the brook in the park....

     For there it is, friend, the whole infinite miracle of nature in every tuft of grass, if we have only eyes to see it, and can disabuse our minds of that tyrannous phantom of size. Only recollect that great and small are but relative terms; that, in truth, nothing is great or small save in proportion to the quantity of

(25) creative thought which has been exercised in making it; that the fly who basks upon one of the trilithons of Stonehenge is, in truth, infinitely greater than all Stonehenge together, though he may measure a tenth of an inch, and the stone of which he sits five-and-twenty feet....

_____

[1] To huddle and shiver
[2] In Christian liturgy, a short general prayer
[3] A prehistoric structure consisting of two standing stones supporting a third lain across them.

Scoring Guide for Free-Response Question One:
From Charles Kingsley's "My Winter Gardens"

9   Essays earning a score of 9 meet all the criteria for 8 papers and in addition are especially thorough in their analysis or demonstrate a particularly impressive control of style.

8   Essays earning a score of 8 effectively discuss what the passage reveals about the way(s) in which aging has modified the author's youthful attitude towards life and show how his rhetorical strategies convey this. They present a carefully reasoned argument in support of their position and enlist appropriate evidence from their reading. Their prose demonstrates an impressive control of the elements of effective writing, though it is not flawless.

7   Essays earning a score of 7 fit the description of 6 essays but feature either more purposeful arguments or a greater command of prose style.

6   Essays scoring 6 accurately discuss what the passage reveals about the way(s) in which aging has modified the author's youthful attitude towards life and show how his rhetorical strategies convey this. Their arguments, while generally sound in nature and adequately supported, are nevertheless not as persuasive as papers earning a score of 7 or better due to their being less developed or less cogent. Though these papers may also feature lapses in diction or syntax, they nevertheless contain the insight and composition skills that characterize a paper in the upper-half.

5   Essays scoring 5 generally understand the task, but are either limited in scope or insufficiently developed. Though they may be marked by errors in syntax or in diction, they nevertheless reflect a certain level of competence.

4   Essays scoring 4 respond inadequately to the question's task, struggling to discuss what the passage reveals about the way(s) in which aging has modified the author's youthful attitude towards life and/or how his rhetorical strategies convey this. Though their prose is often adequate enough to convey their writers' claims, it generally suggests a limited control over organization, diction, or syntax.

3   Essays earning a score of 3 meet the criteria for a score of 4, but are either less persuasive or display a more limited control over the elements of effective composition.

2   Essays scoring 2 achieve little success in discussing what the passage reveals about the way(s) in which aging has modified the author's youthful attitude towards life and/or in showing how his rhetorical strategies convey this. They may fail to develop their arguments to any substantive level or display significant weaknesses in organization, clarity, fluency or mechanics.

1   Essays earning a score of 1 meet the criteria for a score of 2 but are either overly simplistic or marred by severe deficiencies in the elements of composition.

0   Essays scoring 0 offer an off-topic response that receives no credit, or a mere repetition of the prompt.

—   Indicates a blank or completely off-topic response.

Sample Student Essay One

In life many things are taken for granted, especially things that seem almost mundane to the eye. Why would anyone take a second look at their lawn, or why would they even care about the small pebbles that line their driveway? One author addresses this issue very clearly in his essay that pertains to his lost life in which he initially looked at the big things and forgot about the little things. The use of a mournful tone as well as the close attention to detail truly show this author's feelings about how his aging has changed his views of the world.

The author speaks mournfully about his childhood as he constantly looks for the big things such as the Himalayas, and the Alps. He notes that his childhood he spent longing after the pursuit of the large and wonderful things and spent less time looking at the small things that were just outside his door. As he speaks about all of this, the reader can sense a level of distress that he had not chosen to look at the small things earlier on. It seems to greatly upset him that when he was younger he was so discontented with the house he lived in and the lawns outside his house. He mourns the fact that he did not appreciate what he had in front of him until he became older when he was unable to do things on his own anymore. The author speaks about how he wishes that he could have truly looked at the little things around him that were far more valuable to him now than the places he would never get to. He laments that he is as glad looking at the little pebbles that form small Stonehenges and admiring their beauty as he might be traveling all the way to Stonehenge to admire it there. What he is most upset about is the fact that everything was right there in front of him and he chose not to take advantage of it until he was unable to properly move about and function. He becomes more appreciative of things such as the brook in the park and the turf on the lawn, and he realizes that he is truly happy where he is and not wishing he was an eagle flying off to some foreign and mysterious place.

Also the author uses incredible detail to describe every aspect of his wants and need as he ages. When a young man, he was enthralled by the palaces and picture galleries of Italy and not with the prison that was his home. His view of his house is incredibly detailed as he describes the prison that he was unable to escape as if he were locked in and could not get out. It is as if he doesn't even acknowledge that it is a place that gives him shelter and provides him with a home. When he speaks about the wonders of the world, it is clear to the reader that these places are magnificent and grand, yet it is possible to see that as he grows older his attention to detail switches to the plants and rocks in his backyard. These little things he starts to describe as magnificent, not the grand Alps or Himalayas but rather the rocks or the lawn. His shift in detail shows a shift in attitude as he ages. It also shows his overall appreciation of more things as he ages and a better outlook on life. He has truly changed as a person as he has aged.

With age comes perspective. The author of this essay truly proves that as he changes his attitude throughout the essay using his mournful tone and in detail description of everything around him. It is possible to see a change in attitude as he ages and a greater appreciation for everything as well as a level of happiness as he gets older unparalleled by anything else in his life.

Sample Student Essay Two

As children, one dreams of the great unknown and wishes to leave the confines of one's backyard. The author of the given essay deals with this topic of reflection of childhood expectations and compares it to the realities that one faces as they grow older. Through his change in tone and use of details, he shows that he has reached a Zen mindset even though he still harbors regrets about his life.

Initially, the author's tone gives the impression that he is resentful of those who were able to leave and explore while he remained at home. However, he speaks about the past with a peaceful calm that shows that he came to terms with his past. The initial rush of resentment gives hints that for most of his life he had harbored these feelings. Perhaps, in some part of him, it is still there. Therefore, he is content with where he is in life but not happy. This change in tone is due to the change in perspective and a new-found appreciation for the little miracles in everyday occurrences.

Through details, he gives the impression of an adventure by mentioning far off places and peoples. He then changes to minutia which draws the reader toward the same conclusion reached by the author. The comparison between the fly and Stonehenge symbolically draws the parallel of a single person in the vast unknown world. Accumulatively, the details give the impression of the contentment of the author. However, when listing the various maladies that strike as one grows old, he demonstrates an uneasiness and lack of happiness in his life. He acknowledges that he is missing something from his life but not something important.

In the author's reflection of his life, he talks about the hopes he once had for the future and how they remained unfulfilled. He also talks about the way he once viewed the world and how it changed to the calm and watchful perspective of the here and now. His overall tone emits a calm serenity with underlying past resentment seeping in at times. The attention to details reiterates the feelings of the essay overall and makes the reader identify with the author's past and present.

Sample Student Essay Three

Time often erases childhood ambitions and dreams, causing an adult either to become cynical and hardened towards the rest of the world or to become realistic about life in this world. In this particular passage, the speaker has given up some of his wildest dreams in return for a simple, average life in England. Although his older age has helped him to realize that true greatness often lies in some of the smallest objects or ideas, which he reveals through the juxtaposition of a variety of larger and smaller animals, plants, and locations, and has helped him to develop a certain contentment in his life, revealed by his comparison of England to a palace and his comparison of himself to a tree, he also feels a sense of disparity about what he has given up and about old age itself, both of which he reveals through his tone.

At a younger age, even at the age of twenty-one, the speaker felt thirsty for adventure and excitement. In the "first heats of youth," he often looked upon England as a prison from which he wished he could fly like an eagle and "swoop away over land and sea, in a rampant and self-glorifying fashion." The speaker's romantic, idealistic tone, which stems from his hope to fly away and see the new worlds of the West, the bison and grizzly bear or perhaps the Alps and Apennines, seems highly unrealistic and largely blown out of proportion. In fact, the speaker himself, at an older age, realizes that his old dreams were "unwholesome and undesirable." As multiple years passed, he began to learn that one must appreciate his or her designated place in the world because one must love the "thing which is commanded." This idea has allowed the speaker to no longer look for wonders among the "Himalayas or Lake Ngami," but to rather look for wonders in the turf on his lawn or in a small brook. He juxtaposes these large wonders of the world and gallant animals which soar high above others with much smaller miracles in nature, such as tufts of grass and flies sitting on a large stone in the middle of Stonehenge. These juxtapositions between wonders that seem great, but turn out to be unrealistic, and a small, marvelous creature emphasize his belief that "nothing is great or small save in proportion to the quantity of creative thought which has been exercised in making it." Although it took years for him to learn such a lesson, age finally allows the speaker to appreciate the small pleasures in life and to rejoice in his position rather than long for change and for adventure.

Despite the lessons he learns and the small sense of satisfaction which the speaker develops in England, there is also an evident sense throughout the passage a disparity and sadness which can be sensed in the speaker's tone. Initially, he speaks with such fervor about his lost dreams of "bison and grizzly bear [...] and hopes of wild adventure in the Far West, which [he] shall never see." The finality of the word "never" places a damper on the wonder and magnitude of these visions, creating the initial melancholic undertone. In addition, although the speaker recognizes that his young heart was "foolish" or even "unwholesome," he also cannot fully grasp the reason why his friends could explore the world, yet he could not, as emphasized by his repetition of the rhetorical question "why should not I?" This lack of full understanding ultimately continues the underlying gloomy tone and prevents the author from fully reaching a stage of contentment. In addition to this sadness about giving up old dreams, the speaker also feels a sense of disparity about growing old. He mentions that as one reaches forty, "one can no longer jump as high as one's third button" and has "innumerable sprains, bruises, soakings, and chillings." Although knowledge and understanding comes with age, both of which have allowed the speaker to reach a sort of self-contented stage in life, other complications come with age as well. As the speaker mentions such health-issues and such loss of adventurous and fervent youth, the reader senses sadness in his tone as if the speaker has partially found contentment among smaller pleasures in life because of a new understanding and partially found contentment in such things out of necessity, since he no longer has the ability to go out and explore the world. These conflicting views about life ultimately prevent the speaker from reaching a full sense of satisfaction and create some leftover feelings of unhappiness.

Although the speaker's age has allowed him to reach new knowledge about adventure and greatness in the world, revealed through his juxtaposition of his once grandiose dreams and his now simple pleasures, and has helped him to obtain some contentment in his new palace-like England where he has planted his roots, he also feels a moroseness about his loss of his younger, more adventurous self, revealed through an underlying gloomy tone. Despite this incomplete sense of contentment, the speaker does rejoice in the idea that one need not travel the world to find miracles. One must simply forget the idea that miracles are found only in things with a "tyrannous phantom of size" and open one's mind to the grandeur of the fly sitting on the stone.

**Assessment of Student Responses to Free-Response Question One:
From Charles Kingsley's "My Winter Gardens"**

Sample Student Essay One:

A. Assessment of Reader One

The writer of this essay tends to say the same thing over and over without citing lines from the text to back up the assertions or analysis. In the first paragraph the tone is misrepresented as "mournful," but, finally, in the second paragraph the writer does get the gist of the passage: "He becomes more appreciative of things…". There is so much repetition, I was at first thinking this would score a 5, but upon reading the final paragraph, even with the repetition of the "mournful" tone, the student was able to show a basic understanding of the passage with the final sentence. Lower-half 6.

B. Assessment of Reader Two

Sample Student Essay One has merit in that it gets the general gist of Kingsley's passage and examines how its tone and choice of detail reflect the new perspective the author has achieved. However, it wrong-headedly determines this tone to be "mournful" and either does not see or fail to pick up on the rich figurative language contained in the passage. The sentence structure is at times repetitive. I rate this as an upper-half paper, but not far up the rubric: a 6, no more.

Sample Student Essay Two:

A. Assessment of Reader One

Sample essay two is a prototypical 5. The writer seems to understand the task (though he questionably interprets the author's list of age-related maladies as a sign of discontent) and makes reasonable comments about the tone and the contrast of the pillars and the fly. It is written lucidly and coherently, but it is very underdeveloped for forty minutes.

B. Assessment of Reader Two

The introduction for this essay shows real promise, if only these ideas had been supported within the body of the essay. But sadly they are not. There are no lines at all to support the brief analysis, and at one point in paragraph 3 the analysis breaks down completely. The essay does discuss the imagery with the fly and the stones from Stonehenge, but then throughout the remainder of the essay—what little there is—the same ideas are repeated over and over, and many times the analysis is contradictory. 4.

Sample Student Essay Three:

A. Assessment of Reader One

It is hard to believe that this was composed in 40 minutes or less. It is beautifully written and includes lines from the original text for support. This writer sees and understands the depth of the piece, by adding his/her own ideas about "palace" and "prison" being somewhat the same thing to the author. The conclusion is masterful. A lovely 9.

B. Assessment of Reader Two

This paper displays all the qualities of a 9 range-finder, It is perhaps overwritten (the most salient example being the sprawling construction that closes the initial paragraph) but it touches upon and merges fluidly all the essentials of content and language that a 9 paper could possibly hope to include. The student writer displays a deep understanding of Kingsley's intent and a keen eye for diction, rhetorical questions, juxtaposition and other literary techniques, all of which are seamlessly imbedded into the argument. Though the student seems to mistake "despair" for "disparity," it is nevertheless understandable what he/she means.

Précis and Explication of Free-Response Question Two: Citation from Hannah Arendt's "Ideology and Terror"

The key words in the citation from Hannah Arendt's essay are "greatness" and "perplexity." The former alludes to the great freedoms afforded the individual by democratic societies which, unlike their totalitarian counterparts, allow for the exercise of free will. The latter derives from the conundrum caused by that freedom: namely, how can one ever expect individuals to follow society's rules if its philosophy tolerates a breach of them? As Aunt Lydia tells Offred in Margaret Atwood's *The Handmaid's Tale*, there is "freedom from" and "freedom to." Atwood's fictional totalitarian society insures the first, denies the second. Thus, the handmaids are shielded from lewd commentary and exploitative pornography but are forced to wear nun-like habits and to live an extremely cloistered existence. Arendt's observation, however, goes one step further by suggesting that the laws in a democracy do not necessarily provide a definitive moral compass; that they forbid certain unacceptable actions but fail to inform one of the proper courses of action or conduct. This contradiction places the burden of moral conduct squarely on human shoulders.

Students responding successfully to this prompt should likely seek a real or fictional situation that reflects this contradiction, a situation in which an individual must consider what Emerson labels "higher laws" over those legislated by humans. One example might be the capture and killing of Osama Bin Laden. Though clearly the architect of the World Trade Center catastrophe who been had pursued for years by the U.S. military and C.I.A. for the murder of over three thousand U.S. citizens, Bin Laden evaded capture until after years of fruitless pursuit he was finally located in a fortified safe house in Pakistan. For the United States government, this posed an acute moral dilemma: whether to inform the Pakistani government and risk losing Bin Laden due to security leaks by sympathizers, or to cross the border in a brazen night raid intended to capture him and bring him to justice. In the end President Obama opted to follow his moral conscience and okay the raid despite the fact that it violated Pakinstani airspace.

An interesting counter-example might be Herman Melville's novella *Billy Budd* in which Captain Vere is forced to adjudicate Billy's shipboard murder of Claggart. Though Claggart's death might well be deemed manslaughter since Billy strikes him in response to a mendacious charge that he is involved in a planned mutiny, the strict language of the Mutiny Act demands that anyone found guilty of a shipboard murder be hanged. Though Vere is aware of Billy's gentle nature and beloved status among the ship's crew, as well as the fact that Billy's physical violence was a frustrated response to his inability to defend himself due to his characteristic stutter, the captain opts to follow the letter of the law, condemning the Handsome Sailor to death. This instance actually contradicts Arendt's premise since the law clearly tells Captain Vere what he has to do, leaving him little guidance as to how to interpret it under extenuating circumstances.

Arendt's interesting claim should permit students plenty of latitude in responding to the question whether they opt for real-life or fictional examples with which to do so.

This question has been reprinted for your convenience.

<u>Question Two</u>

(Suggested time—40 minutes. This question counts as one-third of the total essay section score.)

Hannah Arendt, in her essay "Ideology and Terror: A Novel Form of Government," makes the following observation: "…the greatness, but also the great perplexity, of laws in free society is that they only tell what one should not, but never what one should do."

Take a moment to reflect on the preceding observation. Then, in a well-organized essay, examine both the contradiction and the moral dilemma inherent in Arendt's claim. Use your reading, studies, experience or observations to develop your argument.

Scoring Guide for Free-Response Question Two:
Citation from Hannah Arendt's "Ideology and Terror"

9   Essays earning a score of 9 meet all the criteria for 8 papers and in addition are especially thorough in their analysis or demonstrate a particularly impressive control of style.

8   Essays earning a score of 8 effectively explore both the contradiction and the moral dilemma inherent in Arendt's claim. They present a carefully reasoned argument in support of their position and enlist appropriate evidence from their reading. Their prose demonstrates an impressive control of the elements of effective writing, though it is not flawless.

7   Essays earning a score of 7 fit the description of 6 essays but feature either more purposeful arguments or a greater command of prose style.

6   Essays scoring 6 accurately explain the contradiction and the moral dilemma inherent in Arendt's claim. Their arguments, while generally sound in nature and adequately supported, are nevertheless not as persuasive as papers earning a score of 7 or better due to their being less developed or less cogent. Though these papers may also feature lapses in diction or syntax, they nevertheless contain the insight and composition skills characterize a paper in the upper-half.

5   Essays scoring 5 generally understand the task, but are either limited in scope or insufficiently developed. Though they may be marked by errors in syntax or in diction, they nevertheless reflect a certain level of competence.

4   Essays scoring 4 respond inadequately to the question's task, struggling to understand the citation from Hannah Arendt, the contradiction and/or the moral dilemma inherent in Arendt's claim. Though their prose is often adequate enough to convey their writers' claims, it generally suggests a limited control over organization, diction, or syntax.

3   Essays earning a score of 3 meet the criteria for a score of 4, but are either less persuasive or display a more limited control over the elements of effective composition.

2   Essays scoring 2 achieve little success in comprehending the citation from Hannah Arendt or the contradiction and the moral dilemma inherent in it. They may fail to develop their arguments to any substantive level or display significant weaknesses in organization, clarity, fluency or mechanics.

1   Essays earning a score of 1 meet the criteria for a score of 2 but are either overly simplistic or marred by severe deficiencies in the elements of composition.

0   Essays scoring 0 offer an off-topic response that receives no credit, or a mere repetition of the prompt.

—   Indicates a blank or completely off-topic response.

Sample Student Essay One

Hannah Arendt's assertion on laws, that they are great and perplexing in free society, is one that while difficult to come to terms with is most certainly true. The contradiction and moral question relating to free will presented by this statement inevitably make it one which is hard to swallow.

To understand whit this is and why Arendt's statement is, in fact, true, one must look at a free society. A "free society" is somewhat contradictory by its very nature because in order to maintain freedoms within a society there must be some force used to assert and maintain law and order. This not a fact which is new to society, it has been clear to many throughout history, amongst them John Stuart Mill who wrote in his <u>On Liberty</u> that the power of a government was derived from it's ability to use force on it's territory.

This inevitably leads to a question relating to that thing which is both mankinds' greatest and most dangerous trait: free will. There are always those in a free society who will assert that a society must be totally free, which is to say without any semblance of law and order. So the question presented is whether it is better to have no law and order or a modicum of law and order designed to safeguard the freedom of the people. History has shown us through examples, such as the period of anarchy that blanketed Europe following the fall of the Roman Empire and the subsequent ages of feudalism and absolutism which resulted from said period, that human nature is incapable of handling a completely and utterly free society. It is not for no reason that a large part of the era described above is known as "the Dark Ages".

Thus, Arendt describes laws in a free society as great, but also perplexing. Our tendency as humans to rationalize life makes the concept of laws in a "free society" difficult to comprehend. However, a starkly different aspect of that same nature, free will, and may be done with it when there are now laws whatsoever, makes laws not only a necessary but a great part of any free society.

Sample Student Essay Two

In free societies, laws exist to prevent actions deemed a threat to the well being of the population. They do not tell one what they must do, but rather what is prohibited. In "Ideology and Terror" Hannah Arendt discusses the problems with laws. She identifies the moral dilemma of having limitations in a society that is "free". Too many laws would create a civilization reminiscent of that described by George Orwell in 1984. Too few laws world create anarchy similarly as dangerous to the well-being of the population. Laws that tell one what they must do seem more limiting to someone's freedom; one could not choose what they deem is best for themselves. Laws that prohibit bestow the freedom to choose what one wants to do as long as it is not a danger to themselves and/or others. Laws that prohibit allow for the existence of something seeming impossible: a free society.

Throughout the course of any history class, many different types of societies are accessed. Everything from democracies to dictatorships are covered, whether they are corrupt, evil or revolutionary. However, few, if any, lawless societies are ever studied. This not because they are unimportant or boring, but rather that they can not exist. Because none of them can possibly last for any significant amount of time, they have no opportunity to make a mark in history. The lack of any anarchical societies in almost all history textbooks is a testament to the failure of societies without government in laws. The historical lack of these types of societies is evidence of how societies need laws to exist.

The need for laws can also be seen in The Lord of the Flies. In the novel, the children struggle to establish a sustainable society on the island. They create a few "laws" but the central government (Ralph) is not powerful enough to keep the subjects under control. After a short while this lack of restrictions brings the children out of control. First the children break some of the small rules; for example some of the younger children defecate near the food supplies. Later, this lack of laws leads to the total degeneration of the society, which culminates in the murder of Simon and Piggy. Ralph's government falls apart as Jack brings most of the children to his new tribe. The collapse of society due to a lack of rules and enforcement shows that laws are necessary for a group of people to exist in a sustainable manner.

Anarchy has little success, but forms of government that use laws to tell one what they must do are often oppressive and unpopular. In 1984, George Orwell paints a portrait of a society with too many laws. The Thought Police are designed to prevent people from thinking bad thoughts. The lack of privacy (due to the monitors in everyone's rooms) totally strips many of the people of their dignity. For the protagonist of the novel, Winston, this world is a nightmare. The laws of the land limit him so much that he is able to make few decisions for himself. The total lack of hope throughout the entire novel shows how a society with too many laws is anything but free.

In history, societies with too many laws fail to succeed. A good example of this is the failure of many communist nations. In the USSR, there were many restrictions. People could only do what the laws dictated. This society was far from free because it contained laws that told one what they must do. After many years, this government eventually fell apart. It started with rebellions in satellite states, where people grew tired of the oppression. Eventually (in combination with Gorbachev's domestic policies) the USSR crumbled.

Throughout history and literature, there have been many examples of societies with too few or too many laws. These societies are not sustainable and soon collapse. The great problem when creating society is balancing the amount of laws. Too few will lead to just as many problems as too many. Great societies are those that have been able to find this balance and remain powerful for long periods of time.

Sample Student Essay Three

Americans prize their status as citizens of the "land of the free and the home of the brave," cherishing their individual rights and civil liberties. However, Hannah Arendt, in her essay "Ideology and Terror: A Novel Form of Government," challenges this assertion, suggesting that "the greatness, but also the great perplexity, of laws in free society is that they "only tell what one should not do, but never what one should do." In this way, Arendt sets up a contradiction: is a free society really free if laws limit the actions of its citizens? Political theorists would defend this moral dilemma by contending that laws that "tell what one should not to do" serve to protect citizens from each other. In essence, the beauty of a free society lies in the fact that individuals retain the freedom to express their own opinions without fear of repercussions.

The early political scientist Thomas Hobbes described life in a state of nature as "nasty, brutish and short." He maintained that people should give some of their rights to an absolute ruler, a Leviathan, in exchange for protection. While Hobbes did not advocate a free society, he did establish one of the key features of democratic government: to provide for the defense and general welfare of its people. Without laws to protect us from our fellow humans, chaos would quickly ensue. Anarchy would certainly result without a government to keep us in line. Laws exist that outlaw certain actions altogether, but they also set limits on our freedoms. For example, in Schenk v. U.S., the Supreme Court held that you cannot shout "Fire!" in a crowded theater since a stampede might ensue, presenting a danger to the safety of others. To protect the sanctity of information and the reputations of others, one cannot slander another. Although Americans reserve the right to bear arms under the Second Amendment, background checks and a license are required to purchase a firearm in many states, all in the name of protecting citizens. While citizens many point to a seemingly extensive list of checks on personal freedoms, these measures are necessary to public safety.

Despite these limitations, by no means are these restrictions intended to govern individual behavior. Unlike many countries, free societies such as the U.S. grant their citizens the right to criticize their government and elect their leaders. Countries with a more dictatorial structure often seek to influence the actions and opinions of their citizens, stifling the voices of activists or censoring Google, for example. In Hitler's time, he indoctrinated the idea of Aryan supremacy into the minds of the German people, telling them to turn upon their Jewish neighbors. During the Cultural Revolution, Chinese dictator Mao Zedong suppressed intellectuals, mandating that all Chinese return a primitive agricultural lifestyle. In free societies, the government does not attempt to infiltrate the private lives of its citizens. Individuals reserve the right to make their own decisions regarding career path, family structure or education. Although the government may try to sway opinions, they never mandate voting for a certain candidate while holding a gun to someone's head. In spite of the necessary restrictions on our liberties, individuals in free societies retain a great deal of freedom.

Although it seems contradictory, free societies must curtail the rights of their citizens in some fashion simply to maintain order. While the society may not fit the textbook definition of "free," most citizens would contend that they prefer limitations designed to preserve their safety in lieu of a completely "free" lawless anarchy. In this way, individuals lead lives free from harm and free to make their own decisions.

**Assessment of Student Responses to Free-Response Question Two:
Citation from Hannah Arendt's "Ideology and Terror"**

Sample Student Essay One:

A. Assessment of Reader One

This essay seems to understand the issue of the prompt and states the important two words/ideas (great, perplexing) in the opening paragraph. Sadly this essay stays "on the surface" of both ideas almost entirely, with little support other than a passing reference to *On Liberty* by John Stuart Mill. The briefness and the lack of depth earns this essay a score of 4.

B. Assessment of Reader Two

Though a more charitable grader might give this a 5, I believe it is a prototypical 4. The writing, apart from the final convoluted sentence, is competent, and the writer does provide some reasonable examples to back his thought. At the same time, the paper is rather brief and does not ever display a firm grasp of the essence of Arendt's observation. It displays characteristics that are common to most 4 essays.

Sample Student Essay Two:

A. Assessment of Reader One

This essay certainly is competent and is supported by the student's reading and knowledge of current events, but it does not use examples from free society. Paragraph two seems almost wasted space as the writer deals in great generalities about the lack of study in history class of the "lawless" society—which seems to be a bit far afield from the prompt. However, competent writing and passable examples earn this essay a 6.

B. Assessment of Reader Two

Sample essay two was appreciably better in all aspects. It shows a clear understanding of Arendt's claim and is thoroughly developed through examples from history and literature. It makes some insightful commentary about the absence of lawless societies from history books and answers the question thoroughly and fluently. The writing itself has some problems (most noticeably, with agreement in number), but these are not fatal distractions to the paper's argument. Though the time spent on the historical and literary examples is limited, collectively they buttress the author's points with conviction. I would score this response a 7.

Sample Student Essay Three:

A. Assessment of Reader One

This essay is very good—clearly a 9. Examples are rich and well-supported; the prompt is addressed insightfully, and the writing is superior.

B. Assessment of Reader Two

There is precious little to be said here. This student's response reflects firm control of the topic and of the elements of composition. The impressive array of historical and political allusions merge seamlessly from start to finish, effectively defending the writer's thesis. This is a clear-cut 9.

Précis and Explication of Free-Response Question Three: Synthesis Essay on Insuring School Safety

Every since the tragic incident at Columbine and several others like it, insuring the safety of school children has become a significant school concern. While educating students remains the number one priority, providing them with a safe environment in which to learn has achieved an almost equal status. Many schools now feature security cameras, prominent signs directing visitors to check in at the school office, more limited access points, school security officers, student profiling, and, in the most at-risk environments, metal detectors that screen for weapons.

While no one can argue that insuring student safety is part of a new reality in education, this brave new world of Orwellian surveillance intrudes upon privacy, treating every member of the school community as a potential suspect. Free-Response Question One posed these two essential questions: "Is ensuring a safe educational environment for America's students a technological issue or a social one?" and "Is vigilance best served by screening for weapons or screening for potentially unstable students?" Students were given five articles and a cartoon on this topic and asked to take a position that "defends, challenges or qualifies the claim that insuring students the right to a secure learning environment is less an issue of technological deterrence than one of social deterrence, and that true security can only be assured by identifying and monitoring students who pose a potential threat to the greater school community."

As is to be expected of a good synthesis question, students were provided with a variety of sources. Document A, from a book called *The Causes of School Violence*, agreed that screening for weapons, by mechanical or human means, was an evil necessitated by circumstance but openly wondered if such a *stalag* mentality created an environment that might inversely encourage violence. Document B, an article from *The Chronicle of Higher Education*, questioned the wisdom in destroying student records, suggesting that prior incidence of violent or potentially violent behavior should be made public so as to avoid a future catastrophe. Such transparency, it notes, clashes with legislation protecting students' privacy. Document C, an amusing but ominous cartoon, shows two students with their arms on the wall being frisked by campus security while a metal detector and a sign insisting on everything from a fingerprint scan to a FBI background check looms in the background.

Document D, a lengthier selection from a book called *Violence in America's Schools: Understanding, Prevention and Responses*, is a more technical article that offers a checklist of things that schools might do to improve security: some pragmatic (two-way locks on classroom doors), some seemingly histrionic (minimizing the number of flat roofs from which a sniper could fire a gun). Source E, from a book called *Comprehending Columbine*, briefly references the two troubled youths who initiated the carnage before looking at the effectiveness of student profiling. It ultimately concludes that the latter tactic is unreliable because it can cast too broad a net, targeting any student who feels alienated. Finally, Source F, an article called "Proactive Prevention," focuses mostly upon the merits of video surveillance while conceding that vigilant parents are the best frontline against potential school violence. Collectively, these six sources provide thoughtful fodder for student essays on the topic.

This question has been reprinted for your convenience.

<u>Question Three</u>

Reading Time: 15 minutes
Suggested Writing Time: 40 minutes

(This question counts as one-third of the total essay section score.)

Directions:

The following prompt is based on the accompanying six sources.

This question requires you to integrate a variety of sources into a coherent, well-written essay. *Refer to the sources to support your position; avoid paraphrase or summary. Your argument should be central; the sources should support this argument.*

Remember to attribute both direct and indirect citations.

Introduction:

Over the last decade schools across America have been forced to confront an increasing incidence of violence, ranging from bullying to bias-motivated crimes to tragic shootings on school campuses. The resultant clamor for greater school security has included calls for everything from increases in security personnel to the installation of surveilliance cameras and metal detectors, from training in conflict resolution to the psychological profiling of students. However, is ensuring a safe educational environment for America's students a technological issue or a social one? Is vigilance best served by screening for weapons or screening for potentially unstable students?

Assignment:

Read the following sources (including any introductory information) carefully. **Then, in an essay that synthesizes at least three of the sources for support, take a position that defends, challenges or qualifies the claim that insuring students the right to a secure learning environment is less an issue of technological deterrence than it is of social deterrence, and that true security can only be assured by identifying and monitoring students who pose a potential threat to the greater school community.**

Scoring Guide for Free-Response Question Three: Synthesis Essay on Insuring School Safety

9   Essays earning a score of 9 meet all the criteria for 8 papers and in addition are especially thorough in their analysis or demonstrate a particularly impressive control of style.

8   Essays earning a score of 8 effectively defend, challenge or qualify the claim that insuring safety is less an issue of technological deterrence than one of social profiling, and that true security can only be assured by identifying and monitoring students who pose a potential threat to the school community. They present a carefully reasoned argument in support of their position and enlist appropriate evidence from their reading. Their prose demonstrates an impressive control of the elements of effective writing, though it is not flawless.

7   Essays earning a score of 7 fit the description of 6 essays but feature either more purposeful arguments or a greater command of prose style.

6   Essays scoring 6 accurately defend, challenge or qualify the claim that insuring student safety is less an issue of technological deterrence than one of social profiling, and that true security can only be assured by identifying and monitoring students who pose a potential threat to the school community. Their arguments, while generally sound in nature and adequately supported, are nevertheless not as persuasive as papers earning a score of 7 or better due to their being less developed or less cogent. Though these papers may also feature lapses in diction or syntax, they nevertheless contain the insight and composition skills characterize a paper in the upper-half.

5   Essays scoring 5 generally understand the task, but are either limited in scope or insufficiently developed. Though they may be marked by errors in syntax or in diction, they nevertheless reflect a certain level of competence.

4   Essays scoring 4 respond inadequately to the question's task, struggling to take a position that defends, challenges or qualifies the claim that insuring student safety is less an issue of technological deterrence than one of social profiling. Though their prose is often adequate enough to convey their writers' claims, it generally suggests a limited control over organization, diction, or syntax.

3   Essays earning a score of 3 meet the criteria for a score of 4, but are either less persuasive or display a more limited control over the elements of effective composition.

2   Essays scoring 2 achieve little success in defending, challenging or qualifying the claim that insuring student safety is less an issue of technological deterrence than one of social profiling. They may fail to develop their arguments to any substantive level or display significant weaknesses in organization, clarity, fluency or mechanics.

1   Essays earning a score of 1 meet the criteria for a score of 2 but are either overly simplistic or marred by severe deficiencies in the elements of composition.

0   Essays scoring 0 offer an off-topic response that receives no credit, or a mere repetition of the prompt.

—   Indicates a blank or completely off-topic response.

Sample Student Essay One

The increased prevalence of violence on school campuses poses a disturbing dilemma to school administrators. Even minor violence can disrupt every aspect of a school community, and in the worst cases, end in tragedy. Technology may help increase security in schools, but the issue of violence among students is essentially social, and this problem will never be solved unless the social aspect is addressed.

There is no doubt that requiring each student to pass through metal detectors and a security checkpoint each day would reduce the amount of weapons brought to school. Such intrusive security measures, however, bring their own set of problems, as mentioned in document A. The mere presence of such rigorous security would disrupt the school community by instilling fear in the student body. It also creates an environment in which the students are alienated by the administration, increasing resentment and decreasing the likelihood of communication and collaboration. Furthermore, security measures such as these would only prevent the entrance of weapons into the school and do nothing to discourage bullying. Document D outlines the benefits of surveillance cameras, but this measure would have little effect in preventing violence among students, though it would be useful after the fact to persecute wrongdoers. Installing cameras and monitoring school entrances would minimize the threat from outside the school, but that is another issue entirely. All things considered, even the most effective technology remedies only the surface issue of school violence. The real problem is social and physiological, and must be treated as such.

Don Frazier states that "Technology alone will not stem the threat of violence in schools," and he could not be more correct. Any child or young adult who is motivated to initiate severe violence in school is seriously emotionally and perhaps mentally disturbed, and psychological profiling may help to detect warning signs before a tragedy occurs. As document E mentions, most students with psychological issues will not end up in the middle of a school shooting, but seeking out help for these students would certainly do no harm, and may prevent a desperate child from turning to violence. Larkin writes that school shooters were often isolated in school and "perceived themselves as punishing peers or teachers who had done them wrong." This brings up another vital component in preventing school violence, and that is relationships among students. The student body has a responsibility to remain aware and make an effort to include socially marginalized peers. Administrations should regularly discourage teasing and bullying and encourage tolerance and inclusion. If students feel less threatened by their peers, they will be less likely to lash out with violence. Technology may increase security, but school violence is an extremely complex social and psychological issue, and it will only be remedied when it is treated as such.

Sample Student Essay Two

In this fast paced world, danger appears to be lurking around every corner especially in the places least suspected: the schools that little boys and girls hurry off to every morning. In the past years, there have been numerous incidents involving school violence, the most obvious being Virginia Tech. The best way to prevent future problems is to screen the student body for potential threats because a technology lockdown fosters a prison mentality, is too expensive and less effective than acknowledging past events in a child's life that may prove dangerous to their peers. Information about students has previously been kept under lock and key in a permanent file when, instead, important information should be distributed to school administrators.

The main problem with setting up a lockdown setup at a school with a million security cameras, metal detectors, and a brute security guard who looks like he/she belongs as a bouncer at a club downtown, is that schools end up looking like prisons. As Helga Schier says in <u>The Causes of School Violence</u>, "lockdown mentality better suits a prison than an educational institution meant to foster creativity and curiosity". It's been proven that if people are treated a certain way, they'll start acting like it. Students will live up to the expectations set upon them which can help them toward a good college or hurt them by sending them to Juvie. Schools were established to give children the opportunity to explore their possibilities in a sheltered environment and they shouldn't be replaced with a stifled and restrictive atmosphere resembling a prison.

Technology has a second set of problems of which the rest of the world is already aware. It is tremendously expensive to install all this equipment which makes it unaffordable for most public schools. Whereas, hiring an effective guidance counselor is more affordable and reasonable than spending billions in technology that might not even work. Equipment may have bugs or glitches. Children are very crafty.] if they want something, they will find a way around a camera. Besides childish ingenuity, there is always other technology which could neutralize the installed machinery. Every time a defense weapon is introduced to the market, someone else is inventing a way to get around it. It becomes a constant arms race similar to the Cold War. It's unnecessary to pay billions for technology that might work and may or may not be effective against human cunning or against its technological counterpart.

Under the current system there are rules in place "to protect a student's privacy or avoid influencing next year's teachers with news of this year's infractions", as Katherine Newman states in <u>Before the Rampage: What Can be Done</u>. This prevents teachers/principals from having access to disciplinary records or permanent files in order to give kids another chance. This is good in theory but has had poor results as DeAngelis, principal at Columbine High School, discovered. In "Comprehending Columbine," Ralph W. Larkin says that DeAngelis "had no information about Dylan Klebold and Eric Harris's arrest and remand to a diversion program....he was unaware of the existence of Eric's Trenchcoat Mafia website that contained threats directed at the school." If he had access to this information, he would have been able to keep an eye on these kids and would have been able to act before things got out of hand. There is a solution to this current dilemma. Give administrators access to this information so they can keep their eyes out for any other examples of dangerous behavior. If things get worse after an isolated incident or if things repeat themselves, then it is time to take action and intervene on behalf of the rest of the student body.

The responsibility of school administrators is to protect their students against outside forces and against each other on a budget. It's a tall order to fill and the only way to accomplish this feat is to carefully watch students and take action when there appears to be a potential problem. Children deserve a second chance, but not at the expense of another person's life.

Sample Student Essay Three

In recent years school safety has become a huge problem to not only the safety of the student but to the learning process. Many students are subjected to metal detectors, pat downs, and other physically unnecessary cautions. But in reality what is the true problem with the students, and how is it possible to avoid the shootings that occurred in places such as Columbine High School? The problem lies more in the mindset of the students, and less in the physical presence of guards at schools. The students who ended up going on shooting rages were students who were upset and often times were students that had recently moved into the school district. In order to increase the security in schools there must be some sort of psychological screening, background checks on kids moving into the school district, and a decrease in physical screening.

The first sign that a student would likely go on any sort of shooting rage would be if they are depressed. But how is anyone supposed to know if a student is depressed if the most contact they have with them is standing in front of a classroom and lecturing to them? What truly needs to happen is some sort of screening process put into place so that at least every month students will go in and talk to a psychologist and they can evaluate their level of contentedness with the school. If they are upset then they can have counseling instead of being left to brood, as unhappy teenagers seem to do. In the case of Columbine the school guidance counselor had absolutely no clue that the students were upset (Doc. E). They were unaware of the problems and thus were unable to either get the students help or even talk to them themselves. The better a student's mindset, the less they would be predisposed to go on a shooting rage. This is fairly straight forward but in almost every school across America it is not instituted. It seems almost effortless to spend time with students to figure out if they are unstable, and not only would it benefit by keeping the school safe but it will weed out kids that are otherwise unhappy and can offer assistance to them. The system would take a while to institute but it would be vital to not only the safety of the schools but also the general level of contentedness at the school.

Also, why are records held at schools when kids move from one city or state to another? There are many cases where students will move from one school to the next and the only thing sent to the new school is their grades (Doc B). Why are schools not also focusing on their records and their history of unstable activity? When a student moves to a new school district their disciplinary record is just as important as their school record. If certain things were to go wrong and the students became unstable, the school would have had no prior warning of this and would not know how to react to this change in character. If a student has a hazy background, then a school should be made aware of this so that they can work with the student if need be or at least be able to track the student. Many teachers complain about a "labeling" effect of these students, but its not actually labeling just merely keeping an eye on the student. The background check would not be for the teachers to then use to judge a student but merely for the teachers to know what to do in case of a problem with the student. If teachers and counselors are forewarned of possible problems, then they will know how to deal with it and they will be able to react in a proper manner as opposed to being blindsided and shocked when the student becomes unstable as they were at Columbine.

Finally, the use of physical measures to determine the instability of a student is overused. If a student walks into a school and is immediately accosted by a police officer and must have his/her bag checked and then go through a metal detector, it certainly puts a bad taste in their mouths (Doc C). If kids aren't forced into these tests than they would be more content going to school, but waking up and thinking about having a complete stranger going through their personal stuff would make it difficult on the students. It would also hinder their performance at school giving them the feeling that they are constantly being watched. The comfort level would go down and they would start feeling edgy about even the slightest thing.

Revoking basic civil rights is not the way to keep students safe. Just knowing what a student brings to school everyday will not protect the school, it is knowing how the person feels on a day to day basis and dealing with their moods appropriately.

School safety is a very important issue in this day and age, and it is not something to be taken lightly. Many school shootings have occurred and in most cases the school involved has been oblivious to the students past record or mental stability. The most important factor in making a school safe is ensuring that all the students are content. This starts with screening the students as much as possible, sending a description of the students disciplinary record to new schools, and less physical intervention. This breakdown in school security comes due to a decrease in attention to students, once the attention goes back up and people start to care more about the actual student and less about their grades, schools will go back to being safe havens for teenagers.

Assessment of Student Responses to Free-Response Question Three: Synthesis Essay on Insuring School Safety

Sample Student Essay One

A. Assessment of Reader One

This essay does the minimum. It is well-written, but that is as far as it goes. Supports could be fleshed out more fully. This essay is competent, but "stays on the surface". 6+

B. Assessment of Reader Two

The first student sample has quite a bit going for it in terms of its fluency and clarity. It addresses the issue by first discounting surveillance cameras as a panacea for school violence and by then advocating for student profiling. The essay is taut and effective though it does lip-service to the documents. I saw this as a very solid 7: a very good paper that was not as persuasive as some higher-scoring ones.

Sample Student Essay Two

A. Assessment of Reader One

Although this writer has moments of "clunky" sentence structure and some grammar and usage errors, this paper supports its position well and fully. The concession is quite well done, and the articles are documented. There is a clear, humorous student voice with the image of "the brute security guard who looks like he/she belongs as a bouncer at a club downtown." The writing skill, however, keeps this from the top scores. 7+

B. Assessment of Reader Two

Though this paper has some minor warts, it is more detailed than the previous sample and features a strong, detailed thesis and an exceptional closing sentence. It does a good job of exploring the financial drawbacks to all this high-tech security and illustrates the harm that can come from a lack of information about potentially troubled students. The occasional fragment and informal tone is vitiated by its confident perspective and strong support. I see this as an 8.

Sample Student Essay Three

A. Assessment of Reader One

This essay is not particularly well written, with a plethora of rhetorical questions, colloquial terms and ideas as well as some grammar and usage problems. Supports are very general with little specifics other than a regurgitation of the documents. The personal supports seem subjective and make assumptions and generalizations. It is a full essay, however, and the writer does cover all the important points, earning a 6-.

B. Assessment of Reader Two

Of the three responses this contains the least mature writing. The paper is laden with rhetorical questions and plagued a bit by a lack of pronoun-antecedent agreement and some issues with awkward syntax. That said, it has a reasonable thesis, is well developed, and achieves nice closure. Though aspects of this push me toward a 6, if I came across it after a bunch of 3s and 4s, I might give it a 7, though a workaday one. This is a 'border' paper: upper-half for sure, but not fluent enough to work its way into the very top numbers.

Sample Examination III

Question 1-14. Refer to the following passage.

In this essay by Wendell Berry, written in 2009, the author questions Americans' belief that they can continue ignoring calls for energy conservation despite the depletion of natural resources.

The general reaction to the apparent end of the era of cheap fossil fuel, as to other readily foreseeable curtailments, has been to delay any sort of reckoning. The strategies of delay so far
(5) have been a sort of willed oblivion, or visions of large profits to the manufacturers of such "biofuels" as ethanol from corn or switchgrass, or the familiar unscientific faith that "science will find an answer." The dominant response,
(10) in short, is a dogged belief that what we call the American Way of Life will prove somehow indestructible. We will keep on consuming, spending, wasting, and driving as before, at any cost to anything and everybody but
(15) ourselves.

This belief was always indefensible—the real names of global warming are Waste and Greed—and by now it is manifestly foolish. But foolishness on this scale looks disturbingly
(20) like national insanity. We seem to have come to a collective delusion of grandeur, insisting that all of us are "free" to be as conspicuously greedy and wasteful as the most corrupt of kings and queens. (Perhaps by devoting more
(25) and more of our already abused cropland to fuel production we will at last cure ourselves of obesity and become fashionably skeletal, hungry, but—thank God!—still driving.)….

Even so, that we have founded our present
(30) society upon delusional assumptions of limitlessness is easy enough to demonstrate. A recent "summit" in Louisville, Kentucky, was entitled "Unbridled Energy: The Industrialization of Kentucky's Energy
(35) Resources." Its subjects were "clean-coal generation, biofuels, and other cutting-edge applications," the conversion of coal to "liquid fuels," and the likelihood that all this will be "environmentally friendly." These hopes,
(40) which can create jobs and boost the nation's security," are to be supported by government

"loan guarantees…investment tax credits and other tax breaks." Such talk we recognize as completely conventional. It is, in fact, a tissue
(45) of clichés that is now the common tongue of promoters, politicians, and journalists. This language does not allow for any computation or speculation as to the *net* good of anything proposed. The entire contraption of "Unbridled
(50) Energy" is supported only by a rote optimism: "The United States has 250 billion tons of recoverable coal reserves—enough to last 100 years even at double the current rate of consumption." We humans have inhabited the
(55) earth for many thousands of years, and now we can look forward to surviving for another hundred by doubling our consumption of coal? This is national security? The world-ending fire of industrial fundamentalism may already
(60) be burning in our furnaces and engines, but if it will burn for a hundred more years, that will be fine. Surely it would be better to attend straightforwardly to contain the fire and eventually put it out! But once greed has been
(65) made an honorable motive, then you have an economy without limits. It has no place for temperance or thrift or the ecological law of return. It will do anything. It is monstrous by definition.
(70) In keeping with our unrestrained consumptiveness, the commonly accepted basis of our economy is the supposed possibility of limitless growth, limitless wants, limitless wealth, limitless natural resources, limitless
(75) energy, and limitless debt. The idea of a limitless economy implies and requires a doctrine of general human limitlessness: *all* are entitled to pursue without limit whatever they conceive as desirable—a license that classifies
(80) the most exalted Christian capitalist with the lowliest pornographer.

This fantasy of limitlessness perhaps arose from the coincidence of the industrial revolution with the suddenly exploitable
(85) resources of the New World—though how the supposed limitlessness of resources can be reconciled with their exhaustion is not clear. Or perhaps it comes from the contrary apprehension of the world's "smallness," made
(90) possible by modern astronomy and high-speed

transportation. Fear of the smallness of our
world and its life may lead to a kind of
claustrophobia and thence, with apparent
reasonableness, to a desire for the "freedom"
(95) of limitlessness. But this desire, paradoxically,
reduces everything. The life of this world is
small to those who think it is, and the desire to
enlarge it makes it smaller, and can reduce it
finally to nothing….

1. The opening paragraph of the essay implies that
the American public has been guilty of all of the
following EXCEPT

   (A) obstinacy
   (B) selfishness
   (C) hoarding
   (D) short-sightedness
   (E) avoidance

2. The author attempts to capture the American
attitude of limitlessness in the opening paragraph
by the

   (A) generalization in lines 1-4
   (B) catalog in lines 4-9
   (C) irony in lines 8-9
   (D) series of gerunds in lines 12-13
   (E) repetition of "any" in line 14

3. The parenthetical comment in lines 24-28—
"(Perhaps by devoting more and more of our
already abused cropland to fuel production we
will at last cure ourselves of obesity and become
fashionably skeletal, hungry, but—thank
God!—still driving.)"—is intended to

   (A) commend our ability to adapt
   (B) satirize the nature of our priorities
   (C) suggest a sensible course of conservation
   (D) address a pressing social concern
   (E) praise the divine for our agrarian bounty

4. The author places the word "summit"
(line 32) in quotation marks to draw attention to
which of the following?

   (A) its parochial perspective on energy
   (B) its vacuously optimistic jargon
   (C) its lack of national publicity
   (D) its factual inaccuracies
   (E) its urgency and importance

5. The author likely cites commentary from the
convocation in Louisville (lines 31-43) in order to

   (A) demonstrate the sincerity with which the
energy crisis is being met
   (B) provide an example of the "limitlessness"
mentioned in line 31
   (C) mock the hackneyed phrases which such
organizations regularly employ
   (D) provide documentation that such claims are
"delusional"
   (E) offset the growing despair that our energy
crisis is unsolvable

6. By labeling these pronouncements "completely
conventional" (line 44), the author is doing which
of the following?

   I. Suggesting that they have become the
normal thing to say at such gatherings.
   II. Acknowledging these statements as
examples of the "common tongue of
promoters, politicians, and journalists"
(lines 45-46).
   III. Absolving those who made these claims
from wrongdoing or deception.

   (A) I only
   (B) III only
   (C) I and II
   (D) II and III
   (E) I, II and III

7. Which of the following is used by the author to reveal the factual insubstantiality of the claims made by the conference speakers?

   (A) "delusional assumptions" (line 30)
   (B) "tissue of clichés" (lines 44-45)
   (C) "common tongue" (line 45)
   (D) "entire contraption" (line 49)
   (E) "rote optimism" (line 50)

8. The tone of the rhetorical questions posed in lines 54-58 is one of

   (A) surprise
   (B) bitterness
   (C) confusion
   (D) defiance
   (E) sarcasm

9. The most striking aspect of the fire image in lines 58-62 is its

   (A) incongruous merger of the apocalyptic and the workaday
   (B) double allusion to the Industrial Revolution and religious fundamentalism
   (C) subtle implication that our present policies will result in spiritual damnation
   (D) symbolic reassurance that the energy potential of coal will never be depleted
   (E) visual exemplification of unbridled energy

10. The complete antecedent of the pronoun "It" (lines 66 and 68) is

    (A) "world-ending fire" (lines 58-59)
    (B) "greed" (line 64)
    (C) "honorable motive" (line 65)
    (D) "economy without limits" (line 66)
    (E) "temperance or thrift or the ecological law" (line 67)

11. In describing in lines 70-81 the "unrestrained consumptiveness" practiced by humans, the author sardonically associates it with the

    (A) ravages of a disease
    (B) ideals of democracy
    (C) growth of industrialization
    (D) fervor of religion
    (E) stigma of pornography

12. In attempting in the fifth paragraph (lines 82-99) to explain how the "doctrine of general human limitlessness" (line 77) came to be, the author employs all of the following EXCEPT

    (A) historical allusions
    (B) speculation about psychological causes
    (C) a red herring
    (D) deductive reasoning to explain antithetical behavior
    (E) a climactic *reductio ad absurdum*

13. The concluding sentence of the passage (lines 96-99) contains a(n)

    (A) paradox
    (B) metaphor
    (C) allusion
    (D) hyperbole
    (E) personification

14. Which of the following does NOT express a similar sentiment as the other choices?

    (A) "willed oblivion" (line 5)
    (B) "dogged belief" (line 10)
    (C) "collective delusion" (line 21)
    (D) "fantasy of limitlessness" (line 82)
    (E) "contrary apprehension" (lines 88-89)

Questions 15-26. Refer to the following passage.

In the following excerpt, from E.B. White's 1954 essay "A Slight Sound at Evening," the author reflects on the hundredth anniversary of the publication of Thoreau's Walden.

....*Walden* is an oddity in American letters. It may very well be the oddest of our distinguished oddities. For many it is a great deal too odd, and for many it is a particular

(5)   bore. I have not found it to be a well-liked book among my acquaintances, although usually spoken of with respect, and one literary critic for whom I have the highest regard can find no reason for anyone's giving *Walden* a

(10)   second thought. To admire the book is, in fact, something of an embarrassment, for the mass of men have an indistinct notion that its author was sort of a Nature Boy.

I think it is of some advantage to encounter

(15)   the book at a period in one's life when the normal anxieties and enthusiasms and rebellions of youth closely resemble those of Thoreau in that spring of 1845 when he borrowed an ax, went out to the woods, and

(20)   began to whack down some trees for timber. Received at such a juncture, the book is like an invitation to life's dance, assuring the troubled recipient that no matter what befalls him in the way of success or failure he will always be

(25)   welcome at the party—that the music is played for him, too, if he will but listen and move his feet. In effect, that is what the book is—an invitation, unengraved; and it stirs one as a young girl is stirred by her first big party bid.

(30)   Many think it a sermon; many set it down as an attempt to rearrange society; some think it as an exercise in nature-loving; some find it a rather irritating collection of inspirational puffballs by an eccentric show-off. I think it

(35)   none of these. It still seems to me that best youth's companion yet written by an American, for it carries a solemn warning against the loss of one's valuables, it advances a good argument for traveling light and trying new

(40)   adventures, it rings with the power of positive adoration, it contains religious feeling without religious images, and it steadfastly refuses to record bad news. Even its pantheistic note is so pure as to be non-corrupting—pure as the

(45)   flute-note blown across the pond on those faraway summer nights. If our colleges and universities were alert, they would present a cheap pocket edition of the book to every senior upon graduating, along with his

(50)   sheepskin, or instead of it. Even if some senior were to take it literally and start felling trees, there could be worse mishaps: the ax is older than the Dictaphone and it is just as well for a young man to see what kind of chips he leaves

(55)   before listening to the sound of his own voice. And even if some were to get no farther than the table of contents, they would learn how to name eighteen chapters by the use of only thirty-nine words and would see how sweet are

(60)   the uses of brevity.

If Thoreau had merely left us an account of a man's life in the woods or if he had simply retreated to the woods and there recorded his complaints about society, or even if he had

(65)   contrived to include both records in one essay, *Walden* would probably not have lived a hundred years. As things turned out, Thoreau, very likely without knowing what he was up to, took man's relation to Nature and man's

(70)   dilemma in society and man's capacity for elevating his spirit and he beat all these matters together, in a wild free interval of self-justification and delight, and produced an original omelette from which people can draw

(75)   nourishment in a hungry day. *Walden* is one of the first vitamin-enriched American dishes. If it were a little less good than it is, or even a little less queer, it would be an abominable book. Even as it is, it will continue to baffle and

(80)   annoy the literal mind and all those who are unable to stomach its caprices and imbibe its theme. Certainly the plodding economist will continue to have rough going if he hopes to emerge from the book with a clear system of

(85)   economic thought. Thoreau's assault on the Concord society of the mid-nineteenth century has the quality of a modern Western: he rides into the subject at top speed, shooting in all directions. Many of his shots ricochet and nick

(90)   him on the rebound, and throughout the melee there is a horrendous cloud of inconsistencies and contradictions, and when the shooting dies down and the air clears, one is impressed chiefly by the courage of the rider and by how

(95)   splendid it was that somebody should have ridden in there and raised all that ruckus....

Excerpt from pp. 234-6 {"...WALDEN is an oddity in American letters....ruckus...."} from "A SLIGHT SOUND AT EVENING" FROM ESSAYS OF E.B. WHITE by E.B. WHITE. Copyright, 1954, by E.B, White. Originally appeared in The Yale Review under the title "Walden-1954." Reprinted by permission of HarperCollins Publishers.

15. Which of the following BEST articulates the author's intention in the opening paragraph?

    (A) discussing what makes *Walden* such a peculiar text
    (B) poking fun at Thoreau's character
    (C) dismissing *Walden* as an exercise in tedium
    (D) presenting diverse responses to Thoreau's text
    (E) confessing his embarrassment at having actually read *Walden*

16. Lines 14-34 suggest that *Walden's* appeal is rooted in which of the following?

    I. Its affinity with youthful unrest and zeal.
    II. Its warm invitation and non-judgmental inclusion.
    III. Its suggestion of Thoreau's personal interest in the reader.

    (A) I only
    (B) III only
    (C) I and II
    (D) II and III
    (E) I, II and III

17. Lines 30-34 imply that over time *Walden* has made people perceive Thoreau as all of the following EXCEPT

    (A) an environmentalist
    (B) a social activist
    (C) a moralist
    (D) an oddball
    (E) a seer

18. In lines 34-43 the author expresses his personal feelings about *Walden* through a parallel series of

    (A) independent clauses
    (B) adjectival clauses
    (C) adverbial clauses
    (D) noun clauses
    (E) imperatives

19. In light of the context in which it appears, the auditory image of the flute-note (lines 43-46) is BEST described as

    (A) alluring and mesmerizing
    (B) eerie and haunting
    (C) distinct and nostalgic
    (D) faint and wavering
    (E) primitive and pagan

20. Both the ax and the Dictaphone (lines 50-55) function as

    (A) metonymies
    (B) images
    (C) euphemisms
    (D) hyperboles
    (E) allusions

21. Which of the following would be the BEST substitution for the "chips" mentioned in line 54?

    (A) residue
    (B) ideas
    (C) accomplishments
    (D) attitude
    (E) debts

22. The rhetorical device that dominates the final paragraph of White's essay (lines 61-96) is

    (A) historical allusion
    (B) extended metaphor
    (C) personal anecdote
    (D) ironical understatement
    (E) parallel syntax

23. The author uses the omelette in lines 67-76 to suggest that Thoreau's *Walden*

    (A) is haphazard in both structure and style
    (B) derived from his culinary interests
    (C) offers philosophical sustenance
    (D) reflects his desire to stir things up
    (E) is not to every reader's taste

24. The author's use of language in lines 85-96 implies that Thoreau's criticism of mid-nineteenth century Concord society is simultaneously

    (A) muddled but insightful
    (B) flawed but intrepid
    (C) provincial but universal
    (D) rambunctious but measured
    (E) censorious but introspective

25. Ultimately, the author sees *Walden* as being all of the following EXCEPT

    (A) admonitory
    (B) pragmatic
    (C) spiritual
    (D) sanguine
    (E) infallible

26. Of the following, which BEST conveys the rustic simplicity of Thoreau's text?

    (A) the "music" that invites the reader to tap his feet (lines 25-27)
    (B) the "invitation, unengraved" (line 28)
    (C) the "sermon"-like quality that abets its spiritual message (line 30)
    (D) the "omelette" that provides life sustenance (lines 74-75)
    (E) the rapid-fire volley "in all directions" (lines 87-89)

Questions 27-39. Refer to the following passage.

In this essay entitled "The Great Stupidity," that appeared in the Atlantic Monthly *in 1921, a Scotsman comments upon the British attitude towards America, in particular towards New York City.*

Sheer ignorance and lack of imagination lie at the root of all that is wrong in the British attitude toward America. We do not begin to realize the magnitude and the majesty of the
(5) phenomenon with which we have to deal.

Ask the average Englishman what he associates with the words "New York," what mental picture the name evokes for him, and there are ten chances to one that he will
(10) express himself in terms of vague depreciation and distaste. He will tell you of a noisy, nerve-racking city, whose inhabitants are so intent on the pursuit of the elusive dollar that they habitually bolt their food at "quick-lunch"
(15) counters, and seek to soothe their chronic dyspepsia by masticating either chewing-gum or big black cigars. He has heard of a clattering abomination called the Elevated Railroad; he has probably never heard of the Subway—most
(20) wonderful, if still inadequate, system of urban transit. The word "sky-scraper" is, of course, familiar to him, connoting, in his imagination, a hideous monstrosity, which the Americans have somehow evolved out of the naughtiness
(25) of their hearts. He thanks his stars that such freaks are impossible in England, where municipal wisdom has established a strict correlation between the height of buildings and the width of streets. Furthermore, he has heard
(30) of Tammany,[1] a conspiracy of corruption, which keeps the city ill-paved, ill-lighted, and a prey to the alternate—or simultaneous—tyranny of brutal Irish policeman and indigenous "gunmen," who will shoot you as
(35) soon as look at you. Here, or hereabouts, his knowledge ends; and he will present this meager caricature in a tone of phrarisaism, congratulating himself that London (or Manchester, or Glasgow, as the case may be) is
(40) not crude and corrupt after the manner of New York.

No doubt there are shreds and patches of truth in this picture; but they are wholly

inessential. The essential fact is that by far
(45) New York is the most magnificent and marvelous city in the whole world—a wonder to the eye and an incomparable stimulus to the imagination. Throned between its noble estuaries,[2] it proclaims, in one majestic
(50) symbol, the supremacy of Man over Matter. Here we feel, for the first time in the modern world,—what the Romans of the Empire might have felt to a minor degree,—that, for all our puny proportions, we belong to a race of titans.
(55) The sky-scraper was, in its beginnings, ugly and unimaginative enough; forty years of development have made it a thing of beauty, of power, of grandeur. And it is still—I will not say in its infancy, but—in its adolescence. The
(60) Singer building, the Metropolitan Tower, and the Woolworth building are not likely to be greatly overtopped. The sky-scraper, essentially a street tilted on end, is also inevitably a cul-de-sac; and a too long cul-de-sac is
(65) uneconomic and inconvenient. Besides, the development of the tower form—immense height on a relatively small base—is practically confined to Manhattan Island, with its rock foundations; in few other places would
(70) architects dare to pile up such enormous weights to the square foot. But there is boundless room for the lateral development of the moderately high building—the building of, say, 15 to 25 floors. Every year that passes
(75) adds some new triumph to the cyclopean architecture of New York. Park Avenue, though it contains no buildings of excessive height, will soon be like a boulevard of Brobdingnag[3] —without any of the rude disproportion,
(80) however, that we might look for in the palaces of giants; and it is doubly impressive when we reflect that, unseen and unheard, the railway traffic of half a continent is gliding to and fro beneath its central gardens....

---

[1] name given to the Democratic political machine that dominated New York City politics from the mid-1800s to the 1930s; often associated with corruption.

[2] rivers that empty out into the ocean

[3] a land of giants in which Jonathan Swift's character Gulliver is shipwrecked

27. Lines 3-5, "We do not begin to realize the magnitude and the majesty of the phenomenon with which we have to deal," foreshadow the author's commentary on the

    (A) grand vision that spurs urban development in America
    (B) poor dietary habits of New York citizenry
    (C) deeply ingrained biases maintained by some Englishmen
    (D) pervasive corruption in New York City government
    (E) railway traffic gliding silently beneath Park Avenue

28. All of the following are concrete manifestations of the "vague depreciation and distaste" (lines 10-11) felt by the average Englishman towards New York EXCEPT

    (A) the frenetic pace of its urban lifestyle
    (B) the financial desperation of its residents
    (C) the colossal and ostentatious nature of its architecture
    (D) the aloof manner in which its residents treat foreigners
    (E) the disturbing clamor of its above-ground public transit

29. The "freaks" alluded to in line 26 are

    (A) Americans
    (B) quick-lunch counters
    (C) elevated rail lines
    (D) skyscrapers
    (E) cigars

30. Which of the following MOST plausibly explain(s) why the author labels the average Englishman's impression of New York a "meager caricature" (line 37)?

    I. The fact that the average Englishman lacks the imagination to provide a more colorful depiction.
    II. The fact that the average Englishman has never actually been there and has likely based his opinion upon hearsay.
    III. The fact that the average Englishman unfairly ignores the shortcomings of his own cities.

    (A) I only
    (B) II only
    (C) I and III
    (D) II and III
    (E) I, II and III

31. To establish the typical Englishman's perception of New York, the author predominantly employs diction that depicts the city as

    (A) inspiring and splendid
    (B) venal and nefarious
    (C) cosmopolitan and bustling
    (D) labyrinthine and crowded
    (E) undeveloped and unsanitary

32. By remarking that the average Englishman "has heard of" such things as sky-scrapers, elevated trains, and quick-lunch counters, the author seems most intent upon showing that

    (A) the average Englishman can make an informed judgment about New York
    (B) New York's institutions are world-renowned
    (C) the average Englishman lacks firsthand exposure to these novelties
    (D) the average Englishman believes they are more mythical than factual
    (E) these innovations mirror similar ones in his own country

33. The author compliments our modern sky-scraper by comparing it to all of the following EXCEPT

(A) a monarch
(B) marvels of classical antiquity
(C) mythical giants
(D) perpendicular streets
(E) buildings in Europe

34. The author adds that the Englishman's comments about New York are delivered with a "tone of pharisaism" (lines 37-38) in order to establish the

(A) sanctimonious preference the Englishman holds for his own country
(B) scorn the Englishman harbors for the American metropolis
(C) hypocrisy of the Englishman's condemnatory position
(D) accuracy of the Englishman's social criticism
(E) religious-like fervor of the Englishman's animosity for New York City

35. The words "shreds and patches" (line 42) make what point about the average Englishman's commentary about New York?

 I. That the reasons behind his distaste are threadbare in nature.
 II. That his impressions of the New York metropolis are fragmented and incomplete.
 III. That there is partial validity to his detractions.

(A) I only
(B) II only
(C) I and III
(D) II and III
(E) I, II and III

36. The author of the essay debunks the sweeping pejorative commentary about New York expressed by the "average Englishman" by

(A) using an *ad hominem* approach to discredit his authority
(B) accusing him of being jingoistic
(C) offering a firsthand account that compliments specific edifices and the transit system
(D) responding point by point to the complaints he makes about the New York metropolis
(E) pointing out similar flaws in London and other English cities

37. In levying his criticism of New York, the "average Englishman" follows which of the following organizational patterns?

(A) comparison-contrast
(B) classification
(C) cause-and-effect
(D) climactic order
(E) enumeration

38. Which of the following words, as it is used in the passage, may be said to have two distinct meanings?

(A) "correlation" (line 28)
(B) "meager" (line 37)
(C) "stimulus" (line 47)
(D) "overtopped" (line 62)
(E) "boundless" (line 72)

39. Which of the following MOST accurately expresses the author's attitude towards New York City?

(A) unbridled enthusiasm
(B) respectful tolerance
(C) qualified appreciation
(D) unabashed distaste
(E) total ignorance

Questions 40-52. Refer to the following passage.

….We were silent. The elephant we advanced upon heard nothing—even when the enormous hindquarters of two bulls loomed before us like grey rocks wedded to the earth.

(5) Blix stopped. He whispered with his fingers and I read the whisper. 'Watch the wind. Swing round them. I want to see their tusks.'

Swing, indeed! It took us slightly over an (10) hour to negotiate a semicircle of fifty yards. The bulls were big—with ivory enough—hundred-pounders at least, or better….

One bull raised his head, elevated his (15) trunk, and moved to face us. His gargantuan ears began to spread as if to capture even the sound of our heartbeats. By chance, he had grazed over a spot we had lately left, and he had got our scent. It was all he needed.

(20) I have rarely seen anything so calm as that bull elephant—or so casually determined upon destruction. It might be said that he shuffled to the kill. Being, like all elephant, almost blind, this one could not see us, but he was used to (25) that. He would follow scent and sound until he could see us, which, I computed would take about thirty seconds.

Blix wiggled his fingers earthward, and that meant, 'Drop and crawl.'

(30) It is amazing what a lot of insect life goes on under your nose when you have got it an inch from the earth. I suppose it goes on in any case, but if you are proceeding on your stomach, dragging your body along by your (35) fingernails, entomology presents itself very forcibly as a thoroughly justified science….

By the time I had crawled three feet, I am sure that somewhere over fifty distinct species of insect life were individually and severally (40) represented in my clothes, with Siafu ants conducting the congress.

Blix feet were just ahead of my eyes—close enough so that I could contemplate the holes in his shoes….His legs moved through (45) the underbrush like dead legs dragged by strings. There was no sound from the elephant.

I don't know how long we crawled like that, but the little shadows in the thicket were leaning toward the east when we stopped. (50) Possibly we had gone a hundred yards. The insect bites had become just broad, burning patches.

We were breathing easier—or at least I was—when Blix's feet and legs went (55) motionless. I could just see his head close against his shoulder, and watch him turn to peak upward into the bush. He gave no signal to continue. He only looked horribly embarrassed like a child caught stealing eggs.

(60) But my own expression must have been a little more intense. The big bull was about ten feet away—and at that distance elephant are not blind.

Blix stood up and raised his rifle slowly, (65) with an expression of ineffable sadness.

'That's for me,' I thought. 'He knows that even a shot in the brain won't stop that bull before we're both crushed like mangos.'

In an open place, it might have been (70) possible to dodge to one side, but not here. I stood behind Blix with my hands on his waist according to his instructions. But I knew it wasn't any good. The body of the elephant was swaying. It was like watching a boulder, in (75) whose path you were trapped, teeter on the edge of a cliff before plunging. The bull's ears were spread wide now, his trunk was up and extended toward us, and he began the elephant scream of anger which is so terrifying as to (80) hold you silent where you stand, like fingers clamped upon your throat. It is a shrill scream, cold as winter wind.

It occurred to me that this was the instant to shoot.

(85) Blix never moved. He held his rifle very steady and began to chant some of the most striking blasphemy I have ever heard. It was colourful, original, and delivered with finesse, but I felt that this was a badly chosen moment (90) to test it on an elephant—and ungallant beyond belief if it was meant for me.

The elephant advanced, Blix unleashed more oaths (this time in Swedish), and I trembled. There was no rifle shot. A single (95) biscuit tin, I judged, would do for both of us—cremation would be superfluous.

'I may have to shoot him,' Blix announced, and the remark struck me as an understatement of classic magnificence….

40. Which of the following contributes LEAST to the dramatization of the author's confrontation with the elephant?

    (A) the terse soundlessness maintained by predator and prey for most of the encounter
    (B) the painstakingly deliberate manner in which Blix and the author navigate the perimeter
    (C) the ominous size of the grazing pachyderms
    (D) the body language and cry of the angered beast
    (E) the blasphemous chanting of Blix

41. The figure of speech MOST frequently employed by the author is

    (A) hyperbole
    (B) simile
    (C) understatement
    (D) allusion
    (E) personification

42. All of the following aspects of the 'dialogue' of the passage augment the tension of the episode EXCEPT

    (A) its muted nature
    (B) its urgent imperatives
    (C) its terseness
    (D) its panic
    (E) its paucity

43. The author marks the duration of the encounter by which of the following?

    (A) diction that relates to time
    (B) the distance crawled by Blix and the author
    (C) changes in sunlight and shadow
    (D) the bodily fatigue and hunger exhibited by the duo
    (E) the consumption of flora by the elephants

44. The author's internal response to the instructions given by Blix in lines 6-8 is BEST labeled

    (A) respectfully obedient
    (B) brazenly defiant
    (C) totally perplexed
    (D) unhappily resigned
    (E) mildly sardonic

45. In her description of the insect life that infests her clothing (lines 30-41), the author makes significant use of

    (A) imagery
    (B) onomatopoeia
    (C) implied metaphor
    (D) hyperbole
    (E) personification

46. Blix's look of embarrassment—"like a child caught stealing eggs" (line 59)—and his subsequent look of "ineffable sadness" (line 65) are likely brought on by which of the following?

    I. His realization that he has inadvertently put the author's life in jeopardy.
    II. His grief at having to shoot such a magnificently regal animal.
    III. His disappointment at not being able to see the elephant's tusks adequately.

    (A) I only
    (B) II only
    (C) I and II
    (D) I and III
    (E) I, II and III

47. Which of the following does NOT contribute to the disarmingly passive nature of the elephant?

    (A) "loomed" (line 3)
    (B) "grazed" (line 18)
    (C) "calm" (line 20)
    (D) "casually" (line 21)
    (E) "shuffled" (line 22)

48. The solitary sentence, "It occurred to me that this was the instant to shoot" (lines 83-84), primarily reveals the author's

    (A) sense of anticipation
    (B) admirable decisiveness
    (C) preternatural calm under duress
    (D) high level of marksmanship
    (E) knowledge of elephant behavior

49. Which of the following BEST exemplifies the use of 'gallows' humor?

    (A) "…entymology presents itself very forcibly as a thoroughly justified science" (lines 35-36)

    (B) "…close enough to contemplate the holes in his shoes…." (lines 43-44)

    (C) "But I knew it wasn't any good." (lines 72-73)

    (D) "A single biscuit tin, I judged, would do for both of us…" (lines 94-96)

    (E) "'I may have to shoot him…'" (line 97)

50. All of the following are rhetorical techniques used in lines 92-99 EXCEPT

    (A) parallel structure

    (B) metonymy

    (C) allusion

    (D) black humor

    (E) parenthetical commentary

51. In which of the following is the MOST fatalistic sentiment expressed?

    (A) "…even when the hindquarters of two bulls loomed before us like grey rocks wedded to the earth" (lines 2-4)

    (B) "He would follow scent and sound until he could see us, which, I computed would take about thirty seconds" (lines 25-27)

    (C) "His legs moved through the underbrush like dead legs dragged by strings" (lines 44-46)

    (D) "'That's for me,' I thought. 'He knows that even a shot in the brain won't stop that bull before we're both crushed like mangos'" (lines 66-68)

    (E) "…I felt that this was a badly chosen moment to test it on an elephant…" (lines 89-90)

52. Taken together, the speaker's thoughts and body language suggest that she is most likely a(n)

    (A) big-game hunter

    (B) photographer

    (C) poacher

    (D) native guide

    (E) adventurer

Section II

Question One
(Suggested time—40 minutes. This question counts as one-third of the total essay section score.)

In the following excerpt, from a speech delivered at a 1981 national convention of Native-American women and activists, Dr. Rayna Green, a Cherokee scholar and writer, facetiously proposes the establishment of a "Museum of the Plains White Person." Read the excerpt carefully. Then, in a well-organized essay, discuss the techniques that the author uses to satirize the beliefs of white people about Native Americans. In responding to the question, you may wish to consider such things as diction, tone and choice of detail.

....Let me tell you something of the plans for our museum. First, we will be building the museum over an abandoned ceremonial ballcourt, called a "football field," somewhere

(5) in what the Omaha nation called "Nebraska." Our Indian archaeologists made, as you know, the great discovery of an ancient white ceremonial cult called the Cornhuskers,[1] right there, and this ballcourt was the site of their

(10) annual rites for that once-great religion. Its major gallery, of course, will be a hall of ancestral remains, and that is the major emphasis of our first collecting effort. We have organized collecting expeditions throughout the

(15) country, and, as we speak, Indian backhoes are excavating the sadly abandoned white cemeteries of the United States. We have, through our powers of eminent domain, acquired at least eighty percent of the white

(20) cemeteries in this country.

We have begun our national campaign to acquire the bones of famous white people, since they themselves insisted for centuries that we can all learn so much from studying and

(25) displaying such remains. And, accepting their notions of reverence for the exhibition of the dead and goods from graves, White People will be honored to have the remains of their grandmothers and grandfathers on display. We

(30) have just acquired what I think is quite an important and moving find, the bones of John Wayne,[2] the White Culture Hero, and we plan to acquire the remains of many other famous white persons. You might guess who we have

(35) our sights on. What a great significance this can have for our scholars, as they attempt to interpret the important aspects of white culture from this most American of mythological characters....

(40) Let me tell you about some of the other collections and exhibition plans that I think are quite exciting. There will be a White Foodways Gallery where we examine the great and holy foods of the quintessential white culture—

(45) mayonnaise, white bread, iceberg lettuce, peanut butter, lime Jell-O and little marshmallows. We will reconstruct one of their temples to food, a so-called "McDonald's," in its entirety. We are currently doing a study of some of the

(50) ceremonial foodways of the Cornhuskers, and we are particularly interested in the great Weenie-Burning rites that occurred in the summer, a religious behavior perhaps related to their reverence for the Little Marshmallows.

(55) And, of course, we are doing research on white hunting and foraging techniques, which appeared to be called "making reservations."

We will have several exhibits about their strange but wonderful customs. We have found

(60) a few remaining White People who know fragments of their quaint dances and songs, and we will offer living history programs of their dances, the waltz, the fox-trot, the Texas Two-Step, the disco, frug, bop and polka.

(65) Additionally, we have discovered people who actually remember and can interpret the meaningless vocables—bop-shu-bop, do-wop, and ooooh, ooooh, ooooh baby—of many of their courting songs. We are creating an entire

(70) photographic exhibition on a form of ritual performance revered by white people, a kind of symbolic warfare they called "talk shows."

We are busily acquiring examples of their most important elaborate ceremonial and

(75) shamanistic costumes and instruments of power—a typical chieftain's three-piece suit and briefcase, a medicine man's stethoscope and a Barbie shaman's spike heels and bikini underpants....And finally, we will be

(80) assembling a stellar and major collection of items of costume associated with their centuries-old significant, though puzzling, form of ritual behavior called "playing Indian"....

---
[1] nickname for the Nebraska football team
[2] iconic film star whose roles included several in which he fought against Native American tribes

Excerpted from a speech in 1981 to the National Conference of Native American Women Activists, first printing in IN OUR OWN WORDS: EXTRAORDINARY SPEECHES OF THE AMERICAN CENTURY by Senator Robert Torricelli and Andrew Carroll. Reprinted courtesy of Rayna Green.

Question Two

(Suggested time—40 minutes. This question counts as one-third of the total essay section score.)

At the 1964 Republican Convention, while accepting his party's nomination for President, Republican Barry Goldwater made the following remark:

"Extremism in the defense of liberty is no vice; moderation in the pursuit of justice is no virtue."

Though Goldwater was reacting to the growing specter of communism, his words resonate strikingly in the present day.

Take a moment to reflect on Barry Goldwater's statement. Then, in a well-organized essay, examine the implications of Goldwater's claim upon personal liberties. Use your reading, studies, experience and observations to develop your argument.

Courtesy of the Republican National Committee.

<u>Question Three</u>

Reading Time: 15 minutes
Suggested Writing Time: 40 minutes

(This question counts as one-third of the total essay section score.)

Directions:

The following prompt is based on the accompanying six sources.

This question requires you to integrate a variety of sources into a coherent, well-written essay. *Refer to the sources to support your position; avoid paraphrase or summary. Your argument should be central; the sources should support this argument.*

Remember to attribute both direct and indirect citations.

Introduction:

The inability of Americans to "make ends meet" is a growing problem on both a national and individual level. Though the phrase "keeping up with the Joneses" has become a catchword for many Americans' tendency to want the same material possessions as their neighbors, the combination of downsizing and layoffs, rising consumer costs, and a volatile stock market has made more and more Americans dependent upon credit, resulting in a spike in credit card interest rates and late fees and a rash of foreclosures by banks and mortgage brokers. Such a vise-like economic squeeze has not been felt by Americans since the Great Depression.

However, is the indebtedness of Americans more a product of a "got-to-have it-now" attitude that drives them to purchase things they ultimately cannot afford, or a result of misleading and morally questionable marketing strategies that have lured people into financial waters in which they can no longer stay afloat?

Assignment:

Read the following sources (including any introductory information) carefully. **Then, in an essay that synthesizes at least three of the sources for support, take a position that defends, challenges or qualifies the claim that the blame for the pervasive American indebtedness lies more with individuals than it does with institutions.**

<u>Document B</u>

Theil, Stefan, et al. "The Urge to Splurge." *Newsweek* 156.23: December 6, 2010.

"No interest until 2014," read the massive red sign outside Big's Furniture in Henderson, Nev. It beckoned Diane Lewis to the store's year-end liquidation sale. "I had to pull in," she said as her sons frolicked on mattresses nearby. "We really need to get us a new bedroom set; their old one is kinda beat up. If we can get that financing deal, we can make it work." As with most in this hard-hit region, the economy hasn't been good to Lewis, whose husband just got a new job after being laid off for eight months.

They're two months behind on their mortgage, "but we're gonna catch up," and she figures the family probably owes about $20,000 on various credit cards. "I know I probably ought to wait a little longer," said Lewis, a hairdresser, "but this is a pretty good sale, so I think we might buy something if they'll approve us. I mean, 2014 is a long way off, you know?"

Old habits die hard. It was only last year that shell-shocked consumers were pledging their allegiance to the "New Frugality." Chastened by the brutal lessons of the worst economic downturn in decades, Americans swore off conspicuous consumption and resolved to embrace the thrifty ways of their grandparents who lived through the Great Depression. But as any dieter can tell you, resolutions are made to be broken.

Even as Americans are still struggling to meet mortgage payments, pay off credit cards, and replenish savings, they're also starting to spend again--whether they have the money or not. Last week, fresh numbers showed household spending rising for the fifth month in a row and consumer confidence reaching its highest level since June. Per capita retail sales are now back up to where they were in the fall of 2008, just before the collapse of Lehman Bros. tore the bottom out of the economy. If you factor out spending on cars, which is still 18 percent below its 2005 peak, Americans' total spending on goods and services has now passed pre-crisis highs....

Document C

Manning, Robert D. *Credit Card Nation: The Consequences of America's Addiction to Credit.* New York: Basic Books, 2000: 22-23, 27.

As millions of Americans endured the social consequences of industrial restructuring—job relocations, temporary assignments, part-time employment, layoffs, buyouts (for the lucky few)—in the 1980s, the credit card industry appeared oblivious to their needs but carefully cultivated the desires of its rapidly growing lower- and middle-income members. Emphasizing financial independence and social indulgence, banks enabled cardholders to maintain the image of middle-class respectability and the material accoutrements of economic success even as they struggled simply to stay afloat. For instance, a 1980 advertisement in *Time* exulted, "You can have it the way you want it with Visa. Only Visa gives you so many ways to pay. Worldwide." With its emphasis on consumption, Visa's marketing campaigns of the mid- and late-1980s highlighted cultural sophistication, social elitism, and the accessibility of an affluent lifestyle.

By presenting examples of credit card use in luxurious and often exotic settings, Visa subliminally offered its members the vicarious experiences of being "everywhere you want to be." Advertisements in 1986 featured adventurous excursions such as "shopping north of London in George Hadfield's 18th-century farmhouse…[for a] meticulously restored grandfather clock:" or to Lew Anfanger's Western Hat Works in downtown San Diego where "you can still buy a hat from a man whose father was a haberdasher to royalty…[and] will custom, design a masterpiece for you"….

These marketing campaigns conjure popular stereotypes of reckless shopping sprees, impulsive consumption, and out-of-control shoppers who end up "staring into the abyss of personal bankruptcy." Images of credit card debt, moreover, provide banks with further justification to raise the financial penalty….

Document D

"The New Loan Sharks." *Atlantic Monthly* 293.1 (Jan/Feb 2004): 48.

Americans owe credit-card companies more than $730 billion, more than four times what they did just fifteen years ago, and credit-card-company profits shot up by 20 percent in 2001. Researchers at Demos, a nonpartisan think tank, recently documented this remarkable growth. Among their findings: industry deregulation has made credit so easy to get that three out of four families now wield at least one credit card, and average credit-card debt is 53 percent greater than it was a decade ago. More people having more access to more credit would appear to be a good thing — but the dark side of the story is that credit-card interest rates (currently averaging 13 percent) and fees (averaging $29 for late payments) have stayed high, even through this era of record-low general interest rates. These punitive rates fall particularly hard on the poor and the elderly: very low-income families (those earning less than $10,000) and seniors are increasingly swimming in debt. From 1989 to 2001 the credit-card debt carried by these poor families increased on average by 184 percent, while seniors' debt increased by 149 percent. The industry now extends as much credit to people in the bottom two quintiles as it did to those in the top two at the beginning of the 1990s.

—"Borrowing to Make Ends Meet," Demos: A Network for Ideas and Action

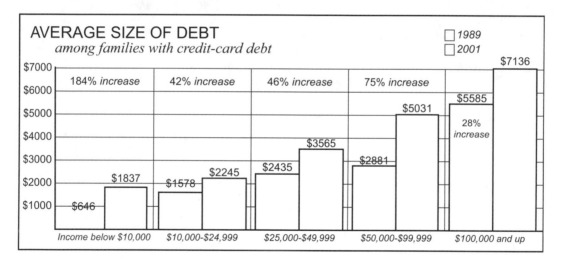

*AVERAGE SIZE Of DEBT among families with **credit-card** debt.*

Document E

Sullivan, Theresa, et al.. *The Fragile Middle Class: Americans in Debt*. New Haven: Yale UP, 2000: 134-135; 137.

How easy are credit cards to obtain? Aside from the anecdotes that regularly dot the filler sections of the local newspaper about a cat or dog that received a preapproved credit card, anyone who picks up the daily mail knows that credit cards are readily available. In 1980 credit card industry experts estimated that the retail credit card market was 84.7 per cent saturated, while the bank card market was not far behind at 80.5 per cent. Four out of five of the people with reasonable incomes and reasonable credit histories already had as many credit cards as they wanted or needed, said the experts. During the following decade, however, the number of cards in circulation nearly doubled from 116 million to 226 million. Nor does the growth show any sign of abating; there are now well over a billion cards in circulation. The amount of credit card debt outstanding at the end of 1997 was $422 billion, twice as much as the amount in 1993.

The credit card industry did not grow by being cautious about distributing credit cards. It grew because it solicited a broad range of debtors, and when they didn't take cards the first time or the second time they were offered, the companies sent mailings ten, eleven, and twelve times. So saturated is the market with credit cards that the typical credit card issuer spends about $100 in solicitation costs to acquire each new cardholder. From 1994 through 1996 credit card issuers sent out more than two and a half billion card solicitations each year.... The results of the industry's extraordinary marketing efforts have paid off. Credit card usage has grown fastest in recent years among debtors with the lowest incomes. Since the early 1990s, Americans with incomes below the poverty level nearly doubled their credit card usage, and those in the $10,000-25,000 bracket come in a close second in the rise in debt. The result is not surprising: 27 percent of the under-$10,000 families have consumer debt that is more than 40 percent of their income, and nearly one in ten has at least one debt that is more than sixty days past due.....

Document F

Royal, Leslie E. "In Too Deep." *Black Enterprise* 36.8 (Mar 2006): 89-93.

Credit counseling agencies offer solutions and obtain reductions in interest rates. Williams reached out to CCCS of Greater Atlanta (www.cccsatl.org). "I pay CCCS a $50 fee per month. When I look at what I save, it is well worth it," says Williams, who had been paying $1,000 more per month in finance charges, late payment charges, over-the-limit charges, and automatic default charges.

In arrears for the last seven years. Williams began a debt consolidation program in April 2005 and will complete it in five years. In exchange for destroying all of his credit cards and committing to a payment plan, Williams negotiated a plan with CCCS to erase late fees, over-the-limit fees, and no-payment fees, and substantially reduced all of his interest rates. They also worked aggressively to make the phone calls from creditors cease. Although he won't disclose exactly how much be pays monthly in addition to the $50 fee. Williams has paid off approximately 10% to 15% of his total balance.

"CCCS provides free credit, budget, and housing counseling. After looking at income, expenses, and debts and helping the client formulate a monthly budget, a counselor may recommend a debt management plan," says Sue Hunt, certified counselor and counseling manager of CCCS of Atlanta. "This gives the client some breathing room to work to pay off the debt, usually in three to five years."

However, many credit counseling organizations are paid by creditors to collect from you. In an industry that has very little regulation, there's room for unscrupulous companies to prey upon your vulnerability. This has been so pervasive that the U.S. Senate Permanent Subcommittee on Investigations released a report April 13, 2005. that examined the credit counseling industry and exposed abusive practices committed by certain credit counseling agencies. Likewise, on Oct. 14, 2003, the Internal Revenue Service, Federal Trade Commission, and state regulators issued a consumer alert for those seeking assistance from tax-exempt credit counseling agencies....

Sample Examination IV

Questions 1-11. Refer to the following passage.

In the following sermon, delivered during the era of Prohibition, famed evangelical preacher Billy Sunday discourses on the evils of drinking.

In these days when the question of saloon or no saloon is at the fore in almost every community, one hears a good deal about what is called "personal liberty." These are fine,
(5) large, mouth-filling words, and they certainly do sound first-rate. But when you get right down and analyze them in light of common old horse sense, you will discover that in their application to the present controversy they
(10) mean just about this: "Personal liberty" is for the man who, if he has the inclination and the price, can stand up at the bar and fill his hide so full of red liquor that he is transformed for the time being into an irresponsible, dangerous,
(15) evil-smelling brute.

But "personal liberty" is not for his patient, long-suffering wife, who has to endure with what fortitude she can, his blows and curses. Nor is it for his children, who, if they escape
(20) his insane rage, are yet robbed of every known joy and privilege of childhood, and too often grow up neglected, uncared for, and vicious as a result of their surroundings and the example before them.
(25) "Personal liberty" is not for the sober, industrious citizen who from the proceeds of honest toil and orderly living has to pay, willingly or not, the tax bills which pile up as a direct result of drunkenness, disorder, and
(30) poverty—the items of which are written in the record of every police court and poorhouse in the land. Nor is "personal liberty" for the good woman who goes abroad in the town only at the risk of being shot down by some drink-
(35) crazed creature. This rant about "personal liberty" as an argument has no leg to stand upon....

The saloon comes as near as being a rat hole for a wage earner to dump his wages in as
(40) anything you can find. The only interest it pays is red eyes and foul breath and the loss of health. You go in with money and you come out with empty pockets. You go in with character and you come out ruined. You go in
(45) with a good position and you lose it. You lose your position in the bank, or in the cab of the locomotive. And it pays nothing back but disease and damnation and gives an extra dividend in delirium tremens and a free pass to
(50) Hell. And then it will let your wife be buried in the potter's field and your children go to the asylum, and yet you walk out and say the saloon is a good institution when it is the dirtiest thing on earth. It hasn't one leg to stand
(55) on and has nothing to commend it to a decent man, not one thing....

The saloon is a coward. It is a thief. It is not an ordinary court offender that steals your money, but it robs you of manhood and leaves
(60) you in rags, and takes away your friends, and it robs your family. It impoverishes your children, and it brings insanity and suicide. It will take the shirt off your back, and it will steal the coffin from a dead child and yank the
(65) last crust of bread out of the hand of the starving child. It will take the last bucket of coal out of your cellar and the last cent out of your pocket, and will send you home bleary-eyed and staggering to your wife and
(70) children....

1. The tone of the speaker's sermon is BEST labeled

   (A) foreboding
   (B) moralizing
   (C) argumentative
   (D) satirical
   (E) despairing

2. In relation to the concept of "personal liberty," the second sentence (lines 4-6) intends to

   (A) establish its parameters
   (B) compliment its virtues
   (C) question its validity
   (D) qualify its meaning
   (E) defend its importance

3. The speaker provides the LEAST amount of evidence for the deleterious effects of "personal liberty" on which of the following?

   (A) family
   (B) employment
   (C) finances
   (D) friendship
   (E) health

4. The primary rhetorical device used by the speaker to convey his point in the second and third paragraphs is

   (A) ironical understatement
   (B) negation
   (C) analogy
   (D) climactic order
   (E) begging the question

5. Paragraph four (lines 38-56) differs MOST from the paragraphs that precede it in terms of its

   (A) argument
   (B) imagery
   (C) tone
   (D) syntax
   (E) perspective

6. Lines 38-50 contain an implied metaphor drawn from

   (A) banking
   (B) transportation
   (C) medicine
   (D) prison
   (E) matrimony

7. The speaker employs a series of "You" clauses, as well as the possessive pronoun "your," in lines 42-54 to do which of the following?

   I. Shift his rhetoric from a general example to a more personal level.
   II. Instill a subliminal sense of guilt in any member of his audience who may directly or indirectly support the saloon.
   III. Cite and attack the immorality of specific individuals.

   (A) I only
   (B) III only
   (C) I and II
   (D) II and IIII
   (E) I, II and III

8. Lines 42-45 contain examples of all of the following EXCEPT

   (A) anaphora
   (B) parallel structure
   (C) antithesis
   (D) metonymy
   (E) inverted syntax

9. Which of the following contributes MOST to the speaker's dramatization of the saloon's destructive capacity?

   (A) the simile comparing it to a "rat hole" (lines 38-40)
   (B) the bitter sarcasm of "yet you walk out and say the saloon is a good institution…." (lines 52-53)
   (C) the clichés of "It hasn't one leg to stand on…." (lines 54-55) and "It will take the shirt off your back…." (lines 62-63)
   (D) the metaphors comparing it to a "coward" and a "thief" (line 57)
   (E) the anaphora of "last crust" (line 65), "last bucket" (line 66), and "last cent" (line 67)

10. Which of the following is NOT characteristic of the speaker's rhetoric?

   (A) choric repetition
   (B) enumeration
   (C) a series of metaphors
   (D) antitheses
   (E) statistical data

11. All of the following represent the impact upon others of the drunkenness sanctioned by "personal liberty" EXCEPT

   (A) the "insane rage" mentioned in line 20
   (B) the "tax bills which pile up as a direct result of drunkenness, disorder, and poverty…" mentioned in lines 28-30
   (C) the "good woman who goes abroad in the town only at the risk of being shot down…" mentioned in lines 32-34
   (D) the "delirium tremens" and "free pass to Hell" mentioned in lines 49-50
   (E) the allusions to Potter's Field burials and commitments to the asylum mentioned in lines 50-52

Questions 12-20. Refer to the following passage.

Spring is a serenade,[1] but autumn is a nocturne.[2] In the waning of the year, the world is full of somber solemnity and a pathetic sense of old age. I have gleaned this information by
(5) reading poems on the subject.

> The melancholy days have come, the
>   saddest of the year,
> Of wailing winds and naked woods, and
>   meadows brown and sere.[3]

(10)   Accordingly, when I went on a long ramble through the countryside this morning I was fully prepared to observe the sad tokens of Nature's senility and decay.
        But a glorious surprise met me at the
(15) outset, and changed my mood from lamentation to exultation. I passed from the dismal poetic fiction to the actual glowing fact; from mournful reverie to mighty revelry. And all the predictions of the gloomy poets were
(20) scattered like the autumn leaves. For who can look at the blaze of autumn colors and declare them solemn? Who can drink deep draughts of the autumn gales and talk about senility?
        Autumn is youthful, mirthful,
(25) frolicsome—the child of summer's joy—and on every side there are suggestions of juvenility and mischief. While spring is a careful artist who paints each flower with delicate workmanship, autumn flings whole
(30) pots of paint about in wildest carelessness. The crimson and scarlet colours reserved for roses and tulips are splashed on the brambles till every bush is aflame, and the old creeper-covered house blushes like a sunset.
(35)   Why do the poets feel that autumn is ancient? He romps over the earth chasing the puppy-like gales, making them scamper over the mirrored pools, and ruffling their surface till the water-reeds hiss him away. He revels in
(40) boisterous gaiety, playing pranks like a schoolboy on the first day of his holidays. He turns on the raintaps to try the effect; he daubs a few toadstools blood red; he switches on summer sunshine for an hour, and then lets
(45) loose a tempest. He torments the stately trees, tears their foliage off in handfuls, rocks them backwards and forwards till they groan, and then scampers away for a brief interval leaving heavenly peace behind him. The fallen leaves
(50) are set racing down the lane. With madcap destructiveness he wastes his own handiwork, stripping the finery from the woods and forest. The bare trees sigh and shiver but he mocks them with howls and caterwaulings. Then he
(55) sets the bracken afire and pauses to admire the October tints. Finally, with deceptive golden sunshine, he tempts the sage out of doors, suddenly drenches him, and drives him home saturated to the skin. The sage thereupon
(60) changes his raiment, and murmurs about the solemnity of the dying year and the pensive beauties of autumn!

12. Of the rhetorical features of the passage, which is MOST effective in conveying the "glorious surprise" (line 14) that the author encounters on his sojourn through the countryside?

(A) the opening music metaphor
(B) the ubiquitous personification
(C) the rhetorical questions
(D) the pervasive color imagery
(E) the lines from Bryant's poem

13. The lines from William Cullen Bryant's poem do which of the following?

  I. Initially confirm the accuracy of Wray's declaration that autumn is a nocturne.
 II. Exemplify the predictions of the "gloomy poets" (line 19).
III. Set up an important contrast between "dismal poetic fiction" and "actual glowing fact" (line 17).

(A) I only
(B) II only
(C) I and III
(D) II and III
(E) I, II and III

[1] a song sung or played to express love for someone
[2] a pensive dreamy musical composition.
[3] from William Cullen Bryant's poem, "The Death of the Flowers"

14. The contrast between spring and autumn that is metaphorically developed in lines 24-34 is one of

(A) youth and age
(B) meticulousness and abandon
(C) jocularity and solemnity
(D) tranquility and violence
(E) facetiousness and austerity

15. The author's declarative response to his own question, "Why do the poets feel that autumn is ancient?" (lines 35-36), is MOST characterized by

(A) comparisons that imply schoolboy cruelty
(B) symbols that foreshadow decay and death
(C) verbs and participles that depict spry and mischievous behavior
(D) onomatopoeic words that audibly reveal the growing decrepitude of nature
(E) derisive commentary that mocks the poets' misconception

16. In the final paragraph autumn is depicted as all of the following EXCEPT

(A) a patriarch
(B) a reveler
(C) an arsonist
(D) a tempter
(E) a vandal

17. Autumn's actions in lines 36-59 are MOST closely associated with which of the following?

(A) "the waning of the year" (line 2)
(B) "a long ramble through the countryside" (lines 10-11)
(C) "the sad tokens of Nature's senility and decay" (lines 12-13)
(D) "suggestions of juvenility and mischief" (lines 26-27)
(E) "delicate workmanship" (line 29)

18. The diction of the final paragraph suggests that autumn shifts from exuberance and whimsy to

(A) disinterest and exhaustion
(B) ravaging and frenzy
(C) insidiousness and stealth
(D) lethargy and tedium
(E) serenity and contemplation

19. Which of the following is NOT personified over the course of the passage?

(A) the house (lines 33-34)
(B) the autumn (lines 36-59)
(C) the leaves (lines 49-50)
(D) the trees (line 53)
(E) the bracken (line 55)

20. The sage's "murmur[ing]" (line 60) is likely a reaction to autumn's

(A) approaching end
(B) vibrant colors
(C) capricious weather
(D) mournful solemnity
(E) fallen leaves

Questions 21-33. Refer to the following passage.

In the following passage from Richard Wright's autobiography <u>Black Boy</u>, the young Richard recalls his mother's desperate appeal for child support to his adulterous father.

....My father and a strange woman were sitting before a bright fire that blazed in a grate. My mother and I were standing about six feet away, as though we were afraid to
(5)   approach them any closer.

"It's not for me," my mother was saying. "It's for your children that I'm asking you for money."

"I ain't got nothing," my father said,
(10)   laughing.

"Come here, boy," the strange woman called to me.

I looked at her and did not move.

"Give him a nickel," the woman said.
(15)   "He's cute."

"Come here, Richard," my father said, stretching out his hand.

I backed away, shaking my head, keeping my eyes on the fire.
(20)   "He is a cute child," the strange woman said.

"You ought to be ashamed," my mother said to the strange woman. "You're starving my children."
(25)   "Now, don't you-all fight," my father said, laughing.

"I'll take that poker and hit you!" I blurted at my father.

He looked at my mother and laughed
(30)   louder.

"You told him to say that," he said.

"Don't say such things, Richard," my mother said.

"You ought to be dead," I said to the
(35)   strange woman.

The woman laughed and threw her arms about my father's neck. I grew ashamed and wanted to leave.

"How can you starve your children?" my
(40)   mother asked.

"Let Richard stay with me," my father said.

"Do you want to stay with your father, Richard?," my mother asked.

(45)   "No," I said.

"You'll get plenty to eat," he said.

"I'm hungry now," I told him. "But I won't stay with you."

"Aw, give the boy a nickel," the woman
(50)   said.

My father ran his hand into his pocket and took out a nickel.

"Here, Richard," he said,

"Don't take it," my mother said.
(55)   "Don't teach him to be a fool," my father said. "Here, Richard, take it."

I looked at my mother, at the strange woman, at my father. I wanted to take the nickel, but I did not want to take it from my
(60)   father.

"You ought to be ashamed," my mother said, weeping. "Giving your son a nickel when he's hungry. If there's a God, He'll pay you back."

(65)   "That's all I got," my father said, laughing again and returning the nickel to his pocket....

A quarter of a century was to elapse between the time when I was to see him again, standing alone upon the red clay of a
(70)   Mississippi plantation, a sharecropper, clad in ragged overalls, holding a muddy hoe in his gnarled, veined hands—a quarter of a century during which my mind and consciousness had become so greatly and violently altered that
(75)   when I tried to talk to him I realized that, though ties of blood made us kin, though I could see a shadow of my face in his face, though there was an echo of my voice in his voice, we were forever strangers, speaking a
(80)   different language, living on vastly different planes of reality. That day a quarter of a century later when I visited him on the plantation—he was standing against the sky, smiling toothlessly, his hair whitened, his body
(85)   bent, his eyes glazed with dim recollection, his fearsome aspect of twenty-five years ago gone forever from him....I stood before him, poised, my mind aching as it embraced the simple nakedness of his life, feeling how completely
(90)   his soul was imprisoned by the slow flow of the seasons, by wind and rain and sun, how fastened were his memories to a cruel and raw past, how chained were his actions and emotions to the direct, animalistic impulses of
(95)   his withering body....

21. What the young Richard seemingly detests MOST about his father is his

    (A) affluent new lifestyle
    (B) shameless betrayal of Richard's mother
    (C) unwillingness to talk to his wife
    (D) tempting offer to Richard to live with him
    (E) inability to take anything seriously

22. The blazing fire that the author mentions in line 2 and again in lines 18-19 functions as which of the following?

    I. A symbol of domestic warmth that Richard desires and envies.
    II. A means by which Richard can avoid eye contact with his father.
    III. A symbol of the passion between Richard's father and his mistress.

    (A) II only
    (B) III only
    (C) I and II
    (D) I and III
    (E) I, II and III

23. The response of Richard's father to his wife's appeal (lines 9-10) is BEST classified as

    (A) dismissive
    (B) flippant
    (C) belligerent
    (D) sympathetic
    (E) procrastinating

24. In the course of the passage, Richard's father laughs at all of the following EXCEPT

    (A) his wife's request for money (lines 6-8)
    (B) the friction between his wife and mistress (lines 22-24)
    (C) his son's precociousness (lines 27-28)
    (D) the display of affection by his mistress (lines 36-38)
    (E) his wife's closing threat (lines 63-64)

25. Which of the following BEST articulates the difference in the motivation behind Richard's mother's admonition, "'Don't take it'" (line 54), and his father's retort, "'Don't teach him to be a fool'" (line 55)?

    (A) concern vs. disinterest
    (B) adamancy vs. accommodation
    (C) threat vs. appeal
    (D) counsel vs. censure
    (E) pride vs. pragmatism

26. Lines 57-58, "I looked at my mother, at the strange woman, at my father," exemplify which of the following?

    (A) climactic order
    (B) inverted syntax
    (C) parallel structure
    (D) non sequitur
    (E) spatial ordering

27. The change in Richard's father over the past quarter century is evidenced LEAST by the

    (A) color of his hair
    (B) slowness of his recall
    (C) stooped nature of his posture
    (D) condition of his financial lot
    (E) absence of his teeth

28. By the "nakedness of his life" (line 89), Richard likely means his father's

    (A) shameful adultery with the strange woman
    (B) threadbare attire
    (C) punishing exposure to the Mississippi sun
    (D) candid portrait of endured hardship
    (E) refusal to apologize to his son

29. Which of the following verbs BEST connotes a softening of Richard's feelings towards his father?

    (A) "altered" (line 74)
    (B) "visited" (line 82)
    (C) "glazed" (line 85)
    (D) "embraced" (line 88)
    (E) "fastened" (line 92)

30. All of the following are characteristic of the lengthy sentence that comprises lines 67-81 EXCEPT

    (A) repetition of a phrase that emphasizes how much time has elapsed
    (B) participial phrases which help delineate the indelible impression of his father's hopelessness
    (C) a trio of subordinate clauses in which Richard acknowledges physiological similarities to his father
    (D) a climactic epiphany in which Richard realizes any relationship with his father is impossible
    (E) adverbs that convey Richard's anger and vindictiveness towards his father

31. The words "kin" (line 76), "shadow" (line 77) and "echo" (line 78) primarily imply the

    (A) physical toll exacted by life on Richard's father
    (B) lingering resemblance that Richard bears to his father
    (C) enduring impression that the childhood encounter had upon Richard
    (D) profound difference between Richard and his father
    (E) pivotal importance to Richard of retaining family ties

32. Lines 87-95, "I stood before him...his withering body," contain diction that alludes to all of the following EXCEPT

    (A) changes in weather and time
    (B) African-American slavery and poverty
    (C) the circumstances of his father's birth
    (D) the physical decline of Richard's father
    (E) Richard's concluding epiphany

33. Which of the following BEST delineates the change in Richard that takes place over the course of the passage?

    (A) ignorance to understanding
    (B) rebelliousness to conformity
    (C) deprivation to abundance
    (D) resentment to sympathy
    (E) shame to pride

Questions 34-46. Refer to the following passage.

You sit down to dinner and life as you know it ends.
The question of self-pity.
People in grief think a great deal about
(5) self-pity. We worry it, dread it, scourge our
thinking for signs of it. We fear that our actions
will reveal the condition tellingly described as
"dwelling on it." We understand the aversion
most of us have to "dwelling on it." Visible
(10) mourning reminds us of death, which is
construed as unnatural, a failure to manage the
situation. "A single person is missing for you,
and the whole world is empty," Philippe Ariès
wrote to the point of this aversion in *Western*
(15) *Attitudes toward Death*. "But one no longer has
the right to say so out loud." We remind
ourselves repeatedly that our own loss is
nothing compared to the loss experienced (or,
the even worse thought, not experienced) by he
(20) or she who died; this attempt at corrective
thinking serves only to plunge us deeper into
the self-regarding deep. (*Why didn't I see that?*
Why am I so selfish?). The very language we
use when we think about self-pity betrays the
(25) deep abhorrence in which we hold it: self-pity
is *feeling sorry for yourself*, self-pity is *thumb-*
sucking, self-pity is *boo hoo poor me*, self-pity
is the condition in which those feeling sorry for
themselves *indulge*, or even *wallow*. Self-pity
(30) remains both the most common and the most
reviled of our character defects, its pestilential
destructiveness accepted as given. "Our worst
enemy," Helen Keller called it. *I never saw a*
wild thing / sorry for itself, D.H. Lawrence
(35) wrote, in a much quoted four-line homily that
turns out on examination to be free of any but
tendentious[1] meaning. *A small bird will drop*
frozen dead from a bough / without ever having
felt sorry for itself.
(40) This may be what Lawrence (or we) would
prefer to believe about wild things, but
consider those dolphins who refuse to eat after
the death of a mate. Consider those geese who
search for the lost mate until they themselves
(45) become disoriented and die. In fact the
grieving have urgent reasons, even an urgent
need, to feel sorry for themselves. Husbands
walk out, wives walk out, divorces happen, but
these husbands and wives leave behind them
(50) webs of intact associations, however

---

[1] biased, partisan

acrimonious. Only the survivors of a death are
truly left alone. The connections that made up
their life—both the deep connections and the
apparently (until they are broken) insignificant
(55) connections —have all vanished. John and I
were married for forty years, During all but the
first five months of our marriage, when John
was still working at *Time*, we both worked at
home. We were together twenty-four hours a
(60) day, a fact that remained a source of both
merriment and foreboding to my mother and
aunts. "For richer for poorer but never for
lunch," one or another of them frequently said
in the early years of our marriage. I could not
(65) count the times during the average day when
something would come up that I needed to tell
him. This impulse did not end with his death. I
read something in the paper that I would
normally have read to him. I notice some
(70) change in the neighborhood that would interest
him: Ralph Lauren has expanded into more
space between Seventy-first and Seventy-
second Streets, say, or the empty space where
the Madison Avenue Bookshop used to be has
(75) finally been leased. I recall coming in from
Central Park one morning in mid-August with
urgent news to report: the deep summer green
has faded overnight from the trees, the season
is already changing. *We need to make a plan*
(80) *for the fall*, I remember thinking. *We need to*
decide where we want to be at Thanksgiving,
Christmas, the end of the year.
I am dropping my keys on the table inside
the door before I fully remember. There is no
(85) one to hear this news, nowhere to go with the
unmade plan, the uncompleted thought. There
is no one to agree, disagree, talk back. "I think
I am beginning to understand why grief feels
like suspense," C.S. Lewis wrote after the
(90) death of his wife. "It comes from the
frustration of so many impulses that had
become habitual. Thought after thought,
feeling after feeling, action after action, had H.
for their object. Now their target is gone. I
(95) keep on through habit fitting an arrow to the
string, then I remember and have to lay the
bow down. So many roads lead thought to H. I
set out on one of them. But now there's an
impossible frontierpost across it. So many
(100) roads once; now so many cul de sacs."
We are repeatedly left, in other words, with
no further focus than ourselves, a source from
which self-pity naturally flows....

From THE YEAR OF MAGICAL THINKING by Joan Didion,
copyright © 2005 by Joan Didion. Used by permission of Alfred
A. Knopf, a division of Random House, Inc.

34. The italicized statements which open the passage reflect all of the following EXCEPT

    (A) the author's consciousness of being utterly alone
    (B) the harsh epiphany that the author experiences due to a change in the routine or the expected
    (C) the author's understandable reluctance to continue living
    (D) the guilt the author feels about feeling sorry for her circumstance
    (E) the author's seemingly incongruous merger of the apocalyptic and the mundane

35. Of the other individuals cited in the passage, which articulates a sentiment closest in meaning to that which the author herself expresses in lines 1-2?

    (A) Philippe Ariès (lines 12-15)
    (B) Helen Keller (lines 32-33)
    (C) D. H. Lawrence (lines 33-39)
    (D) her mother and her aunts (lines 62-64)
    (E) C.S. Lewis (lines 89-100)

36. The series of "We" clauses (lines 5-9 and lines 16-20) primarily serves to

    (A) support the claim about self-pity that was expressed by the topic sentence (lines 4-5)
    (B) suggest the solace the author has received from the community of mourners
    (C) confirm the bereaved's universal belief that death is "unnatural"
    (D) reinforce the importance of the outward expression of grief
    (E) confess every individual's fear of death and what comes after it

37. Philippe Ariès' remark, "'A single person is missing for you, and the whole world is empty'" (lines 12-13) uses which of the following rhetorical techniques to convey its point about the loss of a loved one?

    (A) paradox
    (B) metonymy
    (C) amplification
    (D) hyperbole
    (E) personification

38. The author likely uses the first-person plural pronoun "we" on the heels of the initial italicized text (lines 1-3) to

    (A) seek consolation for her loss from others
    (B) affirm the sad reality that personal loss is universally experienced
    (C) compare the depth of her sorrow to that experienced by others
    (D) address bereaved family members who share her suffering
    (E) recall her deceased spouse

39. The language used by people to characterize individuals who engage in self-pity (lines 23-29) paints them as

    (A) lachrymose and dejected
    (B) downcast and self-indulgent
    (C) obstinate and infantile
    (D) stoic and composed
    (E) pensive and philosophical

40. The author probably labels Lawrence's poem a "four line homily" (line 35) and the sentiment it expresses "tendentious" (line 37) for which of the following reasons?

    I. Lawrence was a poet, not a naturalist.
    II. Lawrence's claim is seemingly contradicted by other species in nature.
    III. Lawrence too glibly dismisses the importance of the grieving process.

    (A) I only
    (B) II only
    (C) I and III
    (D) II and III
    (E) I, II and III

41. In relation to Lawrence's "four-line homily," lines 40-45—"This may be what Lawrence (or we) would prefer….become disoriented and die"—are BEST labeled a(n)

    (A) concession
    (B) speculation
    (C) affirmation
    (D) aside
    (E) contradiction

42. The author likely inserts the parenthetical comment, "(until they are broken)" in line 54 in order to do which of the following?

    I. Exemplify the "dwelling on it" self-pity of which she speaks in the opening paragraph.
    II. Highlight the irony—that trivial things are not valued until they are gone.
    III. Buttress her earlier comments on divorce (lines 47-48).

    (A) I only
    (B) II only
    (C) I and III
    (D) II and III
    (E) I, II and III

43. The sentiment expressed by the author's mother and aunts in lines 62-63, "For richer for poorer but never for lunch," implies her family's

    (A) initial dislike of John, her husband
    (B) annoyance at her husband's frequent travel
    (C) belief that the couple would struggle financially
    (D) fears that the close working proximity of the couple would create friction
    (E) skepticism about the stability of the couple's marriage

44. Lines 83-87—"I am dropping my keys on the table….There is no one to agree, disagree, talk back"—feature all of the following EXCEPT

    (A) a troubling epiphany triggered by an everyday routine
    (B) participles that convey the author's regret about unfulfilled plans
    (C) an anaphora that reiterates the absence of her deceased spouse
    (D) an onomatopoeia that emphasizes the sudden emptiness of the house
    (E) a trio of verbs that convey the discomfiting void of conversation

45. In attempting to convey the impact of his wife's death upon his daily existence in lines 89-100, C.S. Lewis makes the MOST significant use of which of the following?

    (A) personal anecdotes
    (B) extended metaphors
    (C) parallel structure
    (D) ironical understatement
    (E) philosophical speculation

46. In the parts of the passage that use interior monologue, the author relies upon which of the following?

    (A) stream-of-consciousness
    (B) parenthetical citation and italics
    (C) flashback
    (D) shifting verb tense
    (E) alternating points of view

Questions 47-52. Refer to the following passage.

The following is an excerpt from a speech that was delivered in 1996.

....We have been informed by the [electronics] industry that the march of computers and assorted gadgetry into every home, business, school, library and pocket is *(5)* "inevitable." Microsoft's Bill Gates and his pals tell us we can't fight back because in the very near future everything will be digital. If you aren't hooked up now, your children will be illiterate and your business will be bankrupt. *(10)* Worse yet, you will be cut off from the Internet and therefore from the rest of the world. In short, you will be branded a PONA—Person Of No Account in cyberspeak.

Since the victory of gadgetry is *(15)* "inevitable," you might as well come along quietly and let us smother you in speed and convenience, says the digital mafia.

This is propaganda of the most insidious sort, threatening those of us who don't want *(20)* and don't need contraptions in our lives. If you are the parents of a young child, as I am, you are assaulted with a constant advertising and media onslaught that makes you feel both guilty and terrified if you do not spring for a *(25)* computer immediately. Every time your child comes home with tales of new computers and software on the desks of neighborhood kids, you imagine yourself to be both a cheapskate and crank for insisting on paper, pencil, and a *(30)* mind free from machine programming.

You worry that maybe all of this *is* inevitable. The stock market is in an electronic feeding frenzy. Microsoft made Bill Gates the richest man in the United States in just a few *(35)* years. Steven Jobs collected a billion dollars overnight on the stock offering of his Pixar cartoon animation device. Businesses are desperate to stake a claim on a World Wide Web site. Millions of ordinary folk tap into the *(40)* Internet for sex, info, and chat. The New York Public Library warns of "new Dark Ages in literacy" if it can't raise the funds for computers. School boards trim teachers' salaries and slash programs so they can afford *(45)* new and better computer labs. Teachers worry about the day when they will be terminated so a computer can teach and entertain the kids. No big business today will answer the phone without voice mail or do without e-mail. No

(50) letter can simply be mailed. It must be faxed or we are convinced it will be ignored as unimportant.

The electronics wizards tell us we can't balance our checkbooks without Quicken, *(55)* research a simple fact without a CD-ROM, and we shouldn't even attempt our own handwriting—there is a software program with computer fonts that duplicate handwriting fast and neatly for a mere $39.95. Soon, so Bill *(60)* Gates envisions in his instant best-seller, *The Road Ahead*, we wont dare to stroll the street without a pocket PC that will be a combination fax, stock market monitor, digital cash dispenser, e-mail receiver and sender, storer of *(65)* our kids' photos, and—get this—a Global Positioning System that will let you know within 300 feet exactly where you are on the globe. You didn't know you needed this? Well, you do, and it's "inevitable!" The info highway *(70)* is paving us over....

47. The diction in the passage does which of the following?

   I. Depicts technological advancement as an inexorable invasion of society.
  II. Pejoratively dismisses technological innovation as unnecessary contraptions.
 III. Implies that failing to embrace the digital world will have dire social and economic consequences.

(A) I only
(B) III only
(C) I and II
(D) II and III
(E) I, II and III

48. The tone of lines 7-13—"If you aren't hooked up now....you will be branded a PONA— Person Of No Account in cyberspeak"—is BEST labeled

(A) matter-of-fact and informational
(B) confidential and clandestine
(C) understanding and sympathetic
(D) dire and apocalyptic
(E) frustrated and resigned

Reprinted with permission from Bill Henderson. © Pushcart Press.

49. The author states that pressure on individual consumers to purchase new advancements in technology comes from all of the following EXCEPT

    (A) the media
    (B) employers
    (C) their children
    (D) the electronics' industry
    (E) corporate honchos

50. The type of sentence that comprises most of the fourth paragraph (lines 31-52) is

    (A) declarative
    (B) imperative
    (C) interrogative
    (D) exclamatory
    (E) run-on

51. Which of the following LEAST helps to convey the relentless pressure to embrace the new technology that, according to the author, men like Bill Gates and Steve Jobs apply to everyday consumers?

    (A) "march of consumers and assorted gadgetry …" (lines 2-3)
    (B) "…come along quietly and let us smother you…" (lines 15-16)
    (C) "…propaganda of the most insidious sort…" (lines 18-19)
    (D) "…assaulted with a constant advertising and media onslaught…" (lines 22-23)
    (E) "You didn't know you needed this? Well, you do…" (lines 68-69)

52. Which of the following may NOT be said to be a stylistic trait of the passage?

    (A) a deterministic and occasionally sardonic tone
    (B) diction that connotes totalitarianism
    (C) a catalog of electronic innovation
    (D) use of personal pronouns to enhance the immediacy of the problem
    (E) a timeline for economic and social change

Section II

<u>Question One</u>

(Suggested time–40 minutes. This question counts as one-third of the total essay section score.)

The following article appeared in the *London Times* nine years after the Armistice ending the First World War. Read the article carefully. Then, in a well-organized essay, discuss how the author uses language to persuade his audience of the importance of a particular commemorative day. In addition, indicate to what degree you feel the author's sentiment is or is not shared by the present generation.

To the Dead and To the Living

On this the ninth anniversary of the Armistice which ended the greatest and most fateful of all wars, the heart of this world-wide Empire turns in a special manner to the memory of those whose lives were the price of our deliverance. As there has been no struggle in our annals so terrible and so exacting, no danger so prolonged and imminent, no cause so great, no sacrifices so cruel, and no victory on which larger and more lasting issues hung, so there is no day on our calendar like to this. For over four years we stood on
(5)   the edge of the abyss, of ruin as an Empire, as a nation, perhaps of ruin as a race. The men we commemorate today saved us from that ruin by their death. The appeal is universal. Scarce a home in the land, from the most splendid of ancestral palaces to the humblest cottage or the poorest lodging in our towns, was unvisited in that dread time by the angel of death. He smote the best; a whole generation entering upon life
(10)   in the flower of early manhood, and others already husbands and fathers, the stay and the guardians of the widows and the orphans they have left. To the bereaved, first of all, this is a day of days, dedicated to the memory of their dead, a memory ever living with them, but by time and the everyday duties and occupations of life mercifully softened with the years. The annual testimony to the fallen, celebrated with such solemn and fitting rites as Church and State can give, bears recurring witness to the full measure in
(15)   which Empire and nation share the grief and the gratitude of the mourners. There is no day on which all sorts and conditions of our people are so widely and so deeply moved by thoughts and feelings common to them all. The prayerful congregations in the churches on Sunday, the crowds which will gather round the Cenotaph or attend the services and visit the tomb of the Unknown Warrior today, and those other crowds which will assemble in their own churches or about their own local monuments through the provinces and
(20)   through all lands where the flag flies, are filled according to their gifts and their experiences by the same spirit, the same memories, and the same hopes.

Question Two

(Suggested time—40 minutes. This question counts as one-third of the total essay section score.)

James Baldwin, in his 1985 essay "The American Dream and the American Negro," observed "Unless we can establish some type of dialogue between those people who enjoy the American dream and those people who have not achieved it, we will be in terrible trouble." Surely, the American Dream has for some people been a paradoxical concept—at once alluring in its promise of financial progress and social equality and frustrating in its limited access and dispiriting roadblocks.

Take a moment to ponder Baldwin's observation. Then, in a well-organized essay, discuss the degree to which this social "dialogue" has been established and whether we have averted or courted the "terrible trouble" of which he speaks. Use your reading, studies, experience or observations to develop your argument.

Question Three

Reading Time: 15 minutes
Suggested Writing Time: 40 minutes

(This question counts as one-third of the total essay section score.)

Directions:

The following prompt is based on the accompanying six sources.

This question requires you to integrate a variety of sources into a coherent, well-written essay. *Refer to the sources to support your position; avoid paraphrase or summary. Your argument should be central; the sources should support this argument.*

Remember to attribute both direct and indirect citations.

Introduction:

In recent years more and more emphasis has been placed on individuals' ability to multitask. Whether one is a businessman or a stay-at-home mother, the ability to carry out multiple duties at the same time has seemingly become a valuable asset and is viewed by many as an essential, even necessary skill for the twenty-first century. However, does this ability to do multiple things simultaneously detract from one's ability to execute any one thing well? Moreover, is the practice of doing multiple things at once detrimental to the individual's efficiency, attentiveness and focus?

Assignment:

Read the following sources (including any introductory information) carefully. **Then, in an essay that synthesizes at least three of the sources for support, take a position that defends, challenges or qualifies the claim that the ability to multitask can only benefit the academic or employment career of an individual.**

<u>Document A</u>

Jackson, Maggie. *Distracted: The Erosion of Attention and the Coming Dark Age*. Amherst, NY: Prometheus
    Books, 2008: 18.

....Kids are the inveterate multitaskers, the technologically fluent new breed that is better suited for the
lightning-paced, many-threaded digital world, right? After all, they are bathed in an average of nearly six hours a
day of nonprint media content, and a quarter of that time they are using more than one screen, dial, or channel.
Nearly a third of fourteen- to twenty-one-year-olds juggle five to eight media while doing homework. Yet for all
their high-tech fluency, kids show less patience, skepticism, tenacity, and skill than adults in navigating the Web,
all while overestimating their prowess...Meanwhile, U.S. fifteen-year-olds rank twenty-fourth out of twenty-nine
developed countries on an Organization for Economic Cooperation and Development (OECD) test of problem-
solving skills related to analytic reasoning—the sort of skills demanded in today's work force, Nearly 60 percent
of fifteen-year-olds in our country score at or below the most basic level of problem solving, which involves
using single sources of well-defined information to solve challenges such as plotting a route on a map.
Government and other studies show that many U.S. high school students can't synthesize or assess information,
express complex thoughts, or analyze argument. In other words, they often lack the critical thinking skills that
are the bedrock of an informed citizenry and the foundation of scientific and other advancements....

Document B

Freedman, David H. "Why Interruption, Distraction, and Multitasking are not such awful things after all."
Inc 29.2 (Feb 2007): 67-68.

…. So what gives? Does multitasking really impair our ability to get our jobs done? The answer for most workers is, I think, no. But it's not because multitasking doesn't impair your ability to perform tasks. It does. It's because we're now in a complex, fast-response world in which getting a complete task done in the least amount of time is no longer the priority. Instead, today's top priority is to immediately address whatever fraction of a vast, malleable range of tasks has become most critical—a just-in-time, networked workstyle. Focusing on one task to the exclusion of others isn't even an option anymore. When experts examine the detrimental effects of multitasking on productivity, they're asking the wrong question. We don't need to wonder about the ways in which multitasking and interruption impair our ability to speed through a task. We need to appreciate the ways in which multitasking and interruption have become essential to meeting the increasingly nonlinear demands of our jobs.

That means it's essential not only to put up with but also to embrace multitasking. Fifteen years ago, it was almost impossible to get a fast response in midevening, or even midday, from your head of product development or the CEO of a key supplier. But today, with projects and products being zipped around the globe, chances are you know exactly how to get someone's attention at a moment's notice. And the ability to do so has a direct impact on the bottom line, says Michael McCloskey, CEO of Front Range Solutions, a customer relationship management software and services provider in Dublin, California. "If I'm in a price negotiation with a big customer, and they've got their legal and purchasing people right there, and they want an answer to a question, I better be able to get that answer," he says. "Because I may not be able to get those people in the same room talking about my product again anytime soon."….

Meanwhile, businesses have long been moving away from the sort of stovepipe structure that allowed employees to focus on meeting the demands of a single boss or worry only about a small group of employees or customers. Today the dotted-line relationships form a dense web that extends out to customers, suppliers, and partners. In other words, forget about closing the door and crunching on that one presentation. You've got 20 other people breathing at you just as hard, and each one wants to know that you're making progress….

Document C

Gomolski, Barbara. "Are We Multitasking Ourselves into Chaos?" *Computerworld* 40.21 (May 22, 2006): 59.

…. I've noticed lately that it seems to have become quite acceptable to send instant messages to others in the middle of meetings. So, in addition to listening to multiple speakers at these corporate get-togethers, we now have to juggle instant message input from those same colleagues. Inevitably, during such a meeting someone will be asked a question, and it's apparent that he hasn't been paying attention to the speaker. Rather, he's been reading and responding to comments about said speaker or some other topic entirely.

Let's examine another common IT tableau. Many hard-working IT[1] professionals attend conferences. At these events, attendees are often given the opportunity to sit in on as many as six or seven speaker sessions per day on a variety of complex topics. Attendance at these events often requires travel on the part of the IT employee and an expense of several thousand dollars on the part of the IT professional's employer.

Yet, in spite of the great deal of time and expense associated with this activity, it's becoming common to see half the audience typing away on their computer screens while purportedly listening to the speaker. Since many of these events are now set up with wireless access, attendees can be connected to their offices during sessions. Now, it's certainly possible that the dedicated IT professionals are using their PCs to take notes. My own informal survey suggests, however, that this is rarely the case. Rather, most of the screens I've eyeballed show that their owners are answering e-mail, working on projects or even playing solitaire.

There are two issues here: First, there's an ethical one. Is it fair to attend a conference (at significant expense to an employer) and not devote adequate attention to the content? Most would say no. Second, is it really possible to multitask effectively enough to pay attention to a speaker while participating in one or several e-mail or IM dialogues as well? Perhaps it is, but my gut tells me that bounded rationality kicks in at some point.

Are we multitasking ourselves into chaos? Are we doing so many things at once that we do none well? Or am I just missing some genetic mutation that enables some folks to thrive amid chaos?

---

[1] Information Technology

Document D

Bradley, Karen. "Can Teens Really Do It All? *Independent School* 70.4 (Summer 2011): 92-99.

...People are under the illusion that they literally do things simultaneously when they work and play with multiple interfaces. In fact, however, the brain cannot actually do multiple things simultaneously. Rather, it switches gears, which takes time, reduces accuracy, and inhibits creative thought. In many cases, it is simply less efficient than working on tasks sequentially.

Multitaskers are constantly shifting focus and activities ("I want to do this now instead of that") and activating different brain rules ("I'm turning off the rules for having a social conversation and turning on the rules for analyzing an Excel spreadsheet"). But each shift takes several tenths of a second—which can add up when people switch back and forth repeatedly between tasks. "Whether [we] toggle between browsing the Web and using other computer programs, talk on cell phones while driving, [we]...are rapidly switching between tasks all the time," explain researchers from the FAA and the University of Michigan. These researchers studied patterns in the amounts of time lost when people switched repeatedly between two tasks of varying complexity and familiarity, such as solving math problems or classifying geometric objects. The researchers measured subjects' speed of performance as a function of whether the tasks were familiar or unfamiliar, simple or complex. The measurements revealed that, for all types of tasks, subjects lost time when they had to switch from one task to another, and the amount of lost time increased with the complexity of the tasks.

Given that American cell phone users averaged over 357 text messages per month in 2009, it's no wonder students who text report spending six, seven, or eight hours doing their homework whereas students who don't text get the job done in a fraction of the time...

Document E

© Christos Georghiou - Fotolia.com

Document F

Cowen, Tyler. "Three Tweets for the Web." *Wilson Quarterly* 33.4 (Autumn 2009): 54-58.

....The arrival of virtually every new cultural medium has been greeted with the charge that it truncates attention spans and represents the beginning of cultural collapse--the novel (in the 18th century), the comic book, rock 'n' roll, television, and now the Web. In fact, there has never been a golden age of all-wise, all-attentive readers. But that's not to say that nothing has changed. The mass migration of intellectual activity from print to the Web has brought one important development: We have begun paying more attention to information. Overall, that's a big plus for the new world order.

It is easy to dismiss this cornucopia as information overload. We've all seen people scrolling with one hand through a BlackBerry while pecking out instant messages (IMs) on a laptop with the other and eyeing a television (I won't say "watching"). But even though it is easy to see signs of overload in our busy lives, the reality is that most of us carefully regulate this massive inflow of information to create something uniquely suited to our particular interests and needs—a rich and highly personalized blend of cultural gleanings. The word for this process is multi-tasking, but that makes it sound as if we're all over the place. There is a deep coherence to how each of us pulls out a steady stream of information from disparate sources to feed our long-term interests. No matter how varied your topics of interest may appear to an outside observer, you'll tailor an information stream related to the continuing "stories" you want in your life—say, Sichuan cooking, health care reform, Michael Jackson, and the stock market. With the help of the Web, you build broader intellectual narratives about the world. The apparent disorder of the information stream reflects not your incoherence but rather your depth and originality as an individual....

Many critics charge that multitasking makes us less efficient. Researchers say that periodically checking your e-mail lowers your cognitive performance level to that of a drunk. If such claims were broadly correct, multitasking would pretty rapidly disappear simply because people would find that it didn't make sense to do it. Multitasking is flourishing, and so are we. There are plenty of lab experiments that show that distracting people reduces the capacity of their working memory and thus impairs their decision making. It's much harder to show that multitasking, when it results from the choices and control of an individual, does anyone cognitive harm. Multitasking is not a distraction from our main activity, it is our main activity.

Sample Examination V

Questions 1-12. Refer to the following passage.

Personally, I love Crazy Horse[1] because even the most basic outline of his life shows how great he was; because he remained himself from the moment of his birth to the
(5) moment he died; because he knew exactly where he wanted to live, and never left; because he may have surrendered, but he was never defeated in battle; because, although he was·killed, even the Army admitted he was
(10) never captured; because he was so free that he didn't know what a jail looked like; because at the most desperate moment of his life he only cut Little Big Man on the hand;[2] because, unlike many people all over the world, when
(15) he met white men he was not diminished by the encounter; because his dislike of the oncoming civilization was prophetic; because the idea of becoming a farmer apparently never crossed his mind; because he didn't end up in
(20) the Dry Tortugas;[3] because he never met the President; because he never rode on a train, slept in a boardinghouse, ate at a table; because he never wore a medal or a top hat or any other thing that white men gave him; because he
(25) made sure that his wife was safe before going to where he expected to die; because, although Indian agents, among themselves, sometimes referred to Red Cloud as "Red" and Spotted Tail as "Spot," they never used a diminutive
(30) for him; because, deprived of freedom, power, occupation, culture, trapped in a situation where bravery was invisible, he was still brave; because he fought in self-defense, and took no one with him when he died; because, like the
(35) rings of Saturn, the carbon atom, and the underwater reef, he belonged to a category of phenomena which our technology had not then advanced far enough to photograph; because

no photograph or painting or even sketch of
(40) him exists; because he is not the Indian on the nickel, the tobacco pouch, or the apple crate. Crazy Horse was a slim man of medium height with brown hair hanging below his waist and a scar above his lip. Now, in the mind of each
(45) person who imagines him, he looks different.

1. The author's description of Crazy Horse is BEST labeled a(n)

    (A) soliloquy
    (B) elegy
    (C) panegyric
    (D) exhortation
    (E) obloquy

2. The "because" clause which BEST encapsulates the overall impression that the author is trying to paint of Crazy Horse is contained in

    (A) lines 3-5
    (B) lines 5-6
    (C) lines 10-11
    (D) lines 13-16
    (E) lines 22-24

3. The most singular feature of the passage is its

    (A) figurative language
    (B) tone
    (C) perspective
    (D) imagery
    (E) syntax

---

[1] Famous Lakota warrior who defied the encroachment of U.S. military forces in Wyoming and played a key role in the defeat of General Custer at Little Big Horn. He later was forced to surrender and was killed while in custody.

[2] A Lakota warrior who fought along with Crazy Horse but was also involved in his betrayal. This seemingly alludes to the struggle in which Crazy Horse was killed.

[3] An island in the Florida Keys which contained a prison to which dissidents were sent.

"Crazy Horse" from GREAT PLAINS by Ian Frazier. Copyright© 1989 by Ian Frazier. Reprinted by permission of Farrar, Straus and Giroux, LLC.

4. The passage suggests that the author views Crazy Horse as all of the following EXCEPT

(A) an indomitable warrior
(B) an autonomous spirit
(C) a military strategist
(D) a devoted husband
(E) a mythical figure

5. The point being made in lines 13-16, "because, unlike many people all over the world, when he met white men he was not diminished by the encounter," is MOST similar in sentiment to the point made in which of the following?

(A) "because he remained himself from the moment of his birth to the moment he died" (lines 3-5)
(B) "because he may have surrendered, but he was never defeated in battle" (lines 7-8)
(C) "because he never met the President" (lines 20-21)
(D) "because, although Indian agents, among themselves, sometime referred to Red Cloud as 'Red' and Spotted Tail as 'Spot,' they never used a diminutive for him" (lines 26-30)
(E) "because no photograph or painting or even sketch of him exists" (lines 38-40)

6. That Crazy Horse's "dislike of the oncoming civilization was prophetic" (lines 16-17) likely alludes to his fear of

(A) the railroad
(B) his people's eviction from their homeland
(C) the United States' military
(D) publicity
(E) a legal system he could not fathom

7. Lines 21-22, "because he never rode on a train, slept in a boardinghouse, ate at a table," are BEST interpreted to mean Crazy Horse was

(A) backwards in his ways
(B) unrefined in manners
(C) unspoiled by convenience
(D) reclusive in personality
(E) unexposed to civilization

8. That Crazy Horse "never wore a medal or a top hat or any other thing the white man gave him" (lines 23-24) may be attributed to his

(A) scorn
(B) confusion
(C) humility
(D) suspicion
(E) ingratitude

9. The author likely employs the three similes in lines 34-36—"like the rings of Saturn, the carbon atom, and the underwater reef"—to imply that Crazy Horse was

(A) cryptic
(B) aloof
(C) elemental
(D) immanent
(E) spiritual

10. The author's allusion to Native American images that are featured "on the nickel, the tobacco pouch, [and] the apple crate" (lines 40-41) implies that such representations are

(A) unrepresentative
(B) exaggerated
(C) crude
(D) commemorative
(E) demeaning

11. The author inserts the short declarative sentence in lines 42-44 in order to:

I. Debunk Crazy Horse's legendary status as a brave Lakota warrior.
II. Attempt a physical description that might make up for the lack of any photographs of Crazy Horse.
III. Contrast the simple reality of Crazy Horse with the larger-than-life legend he has become.

(A) I only
(B) III only
(C) I and II
(D) I and III
(E) I, II and III

12. The aspect of Crazy Horse's bravery that the author seems to admire MOST is that he

(A) was audacious in battle
(B) never surrendered to the Army that pursued him
(C) survived a lengthy incarceration
(D) remained stalwart in the most hopeless circumstance
(E) never boasted about his heroic exploits

Questions 13-23. Refer to the following passage.

In the following passage an author reflects on the duties of an early-19th century schoolmaster.

The modern schoolmaster is expected to know a little of every thing, because his pupil is required not to be entirely ignorant of any thing. He must be superficially, if I may so say,
(5) omniscient. He is to know something of pneumatics; of chemistry; of whatever is curious, or proper to excite the attention of the youthful mind; an insight into mechanics is desirable, with a touch of statistics; the quality
(10) of soils, &c. botany, the constitution of his country, *cum multis aliis*[1]....

All these things—these, or the desire of them—he is expected to instill, not by set lessons from professors, which he may charge
(15) in the bill, but at school-intervals, as he walks the streets, or saunters through green fields (those natural instructors), with his pupils. The least part of what is expected from him, is to be done in school-hours. He must insinuate
(20) knowledge at the *mollia tempora fandi*.[2] He must seize every occasion —the season of the year—the time of the day—a passing cloud—a rainbow—a wagon of hay—a regiment of soldiers going by—to inculcate something
(25) useful. He can receive no pleasure from a casual glimpse of Nature, but must catch at it as an object of instruction. He must interpret beauty into the picturesque. He cannot relish a beggar-man, or a gipsy, for thinking of the
(30) suitable improvement. Nothing comes to him, not spoiled by the sophisticating medium of moral uses. The Universe—that Great Book, as it has been called—is to him indeed, to all intents and purposes, a book, out of which he
(35) is doomed to read tedious homilies to distasting schoolboys.—Vacations themselves are none to him, he is only rather worse off than before; for commonly he has some intrusive upper-boy fastened upon him at such
(40) times; some cadet of a great family; some neglected lump of nobility, or gentry; that he must drag after him to the play, to the

Panorama,[3] to Mr. Bartley's Orrery[4], to the Panopticon,[5] or into the country, to a friend's
(45) house, or to his favourite watering-place. Wherever he goes, this uneasy shadow attends him. A boy is at his board, and in his path, and in all his movements. He is boy-rid, sick of perpetual boy.
(50) Boys are capital fellows in their own way, among their mates; but they are unwholesome companions for grown people. The restraint is felt no less on the one side, than on the other.—Even a child, that "plaything for an
(55) hour," tires *always*. The noises of children, playing their own fancies—as I now hearken to them by fits, sporting on the green before my window, while I am engaged in these grave speculations at my neat suburban retreat at
(60) Shacklewell—by distance made more sweet— inexpressibly take from the labour of my task. It is like writing to music....

---

[1]along with many others (Lat.)
[2]at opportune moments for speaking (Lat.)
[3]a series of large paintings designed to make the scene depicted appear continuous
[4]a model of the universe
[5]building with a unique circular structure

13. The author primarily conveys his position on the schoolmaster of his time through which of the following?

(A) personal anecdotes
(B) references to official syllabi
(C) a didactic tone
(D) pervasive irony
(E) local color

14. Of the following, which BEST describes what the author believes a schoolmaster of his day was expected to be?

(A) an intellectual
(B) a generalist
(C) a facilitator
(D) a confidant
(E) a factotum

15. The phrase "superficially...omniscient" (lines 4-5) would MOST accurately be labeled a(n)

(A) euphemism
(B) malapropism
(C) oxymoron
(D) hyperbole
(E) qualification

16. By referring to the green fields as "natural instructors" (line 17), the author likely intends to do which of the following?

    I. Point out the inherent didacticism of nature.
    II. Illustrate his claim that "The least part of what is expected from [a schoolmaster], is to be done in school-hours" (lines 17-19).
    III. Imply the inferiority of traditional education.

    (A) I only
    (B) III only
    (C) I and II
    (D) II and III
    (E) I, II and III

17. The BEST equivalent for the verb "insinuate" (line 19) would be

    (A) impart
    (B) discover
    (C) ingest
    (D) proclaim
    (E) feign

18. In delineating the multiple opportunities that a schoolmaster has to instruct his students (lines 19-25), the author employs

    (A) infinitives
    (B) gerunds
    (C) adjectives
    (D) adverbs
    (E) appositives

19. The author's diction in lines 32-49 reveals that a schoolmaster such as the one described in the passage views his pupils as all of the following EXCEPT

    (A) recalcitrant learners
    (B) disobedient charges
    (C) social albatrosses
    (D) ubiquitous presences
    (E) wealthy scions

20. Which of the following words, in the context in which it appears, expresses a similar thought as does the phrase "fastened upon him" (line 39)?

    (A) "catch" (line 26)
    (B) "board" (line 47)
    (C) "restraint" (line 52)
    (D) "engaged" (line 58)
    (E) "labour" (line 61)

21. The simile that closes the passage is intended to imply which of the following about the playing children?

    (A) that the voices of innocent children soothe the author's distemper
    (B) that their mellifluous rhythms enhance the author's writing
    (C) that the sounds of the playing children are nearly imperceptible
    (D) that the cries of the children provide intermittent distraction
    (E) that the author prefers children to the age-group that he teaches

22. The word/phrase that contributes LEAST to establishing the author's overall attitude towards young people, as expressed by his commentary in the passage, would be

    (A) "doomed" (line 35)
    (B) "boy-rid" (line 48)
    (C) "among their mates" (line 51)
    (D) "tires *always*" (line 55)
    (E) "by distance made more sweet" (line 60)

23. Ultimately, the author perceives the bane of the schoolmaster to be the

    (A) variety of disciplines he is expected to master
    (B) long duration of the school day
    (C) menial compensation he can expect
    (D) limited time for intellectual pursuits
    (E) leech-like companionship of a wealthy schoolboy

Questions 24-36. Refer to the following passage.

A couple leaped from the south tower, hand in hand. They reached for each other and their hands met and they jumped. Jennifer Brickhouse saw them falling, hand in hand.

(5)   Many people jumped. Perhaps hundreds. No one knows. They struck the pavement with such force that there was a pink mist in the air.

The mayor reported the mist.

A kindergarten boy who saw people falling
(10)   in flames told his teacher that the birds were on fire. She ran with him on her shoulders out of the ashes.

Tiffany Keeling saw fireballs falling that she later realized were people. Jennifer Griffin
(15)   saw people falling and wept as she told the story. Niko Winstral saw people free-falling backwards with their hands out, as if they were parachuting. Joe Duncan on his roof on Duane Street looked up and saw people jumping.
(20)   Henry Weintraub saw people "leaping as they flew out." John Carson saw six people fall, "falling over themselves, falling, they were somersaulting." Steve Miller saw people jumping from a thousand feet in the air. Kirk
(25)   Kjeldsen saw people flailing on the way down, people lining up and jumping, "too many people falling." Jane Tedder saw people leaping and the sight haunts her at night. Steve Tamas counted fourteen people jumping and
(30)   then he stopped counting. Stuart deHann saw one woman's dress billowing as she fell, and he saw a shirtless man falling end over end, and he too saw the couple leaping hand in hand.

(35)   Several pedestrians were killed by people falling from the sky. A fireman was killed by a body falling from the sky.

But he reached for her hand and she reached for his hand and they leaped out the
(40)   window holding hands.

The day of the Lord will come as a thief in the night, in which the heavens shall pass away with a great noise, wrote John the Apostle, *and the elements shall melt with a fervent heat, the*
(45)   *earth also and the works that are therein shall be burned up.*

I try to whisper prayers for the sudden dead and the harrowed families of the dead and the screaming souls of the murderers but I keep
(50)   coming back to her hand and his hand nestled in each other with such extraordinary ordinary succinct ancient naked stunning perfect simple ferocious love.

There is no fear in love, wrote John, *but*
(55)   *perfect love casteth out fear, because fear hath torment.*

Their hands reaching and joining are the most powerful prayer I can imagine, the most eloquent, the most graceful. It is everything
(60)   that we are capable of against horror and loss and death. It is what makes me believe that we are not craven fools and charlatans to believe in God, to believe that human beings have greatness and holiness within them like seeds
(65)   that open only under great fires, to believe that some unimaginable essence of who we are persists past the dissolution of what we were, to believe against such evil hourly evidence that love is why we are here.

(70)   *Their passing away was thought an affliction, and their going forth from us utter destruction,* says the Book of Wisdom, *but they are in peace. They shall shine, and they shall dart about as sparks through stubble.*

(75)   No one knows who they were: husband and wife, lovers, dear friends, colleagues, strangers thrown together at the window there at the lip of hell. Maybe they didn't even reach for each other consciously, maybe it was
(80)   instinctive, a reflex, as they both decided at the same time to take two running steps and jump out the shattered window, but they did reach for each other, and they held on tight, and leaped, and fell endlessly into the smoking
(85)   canyon, at two hundred miles an hour, falling so far and so fast that they would have blacked out before they hit the pavement near Liberty Street so hard that there was a pink mist in the air.

(90)   *I trust I shall shortly see thee,* John wrote, *and we shall speak face to face.*

Jennifer Brickhouse saw them holding hands, and Stuart DeHann saw them holding hands, and I hold on to that.

24. Taken as a whole, the passage is BEST described as a(n)

(A) catalog of suffering
(B) discourse on evil
(C) testament to faith
(D) attempt at closure
(E) confirmation of Scripture

25. The predominant stylistic trait of the first half of the passage (lines 1-46) is

    (A) a multiplicity of Biblical allusions
    (B) a matter-of-fact journalistic perspective
    (C) the use of italics to indicate direct citation
    (D) the use of hyperbole to dramatize the height from which people plunged
    (E) the use of numbers to catalog the great human loss

26. The author likely cites the names of specific individuals for all of the following purposes EXCEPT

    (A) to validate the tragic event through eyewitness testimony
    (B) to convey the desperation and despair that the tragedy triggered in trapped individuals
    (C) to indicate the diverse perspectives that people viewing the same event can maintain
    (D) to acknowledge individuals who suffered great personal loss during the tragedy
    (E) to confirm the enduring impact of the tragedy upon the living

27. In the fifth paragraph (lines 13-34), the author endeavors to capture the horrifying spectacle by using

    (A) dramatic adverbs
    (B) participles that convey motion
    (C) onomatopoeic diction
    (D) prepositional phrases
    (E) multiple similes

28. Which of the following BEST explains why the author's focus returns in lines 38-40 to the couple he referenced in the opening sentence of the passage?

    (A) their anonymity
    (B) the uncertainty of their fate
    (C) the lack of a specific witness to their fatal decision
    (D) the intrigue posed by their interlocking hands
    (E) his frustration at their despair of rescue

29. The author cites the first passage from John the Apostle (lines 41-46), found in the Biblical Book of Revelation, in order to do which of the following?

    I. Personify death as a thief.
    II. Compare the tragic event to the apocalypse.
    III. Remind readers of their own fragile mortality.

    (A) II only
    (B) III only
    (C) I and II
    (D) I and III
    (E) I, II and III

30. Lines 47-53 mark a tonal shift in the passage primarily because of the author's

    (A) reverential whisper that marks the solemnity of the moment
    (B) shift to a personal pronoun that conveys the impact of the tragedy on himself
    (C) surprising compassion for both the victims and perpetrators
    (D) string of descriptors that celebrates the selflessness of the couple's act
    (E) more emotional response

31. Lines 57-69 suggest that the author perceives the couple's hands as symbolizing all of the following EXCEPT

    (A) the epitome of prayer
    (B) the uncontrollable paroxysm of fear
    (C) the heroic defiance of evil
    (D) the inherent nobility of human beings
    (E) the enduring nature of the soul

32. The power of lines 57-69 is MOST enhanced by which of the following?

   (A) the declarative repetition of "It is" (lines 59 and 61)
   (B) the alliterative phrase "craven fools and charlatans" (line 62)
   (C) the simile "like seeds that open only under great fires" (lines 64-65)
   (D) the antithesis of "who we are" and "what we were" (lines 66-67)
   (E) the climactic trio of infinitives and noun clauses: "to believe in God….that love is why we are here" (lines 62-69)

33. Which of the following word pairs offers the BEST equivalent for "some unimaginable essence of who we are" and "what we were" (lines 66-67)?

   (A) present and past
   (B) death and life
   (C) spirit and body
   (D) fantasy and reality
   (E) anti-matter and matter

34. The tone of the citation from the Book of Wisdom (lines 70-74) is BEST labeled

   (A) morose and despondent
   (B) confused and disoriented
   (C) bleak and resigned
   (D) reverential and elegiac
   (E) uplifting and reassuring

35. Because of the ambiguity of the couple's relationship and intent, the author reacts to their life-ending decision with

   (A) mild bewilderment
   (B) ineffable sadness
   (C) moral disapproval
   (D) crass indifference
   (E) ironic affirmation

36. The intent of the final sentence of the passage is to

   (A) confirm the identity of the doomed couple
   (B) rue the fatal nature of the couple's decision
   (C) corroborate one eyewitness' account with that of another
   (D) dispel any claims that the couple did not join hands
   (E) link the couple and the author through a mutual 'leap of faith'

Questions 37-44. Refer to the following passage.

    ....I have often been amused at the vain efforts made to define the rights and responsibilities of immortal beings as *men* and *women*. No one has yet found out just *where*
(5) the line of separation between them should be drawn, and for this simple reason, that no one knows just how far below man woman is, whether she be a head shorter in her moral responsibilities, or head and shoulders, or the
(10) full length of his noble stature, below him, i.e., under his feet. Confusion, uncertainty, and great inconsistencies, must exist on this point, so long as woman is regarded in the least degree inferior to man; but place her where her
(15) Maker placed her, on the same high level of human rights with man, side by side with him, and difficulties vanish, the mountains of perplexity flow down at the presence of this grand equalizing principle. Measure her rights
(20) and duties by the unerring standard of *moral being*, not by the false weights and measures of a mere circumstance of her human existence, and then the truth will be self-evident, that whatever it is *morally* right for a man to do, it
(25) is *morally* right for a woman to do. I recognize no rights but *human rights*....It is my solemn conviction, that, until this principle of equality is recognized and embodied in practice, the church can do nothing effectual for the
(30) permanent reformation of the world. Woman was the first transgressor, and the first victim of power. In all heathen nations, she has been the slave of man, and Christian nations have never acknowledged her rights. Nay more, no
(35) Christian denomination or Society has ever acknowledged them on the broad basis of humanity....Now, I believe it is woman's right to have a voice in all the laws and regulations by which she is to be *governed*, whether in
(40) Church or State; and that the present arrangement of society, on these points, are a *violation of human rights*, a *rank usurpation of power*, a violent seizure and confiscation of what is sacredly and inalienably hers—thus
(45) inflicting upon woman outrageous wrongs, working mischief incalculable in the social circle, and in its influence on the world producing only evil, and that continually. *If* Ecclesiastical and Civil governments are
(50) ordained of God, *then* I contend that woman has just as much right to sit in solemn counsel in Conventions, Conferences, Associations, and General Assemblies as man—just as much right to sit upon the throne of England, or in the
(55) Presidential chair of the United States.
    Dost thou ask me, if I would wish to see woman engaged in the contention and strife of sectarian controversy, or in the intrigues of political partisans? I say no! never—never. I
(60) rejoice that she does not stand on the same platform which man now occupies in these respects; but, I mourn, also, that he should thus prostitute his higher nature, and vilely cast away his birthright. I prize the purity of his
(65) character as highly as I do that of hers. As a moral being, *whatever it is morally wrong for her to do, it is morally wrong for him to do.* The fallacious doctrine of male and female virtues has well nigh ruined all that is morally
(70) great and lovely in his character....

37. The author refers to the attempts made to define the respective rights and roles of men and women as "vain efforts" (lines 1-2) because she

    (A) is truly confused where the "line of separation" should be drawn
    (B) believes women will never be afforded proper recognition for their contributions
    (C) believes church and state have conspired together to subjugate women
    (D) believes women to be innately subordinate
    (E) considers this distinction to be a fallacy

38. The author's references in lines 6-11 to physical stature—in particular, the phrase "under his feet"—conveys the author's

    (A) misanthropy
    (B) envy
    (C) ignorance
    (D) sarcasm
    (E) misconception

39. The author's exhortation to "place [woman] where her Maker placed her on the same high level of human rights with man, side by side with him..." (lines 14-16) does which of the following?

    I. Alludes to the account of creation in the Book of Genesis.
    II. Intimates the solemn commitment entered into by men and women in marriage.
    III. Implies that men are responsible for the depreciation of women's status.

    (A) I only
    (B) II only
    (C) I and III
    (D) II and III
    (E) I, II and III

40. The author's claim that "Woman was the first transgressor, and the first victim of power" (lines 30-32) alludes to or foreshadows all of the following EXCEPT

    (A) Eve's eating from the Tree of Knowledge
    (B) Eve's subsequent expulsion from Eden
    (C) the traditional perception of women being inferior to men
    (D) women's lack of a voice in framing the spiritual laws by which they are governed
    (E) women's inability to hold positions of authority in the church

41. The author ratchets up the fervor of her rhetoric primarily by

    (A) a switch to first-person
    (B) forceful and dramatic diction
    (C) a revealing anecdote
    (D) an *ad hominem* diatribe
    (E) the use of italics

42. Which of the following does NOT contribute to the central spiritual-secular juxtaposition established by the author?

    (A) "In all heathen nations, she has been the slave of man, and Christian nations have never acknowledged her rights" (lines 32-34).
    (B) "Now, I believe it is woman's right to have a voice in all the laws and regulations by which she is to be *governed*, whether in Church or State" (lines 37-40).
    (C) "...a violent seizure and confiscation of what is sacredly and inalienably hers" (lines 43-44).
    (D) "*If* Ecclesiastical and Civil governments are ordained of God, *then* I contend that woman has just as much right to sit in solemn counsel in Conventions, Conferences, Associations, and General Assemblies as man..." (lines 48-53)
    (E) "just as much right to sit upon the throne of England, or in the Presidential chair of the United States" (lines 53-55)

43. The passage's culminating irony involves the author's

    (A) claim that women have no interest in positions of power
    (B) joy at the absence of women in the political arena
    (C) admiration for the purity of man's character
    (D) belief that in devaluing women man has sullied himself
    (E) reversal of an earlier avowal made in lines 23-25

44. Words and phrases such as "then the truth will be self-evident" (line 23) and "inalienably" (line 44) are intended to call to mind

    (A) the New Testament
    (B) the Declaration of Independence
    (C) the Book of Revelation
    (D) Magna Carta
    (E) Mary Wollstonecraft's *A Vindication of the Rights of Women*

Questions 45-52. Refer to the following passage.

In the following passage a Canadian artilleryman reflects upon the damaging consequences of modern warfare.

....Once I could say you cannot be disgusted with the war, because it is too big for disgust, that disgust is too shallow an emotion for something involving millions of people.
(5) But I am disgusted now, and I know what I am saying. Once I used to get quite a thrill out of seeing a city destroyed and left an ash heap from end to end. It gave me a vicarious sense of power. I felt the romantic and histrionic
(10) emotion produced by seeing "retribution" done; and an aesthetic emotion produced by beholding ruins; and the childish emotion that comes from destroying man-made things. But it is not that way any more. All I experience is
(15) revulsion every time a fresh city is taken on. I am no longer capable of thinking that the systematic destruction of a city is a wonderful or even a difficult thing, though some seem to think it even a heroic thing. Well, how is it
(20) done? Dozens upon dozens of gun crews stationed some two or three miles away from the city simply place shell after shell into hundreds of guns and fire away for a few hours—the simplest and most elementary
(25) physical and mental work—and then presently the firing stops, the city has been demolished, has become an ash heap, and great praise is bestowed on the army for the capture of a new city.
(30) I am not suggesting that cities shouldn't be captured in this way; actually it saves lives. But it fills me with disgust because it is all so abysmally foolish, so lunatic. It has not the dramatic elements of mere barbarism about it;
(35) it is straight scientific debauchery. A destroyed city is a terrible sight. How can anyone record it?—the million smashed things, the absolutely innumerable tiny tragedies, the crushed life-works, the jagged homes, army tanks parked in
(40) living rooms—who could tell of these things I don't know; they are too numerous to mention, too awful in their meanings. Perhaps everyone should be required to spend a couple of hours examining a single smashed home, looking at
(45) the fragmentation of every little thing, especially the tiniest things from kitchen to attic, if he could find an attic; be required, in fact, to list the ruined contents of just one

home; something would be served, a little
(50) sobriety perhaps honored.
It is disgusting (that it should be necessary, is what galls me to the bones) that a towering cathedral, built by ages of care and effort, a sweet labor of centuries, should be shot down
(55) by laughing artillerymen, because somebody with a machine gun is hiding in a belfry tower. When I see such a building, damaged perhaps beyond repair after one of these "operations," I know only disgust. The matter of sides in this
(60) war temporarily becomes irrelevant, especially if someone at my close elbow says, like a conquering hero: "Well, we sure did a job on the old church, eh?"
A job has been done on Europe, on the
(65) world, and the resulting trauma will be generations long in its effects. It is not just the shock of widespread destruction, of whole cities destroyed, nor the shock which the defeated and the homeless must have suffered,
(70) that I am thinking of: it is even more the conqueror's trauma, the habit of violence, the explosion of values, the distortion of relations, the ascending significance of the purely material, the sense of power, and the pride of
(75) strength. These things will afflict the victors as profoundly and for quite as long a time as the other things will afflict the victims; and of the two I am not sure that a crass superiority complex is the more desirable. Perhaps I
(80) underestimate our ability to return to normal again.

45. Upon reflection, the author admits that his initial reaction to the destruction of cities by long-range artillery bombardment was all of the following EXCEPT

(A) marked by a perverse thrill
(B) oblivious to the human tragedy that accompanies such devastation
(C) justified by the praise and recognition heaped upon the gunners
(D) fueled by a patriotic desire for revenge
(E) characterized by an immature delight at blowing things up

46. The author uses the short declarative fragment "But it is not that way any more" (lines 13-14) to convey which of the following?

    (A) his longing for the thrill of combat
    (B) the cessation of wartime hostilities
    (C) his change in perspective on warfare
    (D) the cities that are now ash heaps
    (E) the guilt he no longer feels for his actions

47. In the contrast presented in lines 33-35, "It has not the dramatic elements of mere barbarism about it; it is straight scientific debauchery," the author argues that enhancements of military technology have done which of the following?

    I. Significantly reduced battlefield casualties by increasing artillerymen's accuracy.
    II. Totally expunged even the most primitive sense of human conflict through their remote means of waging war.
    III. Dramatically exacerbated the losses suffered by besieged peoples.

    (A) I only
    (B) III only
    (C) I and II
    (D) II and III
    (E) I, II and III

48. The author's remark in lines 42-49, that "Perhaps everyone should be required to spend a couple of hours examining a single smashed home…be required, in fact, to list the ruined contents of just one home…," is BEST labeled

    (A) cynical
    (B) imperious
    (C) unrealistic
    (D) morbid
    (E) didactic

49. All of the following details about the destruction of the cathedral irritate the author mightily EXCEPT

    (A) the trivial military rationale for targeting it
    (B) the disregard shown for its stature and workmanship
    (C) the insensitivity and braggadocio of his fellow soldiers
    (D) the disrespect for its sanctity as a house of worship
    (E) the fact that a building that took so long to build can be obliterated so quickly

50. The author likely places the word "operations" (line 58) in quotation marks to convey the

    (A) animus he feels for such sordid work
    (B) surreptitiousness of the military campaign
    (C) surgical precision of the attack
    (D) wartime necessity to communicate in code
    (E) bureaucratic nature of the military

51. The primary difference between the concluding paragraph and the three paragraphs that precede it involves its

    (A) more detailed documentation of collateral damage
    (B) first-person perspective
    (C) shift of focus from victim to victor
    (D) use of hyperbole to dramatize the destruction
    (E) misanthropic tone

52. Upon completion of the passage, the MOST disturbing aspect of the response offered by the author to the rhetorical question posed in lines 19-20 is the

    (A) facility of the author's explanation
    (B) staggering number of gun crews
    (C) long duration of the bombardment
    (D) meticulous description of the procedure
    (E) detachment of the soldiers to the carnage

Section II

Question One

(Suggested time–40 minutes. This question counts as one-third of the total essay section score.)

In the following essay by Ted Kooser, entitled "Hands," an author reflects upon a physical trait passed on to him by his father. Read the selection carefully. Then, in a well-organized essay, discuss how the author uses language to convey the impact of his father's life and values upon his own. In framing your response, you may wish to consider such things as choice of detail, figurative language, and tone.

More and more frequently since I entered my fifties I have begun to see my father's hands out at the ends of my arms. Just now, the left and more awkward one lies curled in my lap while the right one massages the beard on my chin. On the ring finger of the left is the silver wedding band that my wife gave me, not my father's gold ring with its yellow sapphire. But I am not deceived; this wearing of my

(5) ring on his ring finger is a part of my father's respectful accommodation of me and of my life and marriage. Mine have succeeded his, which is, as he would have said, as it should be.

I recognize his hands despite the ring. They are exactly as I remember them from his middle age—wrinkled, of course, with a slight sheen to the tiny tilework of the skin; with knotted, branching veins; and with thin dark hair that sets out from beneath the shirtcuffs as to cover the hand but that within

(10) an inch thins and disappears as if there were a kind of glacial timberline there. There is, as we know, a field of coldness just beyond the reaching tips of our fingers, and this hair has been discouraged and has fallen back.

As a young man my father had been a drapery salesman in a department store and his hands were ever after at their best when smoothing fabric for display—the left one holding a piece of cloth unrolled

(15) from a bolt while the right lovingly eased and teased the wrinkles from it, his fingers spread and their tips lightly touching the cloth as if under them was something grand and alive like the flank of a horse.

Those hands had never done hard physical work, but they are not plump, or soft, or damp and cool. Nor are their nails too carefully clipped or too carefully buffed and polished. They are firm, solid, masculine hands, and other men feel good about shaking them. They have a kind of brotherly warmth

(20) and when they pinch the selvage[1] of the drapery fabric and work it just a little between thumb and finger they do it with power and confidence. There are pairs of hands like these—some brown, some black, some white—in every bazaar in the world—hands easing and smoothing, hands flying like doves through the dappled light under time-riddled canvas.

I would like to be held by these hands, held by them as they were when I was a child and I seemed to

(25) fall within them wherever I might turn. I would like to feel them warm and broad against my back and I would like to be pressed to the breast of this man with his faint perfume of aftershave, with the tiny brown moles on his neck, with the knot of his necktie slightly darkened by perspiration. Now he has taken his glasses off and set them on the mantel and there are small red ovals on the side of his nose. I reach to touch them and find them wet, as if I were touching something deep inside him. Now I hear him

(30) singing, softly singing, the words buzzing deep in his chest.

But these old hands of his are past all that. They lie side by side in my lap, their palms turned up as if to catch this fleeting moment as it falls away. But as I peer down into them they begin to move on their own, to turn and shift. I watch the left hand slowly rise to place its palm against my heart, and watch the right rise swiftly to enfold the other.

---

[1]the edge of a fabric

<u>Question Two</u>

(Suggested time—40 minutes. This question counts as one-third of the total essay section score.)

"What lies behind you and what lies in front of you pales in comparison to what lies inside of you."

The following adage—popularly attributed to Ralph Waldo Emerson (though its origins are somewhat debatable)—implies that what has happened in the past or may happen in the future is less significant than an individual's character, the courage, hope and perseverance he/she can draw upon in response to these challenges.

Take a moment to reflect on this statement. Then, in a well-organized essay, explore the validity of this assertion using examples drawn from your reading, studies, experience and/or observations to develop your argument.

Question Three

Reading Time: 15 minutes
Suggested Writing Time: 40 minutes

(Suggested time—40 minutes. This question counts as one-third of the total essay section score.)

Directions:

The following prompt is based on the accompanying six sources.

This question requires you to integrate a variety of sources into a coherent, well-written essay. *Refer to the sources to support your position; avoid paraphrase or summary. Your argument should be central; the sources should support this argument.*

Remember to attribute both direct and indirect citations.

Introduction:

Within the past year concerns about childhood obesity have come into prominence, with First Lady Michelle Obama establishing a nationwide campaign called "Let's Move" that encourages families and schools to make healthier choices when it comes to nutrition and exercise. Studies have confirmed that Americans in general weigh more than their counterparts from previous generations, and some claim that the number of obese children has reached epidemic proportions.

As to who is to blame for this unprecedented weight gain among young people, fingers have been alternately pointed at parents, schools, corporations, even children themselves since each has seemingly contributed in some way to this problem. However, is one party more or less guilty than another? Is the blame for this problem more institutional than personal?

Assignment:

Read the following sources (including any introductory information) carefully. **Then, in an essay that synthesizes at least three of the sources for support, take a position that defends, challenges or qualifies the claim that the problem of adolescent obesity is due more to environment than to a lack of personal initiative or motivation.**

Document A

Crute, Sheree. "Growing Pains." *NEA Today* (Mar 2005): 22-31.

.... Over the years, schools have been hard-pressed to help. Cash-strapped, many have cut vending deals with soda companies and brought high-fat, high-revenue fare into cafeterias to balance shaky budgets. Even where schools have tried to buck the trend, it's a financial struggle. It still costs a school district more than twice as much to provide a high-fiber, low-fat, veggie burger than it does to provide a higher-fat, fiber-free hamburger, according to a report by the Physicians Committee for Responsible Medicine, a Washington-based group that promotes healthy eating. That's because the federal government subsidizes hamburger and other meats but not alternatives like soy, or in the case of milk, calcium-rich, non-dairy beverages.

It hasn't helped that kids are getting less physical activity—at home and at school. Video games have replaced the playground as kids' favorite pastime, and more than 50 percent of the nation's schools have eliminated physical education classes altogether. Once a regular part of nearly every school day, P.E. programs have become rare to nonexistent in many parts or the country, even though researchers have found that just one additional hour of P.E. per week is significant in addressing obesity for 5- and 6-year-olds, especially girls. Bruce Hanson, a physical education teacher at Fairview Elementary School in Westminster, Colorado, says he's seeing the results of inactivity every day: many of his kids can't run a minute around the track without stopping. "They could do it a decade ago but today's kids can't handle it," he says. "They're struggling."

Compounding matters: the so-called No Child Left Behind law, which has put pressure on schools to spend less time on P.E. and more time preparing students for make-or-break standardized tests. Educators say the shift is ironic given the link between fitness and academic success....

Document B

© Cartoonstock.com

<u>Document C</u>

Schlosser, Eric. *Fast Food Nation: The Dark Side of the All-American Meal*. New York: Harper Perennial, 2004: 47.

Although the fast food chains annually spend about $3 billion on television advertising, their marketing efforts directed at children extend far beyond such conventional ads. The McDonald's Corporation now operates more than eight thousand playgrounds at its restaurants in the United States. Burger King has more than two thousand. A manufacturer of "playlands" explains why fast food operators build these largely plastic structures: "Playlands bring in children, who bring in parents, who bring in money." As American cities and towns spend less money on children's recreation, fast food restaurants have become gathering places for families with young children. Every month about 90 percent of American children between the ages of three and nine visit a McDonald's. The seesaws, slides, and pits full of plastic balls have proven to be an effective lure. "But when it gets down to brass tacks," a *Brandweek* article on fast food notes, "the key to attracting kids is toys, toys, toys."

The fast food industry has forged promotional links with the nation's leading toy manufacturers, giving away simple toys with children's meals and selling more elaborate ones at a discount. The major toy crazes of recent years—including Pokemon cards, Cabbage Patch kids, and Tamogotchis—have been abetted by fast food promotions. A successful promotion easily doubles or triples the weekly sales volume of children's meals....

Document D

Schwager, Tina. "Defeating Childhood Obesity." *American Fitness* 28.6 (Nov-Dec 2010): 18-20.

There was a time when we, as kids, could ask our moms, "Can we go outside and play?" And they would respond, "OK, just be back by dinner time." Then we'd hop on our bikes and off we'd go. And we would play outside... all day long. In those days, we didn't have computers, or video games, or cell phones. Every kid knew how to throw and kick a ball, play a game of tag that could last for hours, and find things to keep busy until it was time to head home.

Things are different now. Today, kids can "play" with friends in a virtual world, and going outside simply to goof around is a rarity. An overabundance of conveniences makes most everything we do easier, faster and more connected with the mere push of a button. But those conveniences are a part of what is helping to destroy our kids.

To be blunt, a large percentage of kids in America are fat and unhealthy. In the past 20 years, "the prevalence of obesity among children ages 6 to 11 years has more than doubled," and more than tripled in adolescents ages 12 to 19. Organizations such as the Centers for Disease Control and Prevention (CDC) and the American Obesity Association (AOA) have amassed the numbers on this disturbing epidemic: 30.3% of kids ages 6 to 11 are overweight, 15.3% are classified as obese, and for adolescents, 30.4% are estimated to be overweight and 15.5% obese. The tendency toward overweight is slightly greater in boys than girls (32.7% to 27.8%) and is an even bigger problem among lower-income and ethnic minority families where African-American, Hispanic and Native-American kids have a particularly high obesity prevalence"....

Call it entertainment, or a learning tool...it doesn't matter what you call it. Media tools such as computers, cell phones, video games, high-tech TVs and hand-held media devices (like music and movie players) are helping make young people fat. In 2007, the national Youth Risk Behavior Survey done by the Department of Health and Human Services, Centers for Disease Control and Prevention, found that 25% of high school kids played "...video or computer games or used a computer for something that was not school work for 3 or more hours per day on an average school day. And as for TV, 35% watched 3 or more hours a day."

Sitting in front of a screen and watching others do things that grown-ups used to get out and actually do; playing with. virtual friends or against foes instead of running around outside; texting instead of riding bikes together—all these tools of convenience lead to a reduction in physical activity and lots of mindless snacking....

Reprinted by permission of Schwager, T., DEFEATING CHILDHOOD OBESITY Nov-Dec 2010 *American Fitness*.

Document E

Ruskin, Gary and Juliet Schor. "Junk Food Nation." *Nation* 281.6 (Aug 21, 2005): 15-17.

In recent months the major food companies have been trying hard to convince Americans that they feel the pain of our expanding waistlines, especially when it comes to kids. Kraft announced it would no longer market Oreos to younger children, McDonald's promoted itself as a salad producer and Coca-Cola said it won't advertise to kids under 12. But behind the scenes it's hardball as usual, with the junk food giants pushing the Bush Administration to defend their interests. The recent conflict over what America eats, and the way the government promotes food, is a disturbing example of how in Bush's America corporate interests trump public health, public opinion and plain old common sense….

Conflict about junk food has intensified since late 2001, when a Surgeon General's report called obesity an "epidemic." Since that time, the White House has repeatedly weighed in on the side of Big Food. It worked hard to weaken the World Health Organization's global anti-obesity strategy and went so far as to question the scientific basis for "the linking of fruit and vegetable consumption to decreased risk of obesity and diabetes." Former Health and Human Services Secretary Tommy Thompson—then our nation's top public-health officer—even told members of the Grocery Manufacturers Association to "'go on the offensive' against critics blaming the food industry for obesity," according to a November 12, 2002, GMA news release.

Last year, during the reauthorization of the children's nutrition programs, Republican Senator Peter Fitzgerald of Illinois attempted to insulate the government's nutrition guidelines from the intense industry pressure that has warped the process to date. He proposed a modest amendment to move the guidelines from the USDA to the comparatively more independent Institute of Medicine. The food industry, alarmed about the switch, secured a number of meetings at the White House to get it to exert pressure on Fitzgerald. One irony of this fight was that the key industry lobbying came from the American Dietetic Association, described by one Congressional staffer as a "front for the food groups." Fitzgerald held firm but didn't succeed in enacting his amendment before he left Congress last year.

By that time the industry's lobbying effort had borne fruit, or perhaps more accurately, unhealthy alternatives to fruit. The new federal guidelines no longer contain a recommendation for sugar intake, although they do tell people to eat foods with few added sugars. The redesigned icon for the guidelines, created by a company that does extensive work for the junk food industry, shows no food, only a person climbing stairs….

For their money, the industry has been able to buy into a strategy on obesity and food marketing that mirrors the approach taken by Big Tobacco. That's hardly a surprise, given that some of the same companies and personnel are involved: Junk food giants Kraft and Nabisco are both majority-owned by tobacco producer Philip Morris, now renamed Altria. Similarity number one is the denial that the problem (obesity) is caused by the product (junk food). Instead, lack of exercise is fingered as the culprit, which is why McDonald's, Pepsi, Coke and others have been handing out pedometers, funding fitness centers and prodding kids to move around….This strategy has been evident in the halls of Congress as well. During child nutrition reauthorization hearings, the man some have called the Senator from Coca-Cola, Georgia's Zell Miller, parroted industry talking points when he claimed that children are "obese not because of what they eat at lunchrooms in schools but because, frankly, they sit around on their duffs watching Eminem on MTV and playing video games." And that, of course, is the fault not of food marketers but of parents….

<u>Document F</u>

Dillon, Thale. "Too Much Junk Food and TV?: 'Obesity Epidemic' On Upward Trajectory." *Montana Business Quarterly* 47.4 (Winter 2009) 16-20.

....When caloric intake exceeds caloric expenditure, the result is weight gain. Yet the message conveyed to today's children is that more is better: super-sized servings of French fries and soda, gigantic buckets of movie popcorn (with free refills) and king-sized candy bars. Today's diet features serving sizes that are often twice as big as they were 20 years ago…and regrettably short on fruits, vegetables, and whole grains. Children may be taught good nutrition in the classroom, but when they find themselves surrounded by food options of poor nutritional quality through vending machines and school stores, the message is diluted. The proximity of fast-food restaurants, either near home or school, further compounds the issue as they become the go-to source for a quick meal on the way home. Unfortunately, our activity levels have not kept up with the changes in our diets. Rather than become more active to compensate for our ballooning caloric intake, we have become more sedentary, and our children learn from our example. They spend less time engaged in active pursuits and more time playing video games, surfing the Internet, or watching TV. The ultimate irony is that you can now play a video game to help you exercise. Soon, we'll have fresh air available by bottle….

Published courtesy of The University of Montana Bureau of Business and Economic Research.

Sample Examination VI

Questions 1-12. Refer to the following passage.

Academics,[1] in my experience, are not inclined to be generous to essayists. They are suspicious about humanism, nervous about too much style, and wary of public celebrations of
(5) the personal. They assume defensive postures and query: do essayists believe in uniqueness? Once, at a meeting to plan a graduate conference in literary studies, the kind of meeting where inclusivity is the aim, and the
(10) group spends three hours and forty minutes worrying about getting enough wheelchairs, ramps, crutches, hearing aids, tofu, baby-sitters, etc., to make "everyone feel welcome" but especially those people who never really
(15) are; once I suggested we open the calls for papers to include creative writing on the conference's theme, and people looked at me as if I had requested a naked boy be hired to roller skate in and serve me cotton candy.
(20) Essayists are thought to be indulgent.
Which means lenient, messy, loose.
This essayist? Undisciplined? Able to set a perfect table but unable to arrange three consecutive thoughts? One might tackle these
(25) accusations in a methodical way, or only pretend to.
The essay seems disorganized, I think, because it has a stake in pretending not to know where it is going. Putting on its hat,
(30) heading for the door, it seems to follow the random movement of the mind itself. This looks like laziness, but it smells like epistemology.[2] Because essays offer a way of thinking—a dramatization of process as
(35) opposed to a curtain unfurled on the final product, all scrubbed and clean as the newborn on TV. Unlike articles, they give form to the streakiest mental processes. I like to call the essayist a sketch artist for thought, since
(40) artistry is an important part of the package. Yes, yeah, right, my thoughts don't really bump along this way, but they do bump

somehow, and it's more honest—more pedagogically useful, more truthful—to arrange
(45) them in a loose, disconnected, provisional way than to deliver only the conclusions.
Another thing that makes the essay seem like a mess is its refusal to decide the things it feels it cannot decide. Like a hotel for
(50) disagreements, like a pillow on which discrepancy can rest her rumpled head. The article likes contradictions too but it starts with them and tries to resolve them; or it starts with something that doesn't look like a
(55) contradiction at all, and methodically shows it to be one. Either way contradictions are cunningly displayed in such a way that the contradiction seems to be located outside—outside in a text, outside in the
(60) culture, most importantly, outside of the author.
Often an essay ends without any contradiction solved. Often an essay doesn't even push toward resolution. It thinks it is interesting without a big bang.

---

[1] members of institutions of higher learning
[2] The branch of philosophy that studies the nature of knowledge, its presuppositions and foundations, and its extent and validity.

1. The author's description of the academics in the first paragraph generally portrays them as

   (A) parochial
   (B) distinguished
   (C) egotistical
   (D) liberal
   (E) inquisitive

2. The author develops the academics' skepticism towards essayists using all of the following EXCEPT

   (A) descriptive adjectives
   (B) ironical understatement
   (C) physical and intellectual reactions
   (D) personal anecdote
   (E) analogy

Reprinted by permission of The Wendy Weil Agency, Inc. First published by Simon & Schuster © 2007 by Sara Levine.

212

3. The author likely repeats the word "Once" (lines 7 and 15) in order to do which of the following?

   I. Suggest the rarity of such inclusive accommodations.
   II. Imply that she will never again make such an unpopular suggestion.
   III. Humorously model her claim that the essay follows the random movement of the mind.

   (A) II only
   (B) III only
   (C) I and II
   (D) II and III
   (E) I, II and III

4. The author chooses the simile in lines 18-19 primarily to underscore the

   (A) inherent absurdity of her proposal
   (B) bizarre novelty of her idea
   (C) sheer impropriety of her suggestion
   (D) uncharacteristic levity of the academics
   (E) overt scorn which her proposal provoked

5. Which of the following BEST describes the function of line 20, "Essayists are thought to be indulgent?"

   (A) It contains the thesis of the selection.
   (B) It provides a strong reason why essayists should be included in the graduate conference.
   (C) It provides the first clue as to why academics are condescending towards essayists.
   (D) It sets up the more euphemistic adjective "disorganized" in line 27.
   (E) It reflects the author's own dislike of the essay form.

6. The author's response to the "accusations" levied at the unnamed essayist in lines 22-24 does which of the following?

   I. Whimsically disassociates her from the more rigid methodology of her fellow academics.
   II. Figuratively explains the seemingly random organization of the essayist's argument.
   III. Passionately attacks the academics' obduracy in refusing to acknowledge the essay's artistry.

   (A) II only
   (B) III only
   (C) I and II
   (D) II and III
   (E) I, II and III

7. In regard to the essay's form, lines 31-33, "This looks like laziness, but it smells like epistemology," do which of the following?

   (A) defend it
   (B) criticize it
   (C) question it
   (D) qualify it
   (E) dismiss it

8. Words such as "seems" (lines 27 and 30), "pretending" (line 28), and "looks like" (line 32) imply that the essay form is deliberately

   (A) pragmatic
   (B) haphazard
   (C) convoluted
   (D) histrionic
   (E) insubstantial

9. The phrase, "a curtain unfurled on the final product…" (lines 35-36), is closest in meaning to which of the following?

   (A) "…open the calls for papers to include creative writing on the conference's theme" (lines 15-17)
   (B) "Able to set a perfect table but unable to arrange three consecutive thoughts?" (lines 22-24)
   (C) "… artistry is an important part of the package" (line 40)
   (D) "…to deliver only the conclusions" (line 46)
   (E) "…displayed in such a way that the contradiction seems to be located outside…" (lines 57-59)

10. Which BEST approximates the role of the trio of affirmatives "Yes, yeah, right" in line 41?

    (A) They constitute the author's sardonic dismissal of the academics' opinion.
    (B) They represent an admission that she herself doesn't always think in the spontaneous manner that essayists do.
    (C) They express her ardent vocal support for the essayists' efforts.
    (D) They reflect a rapidly diminishing conviction in the rightness of her position.
    (E) They reveal an unexpected reversal of an earlier position.

11. The author figuratively depicts the internal contradictions that often characterize the essay through

    (A) the personification of "Putting on its hat, heading toward the door…" (lines 29-30)
    (B) the simile of the "newborn on TV" (lines 36-37)
    (C) the similes of the "hotel" and "pillow" (lines 49-51)
    (D) the anaphora of the three "outside" phrases (lines 59-60)
    (E) the onomatopoeia and alliteration of "big bang" (line 64)

12. As opposed to the article, the author credits the essay with being all of the following EXCEPT

    (A) more instructive
    (B) more candid
    (C) more conclusive
    (D) more spontaneous
    (E) more free-form

Questions 13-21. Refer to the following passage.

The Life of Johnson[1] is assuredly a great, a very great work. Homer is not more decidedly the first of heroic poets, Shakespeare is not more decidedly the first of dramatists,
(5) Demosthenes is not more decidedly the first of orators, than Boswell is the first of biographers. He has no second. He has distanced all his competitors so decidedly that it is not worth while to place them. Eclipse is
(10) first, and the rest nowhere.
We are not sure that there is in the whole history of the human intellect so strange a phenomenon as this book. Many of the greatest men that ever lived have written biography.
(15) Boswell…was, if we are to give any credit to his own account or to the united testimony of all who knew him, a man of the meanest and feeblest intellect. Johnson described him as a fellow who had missed his only chance at
(20) immortality by not having been alive when the Dunciad[2] was written. Beauclerk used his name as a proverbial expression for a bore. He was the laughing-stock of the whole of that brilliant society which has owed to him the
(25) greater part of his fame. He was always laying himself at the feet of some eminent man, and begging to be spit upon and trampled upon. He was always earning some ridiculous nickname, and then "binding it as a crown unto him,"[3] not
(30) merely in metaphor, but literally. He exhibited himself, at the Shakespeare Jubilee, with a placard round his hat bearing the inscription of Corsica Boswell[4]….Servile and impertinent, shallow and pedantic, a bigot and a sot, bloated
(35) with family pride, and eternally blustering about the dignity of a born gentleman, yet stooping to be a tale-bearer, an eavesdropper, a common butt in the taverns of London, so curious to know everybody who was talked
(40) about, that, Tory and high Churchman that he was, he maneuvered, we have been told, for an introduction to Tom Paine, so vain of the most childish distinctions, that when he had been to court, he drove to the office where his book

(45) was printing without changing his clothes, and summoned all the printer's devils to admire his new ruffles and sword; such was this man and such was he content and proud to be. Everything which another man would have
(50) hidden, everything the publication of which would have made another man hang himself, was matter of gay and clamorous exultation to his weak and diseased mind. What silly things he said, what bitter retorts he provoked, how at
(55) one place he was troubled with evil presentiments which came to nothing, how at another place on waking from a drunken doze, he read the prayerbook and took a hair of the dog that had bitten him,[5] how he went to see
(60) men hanged and came away maudlin, how he added five hundred pounds to the fortune of one of his babies because she was not scared at Johnson's ugly face, how he was frightened out of his wits at sea, and how the sailors quieted
(65) him as they would have quieted a child, how tipsy he was at Lady Cork's one evening and how much his merriment annoyed the ladies, how impertinent he was to the Duchess of Argyle and with what stately contempt she put
(70) down his impertinence, how Colonel Macleod sneered to his face at his impudent obtrusiveness, how his father and the very wife of his bosom laughed and fretted at his fooleries, all these things he proclaimed to all
(75) the world, as if they had been subjects for pride and ostentatious rejoicing…
Of the talents which ordinarily raise men to eminence as writers, Boswell had absolutely none. There is not in all his books a single
(80) remark of his own on literature, politics, religion, or society, which is not either commonplace or absurd…. Logic, eloquence, wit, taste, all those things which are generally considered as making a book valuable, were
(85) utterly wanting to him. He had, indeed, a quick observation and a retentive memory. These qualities, if he had been a man of sense and virtue, would scarcely of themselves have sufficed to make him conspicuous; but,
(90) because he was a dunce, a parasite, and a coxcomb, they have made him immortal….

---

[1] James Boswell's biography of Samuel Johnson
[2] Early 18th c. work by Alexander Pope which mock-celebrates the goddess of Dullness to satirize the decline of intellectual discourse.
[3] Ostensibly, an allusion to the Book of Job in which Job asserts that if he was guilty of any wrongdoing, he would display his guilt publicly.
[4] Boswell sympathized with the Corsican resistance to the occupying French and prominently displayed his support for it.

---

[5] Slang for taking a drink to abate a hangover

13. The first paragraph of the selection does which of the following?

    I. Acknowledges Boswell's stature in the literary canon.
    II. Metaphorically affirms Boswell's dominance in the field of biography.
    III. Sets up the incongruity of Boswell's intellectual limitations.

    (A) I only
    (B) III only
    (C) I and II
    (D) II and III
    (E) I, II and III

14. Lines 25-33—"He was always....Corsica Boswell"—in conjunction with the second and third footnotes—provide information that reveals which of the following aspects of Boswell?

    (A) his consciousness of how the gentry derided him
    (B) his emotional hurt at being deemed a laughing-stock
    (C) his belief that he was an undeserving victim of society's mockery
    (D) his ludicrous flaunting of his political alliances
    (E) his foolish sense of self-importance

15. All of the following are accurate observations about the sentence that begins in line 33 and concludes in line 48 EXCEPT

    (A) It uses inversion to dramatic effect.
    (B) It is marked by parallel pairings of nouns and descriptive adjectives.
    (C) It uses anecdotes to depict the antithetical nature of Boswell—part sycophant, part peacock.
    (D) It uses alliterative participles to capture Boswell's supercilious bombast.
    (E) It uses metonymies to detail Boswell's various roles.

16. Lines 49-53, "Everything which another man would have hidden...to his weak and diseased mind," are MOST notable for their use of

    (A) understatement
    (B) anaphora
    (C) simile
    (D) allusion
    (E) satire

17. The reactions of Lady Cork, the Duchess of Argyle and other members of the social elite in lines 65-72 suggest that their attitude toward Boswell was one of

    (A) warm acceptance
    (B) grudging admiration
    (C) bored indifference
    (D) bristling indulgence
    (E) total intolerance

18. The words "dunce" (line 90) and "coxcomb" (line 91) are MOST closely related to which of the following?

    (A) Boswell's ridiculous nicknames
    (B) Boswell's infatuation with Thomas Paine
    (C) Boswell's teary response to the hanging
    (D) Boswell's childish terror at sea
    (E) Boswell's impulsive prodigality towards his infant daughter

19. The concluding paragraph implies that the author would consider Boswell's literary output to be all of the following EXCEPT

    (A) vacuous
    (B) banal
    (C) forgettable
    (D) clever
    (E) prolific

20. Which of the following aspects of Boswell does the author enhance by hyperbole?

    (A) his position as an object of derision (lines 18-25)
    (B) his fawning servility (lines 25-27)
    (C) his unquenchable curiosity (lines 37-42)
    (D) his shameless vanity (lines 42-47)
    (E) his complete lack of traditional literary proficiencies (lines 77-82)

21. Of the following, which BEST articulates the author's overall feelings about Boswell?

    (A) respect for his intellect but disdain for his competence as a writer
    (B) scorn for his character but respect for his singular biographical accomplishment
    (C) chagrin for his social gaffes but bemusement at his impertinence
    (D) delight in his wit but embarrassment at his vanity
    (E) intolerance for his egocentricity but empathy for his insecurity

Questions 22-29. Refer to the following passage.

In the following passage an English novelist/essayist offers a critique of Bottom, the weaver in Shakespeare's A Midsummer Night's Dream, *who, together with other lower-class tradesmen, puts on a play to honor the marriage of Theseus and Hippolyta.*

....Against the background of the whole play, which is only so much gossamer and moonlight, the honest weaver appears anything but romantic, a piece of humorous, bewildered

(5) flesh, gross, earthy. He is a trades-unionist among butterflies, a rate-payer in Elfland. Seen thus, he is droll precisely because he is a most prosaic soul called to a most romantic destiny. But if we view him first among his own

(10) associates, we shall see that he is the only one of them who was fit to be "translated".[1] Puck, who was responsible for the transformation, described him as "the shallowest thickskin of that barren sort," the biggest fool in a company

(15) of fools; but Puck was no judge of his character. Bottom, though he may be the biggest fool (and a big fool is no common person), is really the least shallow and thickskinned of his group, in which he shows

(20) up as the romantic, the poetical, the imaginative man, who naturally takes command. We admit that he is conceited, but he is in some measure, an artist, and artists are notoriously conceited. The company of such

(25) tailoring and bellows-mending souls would make any man of spirit conceited. Old Quince, who obviously owes his promotion to seniority and nothing else, is nominally in charge of the revels...but it is clear that Bottom, and Bottom

(30) alone, is the leader. Quince ("Good Peter Quince," as Bottom, with easy contempt and patronage, calls him) is nothing but a tool in the hands of the masterful weaver, who directs the whole proceedings, the calling of the roll of

(35) players, the description of the piece, the casting of the parts, and so forth, step by step....

When the players are first met together and the parts are being given out, it is not just Bottom's conceit that makes him want to play

(40) every part himself. Of all those present, he is the only one who shows any passion for the drama itself, the art of acting, the enthralling business of moving and thrilling an audience. The others are only concerned with getting

(45) through their several tasks in the easiest and safest manner, with one eye on the hangman and the other on the exchequer. But the creative artist is stirring in the soul of Bottom; his imagination is catching fire; so that no

(50) sooner is a part mentioned than he can see himself playing it, and playing it in such a manner as to lift the audience out of their seats. He is set down for the principal part, that of the lover, but no sooner has he accepted it, seeing

(55) himself condoling and moving storms ("That will ask some tears in the true performing of it: if I do it, let the audience look to their eyes; I will move storms, I will condole in some measure"), than he regrets that he cannot play

(60) a tyrant...and even shows the company how he would deal with it. Then when Thisbe is mentioned, he sees himself playing her too, speaking in a monstrous little voice. The lion is the next part of any importance, and though it

(65) consists of nothing but roaring, Bottom has no doubt that he could make a success of that too, by means of a roar that would do any man's heart good to hear it, or, failing that, if such a full-blooded performance should scare the

(70) ladies, a delicately modulated roar that would not shame either a suckling dove or a nightingale....It is clear that a man cannot play every part, cannot be lover, tyrant, lady, and lion at once; but it is equally clear that every

(75) man of imagination and spirit ought to want to play every part. It is better to be vain, like Bottom, than to be dead in the spirit, like Snug or Starveling.[2] If it is a weakness to desire to play lover, lady, and lion, it is a weakness of

(80) great men, of choice, fiery, and fantastic souls who cannot easily realize or submit to the limitations pressing about our puny mortality....

---

[1] Bottom's head is magically turned into that of an ass by the mischievous Puck.

[2] Two other members of the company

22. The author's attitude toward Bottom is BEST described as

    (A) qualified admiration
    (B) unbridled disdain
    (C) reverential awe
    (D) grudging tolerance
    (E) sheer bewilderment

23. The author's description of the play as "only so much gossamer and moonlight" (lines 2-3) is likely intended to do which of the following?

    I. Dismiss the play's content as insubstantial.
    II. Depict the magical ambience of the play's nocturnal setting.
    III. Contrast the world of enchantment with Bottom's mundane profession.

    (A) I only
    (B) III only
    (C) I and II
    (D) II and III
    (E) I, II and III

24. That the pedestrian Bottom is out of place in this enchanted environment is implied by all of the following EXCEPT

    (A) "…piece of humorous, bewildered flesh, gross, earthy" (lines 4-5)
    (B) "a trades-unionist among butterflies, a rate-payer in Elfland" (lines 5-6)
    (C) "…a most prosaic soul called to a romantic destiny" (lines 7-8)
    (D) "…the only one of them that was fit to be 'translated'" (lines 10-11)
    (E) "'the shallowest thickskin of that barren sort'" (lines 13-14)

25. Which of the following contributes LEAST to justifying the author's claim in line 22 that Bottom is conceited?

    (A) That Bottom is the biggest fool of the company of tradesmen.
    (B) That Bottom has an artistic personality.
    (C) That Bottom is superior in imaginative vision to his fellow tradesman.
    (D) That Bottom looks down upon Old Quince.
    (E) That Bottom wishes to play every part in the drama.

26. Lines 44-47, "The others are only concerned with getting through their several tasks in the easiest and safest manner, with one eye on the hangman and the other on the exchequer," suggest that the attitude of the other players is

    (A) rote and perfunctory
    (B) bored and negligent
    (C) pragmatic and self-preservational
    (D) embittered and greedy
    (E) responsible and meticulous

27. Of the following, which BEST reflects what the author perceives as the reason behind Bottom's desire to play every role in the production?

    (A) his lack of trust in his fellow actors
    (B) his yearning for public acknowledgment of his talent
    (C) his enormous versatility as a thespian
    (D) his irrepressibly creative spirit
    (E) his lamentable indecision

28. Bottom's parenthetical comment, "…let the audience look to their eyes" (line 57), is BEST paraphrased by which of the following?

    (A) wipe away tears
    (B) follow the play's action
    (C) endeavor to remain awake
    (D) question what they are seeing
    (E) wonder who is playing the part

29. Ultimately, the author's primary goal in this essay is to persuade the reader that Bottom is

    (A) passionately quixotic
    (B) insufferably conceited
    (C) embarrassingly unrefined
    (D) ruthlessly ambitious
    (E) severely limited

30. All of the following are stylistic traits of the passage EXCEPT

    (A) the use of lines from the play and parenthetical comments to buttress his argument
    (B) a reference to another prominent Shakespearean critic
    (C) a contrast between Bottom and other players
    (D) the use of the collective "we" to link author and audience
    (E) a concluding irony that affirms the singular brilliance of Bottom

Questions 31-42. Refer to the following passage.

The following excerpt is from a controversial 1966 book documenting the ethos and activities of an infamous motorcycle gang.

Far from being freaks, the Hell's Angels are a logical product of the culture that now claims to be shocked at their existence. The generation represented by the editors of *Time*
(5) has lived so long in a world full of Celluloid[1] outlaws hustling toothpaste and hair oil that it is no longer capable of confronting the real thing. For twenty years they have sat with their children and watched yesterday's outlaws raise
(10) hell with yesterday's world…and now they are bringing up children who think Jesse James is a television character. This is the generation that went to war for Mom, God and Apple Butter, the American Way of Life. When they
(15) came back they crowned Eisenhower[2] and then retired to the giddy comfort of their TV parlors, to cultivate the subtleties of American history as seen by Hollywood.

To them the appearance of the Hell's
(20) Angels must have seemed like a wonderful publicity stunt. In a nation of frightened dullards there is a sorry shortage of outlaws and those few who make the grade are always welcome….
(25) Now, looking for labels, it is hard to call the Hell's Angels anything but mutants. They are urban outlaws with a rural ethic and a new, improvised style of self-preservation. Their image of themselves derives mainly from
(30) Celluloid, from Western movies and two-fisted TV shows that have taught them most of what they know about the society they live in. Very few read books, and in most cases their formal education ended at fifteen or sixteen. What
(35) little they know of history has come from mass media, beginning with comics…so if they see themselves in terms of the past, it's because they can't grasp the terms of the present, much less the future. They are the sons of poor men
(40) and drifters, losers and the sons of losers. Their backgrounds are overwhelmingly ordinary. As people, they are like millions of other people. But in their collective identity they have a peculiar fascination so obvious that even the

(45) press recognized it, although not without cynicism. In its ritual flirtation with reality the press has viewed the Angels with a mixture of awe, humor and terror—justified, as always, by a slavish dedication to the public appetite,
(50) which most journalists find so puzzling and contemptible that they have long since abandoned the task of understanding it to a handful of poll-takers and "experts."

The widespread appeal of the Angels is
(55) worth pondering. Unlike most other rebels, the Angels have given up hope that the world is going to change for them. They assume, on good evidence, that the people who run the social machinery have little use for outlaw
(60) motorcyclists, and they are reconciled to being losers. But instead of losing quietly, one by one, they have banded together with a mindless kind of loyalty and moved outside the framework, for good or ill. They may not have
(65) an answer, but at least they are still on their feet….The Industrial Workers of the World[3] had serious blueprints for society, while the Hell's Angels mean only to defy the social machinery. There is no talk among the Angels
(70) of "building a better world" yet their reactions to the world they live in are rooted in the same kind of anarchic, para-legal sense of conviction that brought the armed wrath of the Establishment down on the Wobblies.[4] There is
(75) the same kind of suicidal loyalty, the same kinds of ingroup rituals and nicknames, and above all the same feeling of constant warfare with an unjust world. The Wobblies were losers and so are the Angels…and if every
(80) loser in this country rode a motorcycle the whole highway system would have to be modified.

There is an important difference between the words "loser" and "outlaw." One is passive
(85) and the other is active, and the main reason the Angels are such good copy is that they are acting out the day-dreams of millions of losers who don't wear any defiant insignia and who don't know how to be outlaws. The streets of
(90) every city are thronged with men who would pay all the money they could get their hands on to be transformed—even for a day—into hairy, hard-fisted brutes who walk over cops, extort free drinks from terrified bartenders and
(95) thunder out of town on big motorcycles….

[1] A motion-picture film
[2] commander of Allied forces in World War Two; elected to two terms as U.S. President: 1953-1961
[3] A labor organization, dedicated to the overthrow of capitalism, that was especially active in the United States in the early 1900s.
[4] Nickname for members of the I.W.W.

From HELL'S ANGELS by Hunter S. Thompson, copyright © 1966, 1967 by Hunter S. Thompson. Used by permission of Random House, Inc.

31. Taken as a whole, the passage is BEST described as a

    (A) personal memoir of a gang member
    (B) blistering satire of post-war American values
    (C) critique of Hollywood cinema
    (D) social commentary on a motorcycle gang
    (E) political manifesto of anarchical sentiments

32. The opening sentence of the passage does all of the following EXCEPT

    (A) establish a guiding thesis
    (B) dismiss a popular misconception
    (C) invalidate a source
    (D) note an amusing irony
    (E) hint at a disingenuous claim

33. The author implies that the post-war "generation represented by the editors of *Time*" (line 4) became all of the following EXCEPT

    (A) assured of their present safety
    (B) enamored with television
    (C) detached from reality
    (D) less patriotic
    (E) ensconced in an idyllic way of life

34. The words "mom, God and Apple Butter" (lines 13-14) are BEST labeled

    (A) ironies
    (B) metonymies
    (C) personifications
    (D) images
    (E) anachronisms

35. The author likely intends the verb "crowned" in line 15 to do which of the following?

    I. Indicate whom Americans voted into office in the first post-war election.
    II. Illustrate the revered status that Americans regularly bestow upon their military heroes.
    III. Decry the expanding power of the American Presidency.
    IV. Imply that Eisenhower felt this was the penultimate moment of his career.

    (A) I only
    (B) III only
    (C) I and II
    (D) I, II and IV
    (E) I, II, III and IV

36. Lines 23-24, "those few who make the grade are always welcome," refer back to which of the following?

    (A) the "Hell's Angels" (line 1, lines 19-20)
    (B) the "generation represented by the editors of *Time*" (line 4)
    (C) the "world full of Celluloid outlaws…" (lines 5-6)
    (D) the "generation that went to war for Mom, God and Apple Butter…" (lines 13-14)
    (E) the "nation of frightened dullards" (lines 21-22)

37. Which of the following may NOT be considered a legitimate reason for the author's labeling the Hell's Angels "mutants" (line 26)?

    (A) the "Celluloid" nature of their self-image (line 5)
    (B) the "rural ethic" (line 27) behind their urban image
    (C) their "improvised style of self-preservation" (line 28)
    (D) their "overwhelmingly ordinary" roots (line 41)
    (E) their "hairy, hard-fisted" mien (lines 92-93)

38. Lines 41-53—"As people, they are like millions.... to a handful of poll-takers and 'experts'"—express the author's mild scorn for which of the following?

    (A) the pedestrian nature of many individual gang members
    (B) the ability of journalists to recognize a socially significant phenomenon
    (C) the slavish hours demanded by a career in journalism
    (D) the public's insatiable appetite for scandal
    (E) the accuracy of poll-takers and "experts"

39. In lines 54-66 the author seems to express the greatest admiration for the Angels'

    (A) similarity to "other rebels" (line 55)
    (B) resignation to always "losing quietly" (line 61)
    (C) bonding with other gang members in "mindless kind of loyalty" (lines 62-63)
    (D) election to move "outside the framework" and endure (lines 63-64)
    (E) acceptance that the "social machinery" will not change for them (lines 68-69)

40. The singular difference between the Wobblies and the Hell's Angels lies in the latter's

    (A) emphasis on organizational allegiance
    (B) belief in rituals and nicknames
    (C) lack of commitment to social change
    (D) perception as a public menace
    (E) appeal to the ordinary man

41. Which of the following does LEAST to contribute to the author's "anarchic" characterization of the Hell's Angels in the passage?

    (A) "moved outside the framework for good or ill" (lines 63-64)
    (B) "defy the social machinery" (lines 68-69)
    (C) "constant warfare with an unjust world" (lines 77-78)
    (D) "defiant insignia" (line 88)
    (E) "thunder out of town on big motorcycles…" (line 95)

42. The passage's closing sentence (lines 89-95) implies that the average man secretly

    (A) wants to be a gang member
    (B) wishes to be nonconformist and assertive
    (C) craves the spotlight
    (D) desires camaraderie
    (E) is innately violent

Questions 43-52. Refer to the following passage.

In the following selection from an essay by Mark Twain, the author evaluates the merits of an earlier American author, James Fenimore Cooper.

....Cooper's gift in the way of invention was not a rich endowment; but such as it was he liked to work it, he was pleased with the effects, and indeed he did some quite sweet
(5) things with it. In his little box of stage properties he kept six or eight cunning devices, tricks, artifices for his savages and woodsmen to deceive and circumvent each other with, and he was never so happy as when he was
(10) working these innocent things and seeing them go. A favorite one was to make a moccasined person tread in the tracks of a moccasined enemy, and thus hide his own trail. Cooper wore out barrels and barrels of moccasins in
(15) working that trick. Another stage-property that he pulled out of his box pretty frequently was his broken twig. He prized his broken twig above all the rest of his effects, and worked it the hardest. It is a restful chapter in any book
(20) of his when somebody doesn't step on a broken twig and alarm all the reds and whites for two hundred yards around. Every time a Cooper person is in peril, and absolute silence is worth four dollars a minute, he is sure to
(25) step on a dry twig. There may be a hundred handier things to step on, but that wouldn't satisfy Cooper. Cooper requires him to turn out and find a dry twig; and if he can't do it, go and borrow one....
(30)   I am sorry there is not room to put in a few dozen instances of the forest, as practiced by Natty Bumppo[1] and some of the other Cooperian experts. Perhaps we may venture two or three samples. Cooper was a sailor—a
(35) naval officer; yet he gravely tells us how a vessel, driving toward a lee shore in a gale, is steered for a particular spot by her skipper because he knows of an *undertow* there which will hold her back against the gale and save
(40) her. For just pure woodcraft, or sailor craft, or whatever it is, isn't that neat? For several years Cooper was daily in the society of artillery, and he ought to have noticed that when a cannon ball strikes the ground it either buries itself or
(45) skips a hundred feet or so; skips again a

hundred feet or so—and so on, till it finally gets tired and rolls. Now in one place he loses some "females"—as he always calls his women—in the edge of a wood near a plain at night in a
(50) fog, on purpose to give Bumppo a chance to show off the delicate art of the forest before the reader. These mislaid people are hunting for a fort. They hear a cannon-blast, and a cannon-ball presently comes rolling into the
(55) wood and stops at their feet. To the females this suggests nothing. The case is very different with the admirable Bumppo. I wish I may never know peace again if he doesn't strike out promptly and follow the track of that cannon-
(60) ball across the plain through the dense fog and finds the fort. Isn't it a daisy? If Cooper had any real knowledge of Nature's ways of doing things, he had a most delicate art in concealing the fact....
(65)   We must be a little wary when Brander Matthews[2] tells us that Cooper's books "reveal an extraordinary fulness of invention." As a rule, I am quite willing to accept Brander Matthews' literary judgments and applaud his
(70) lucid and graceful phrasing of them; but that particular statement needs to be taken with a few tons of salt...

43. The passage as a whole is BEST described as a(n)

(A) *ad hominem* attack on Cooper
(B) rebuttal of a popular critical perspective
(C) critique of Cooper's literary technique
(D) selection from a biography of Cooper
(E) feminist critique of Cooper's fiction

44. Which of the following BEST captures the attitude Twain displays toward the imaginative craft of James Fenimore Cooper?

(A) utter disdain
(B) reverential admiration
(C) mild bemusement
(D) frustrated perplexity
(E) knowing empathy

---

[1] one of Cooper's well-known protagonists
[2] late nineteenth/early twentieth century literary critic

45. In conveying his opinion of Cooper's literary strategies, Twain makes the MOST use of

    (A) a central metaphor
    (B) the exploits of Cooper's characters
    (C) a literary critic
    (D) sardonic rhetorical questions
    (E) a telling cliché

46. Taken collectively, Twain's allusions to Cooper's moccasin "trick" (lines 11-13), the actions of Cooper's naval captain (lines 34-41), and Natty Bumppo's encounter with the cannon-ball (lines 52-61) do which of the following?

    I. Illustrate Cooper's childish delight in being clever.
    II. Point out the preposterousness of the actions of some of Cooper's characters.
    III. Show how Cooper's own experiences heightened the veracity of his fiction.

    (A) I only
    (B) III only
    (C) I and II
    (D) II and III
    (E) I, II and III

47. In terms of the moccasins and the broken twig, it is not so much Cooper's use of these conventions that Twain dislikes as their

    (A) frequency
    (B) triteness
    (C) insensibility
    (D) histrionics
    (E) archaism

48. The BEST equivalent for "society" (line 42) would be

    (A) fellowship
    (B) proximity
    (C) range
    (D) detail
    (E) barrage

49. The quintet of prepositional phrases—"in the edge of a wood near a plain at night in a fog" (lines 48-50)—serves to

    (A) censure the carelessness of the women by detailing the perils of the environment
    (B) attest to the meticulousness of Cooper's description
    (C) increase via climactic order the incident's dramatic tension
    (D) highlight the absurdity of Bumppo's forest acumen
    (E) anticipate a later stylistic development: stream of consciousness

50. In the phrase, "…give Bumppo a chance to show off the delicate art of the forest…" (lines 50-51), the author

    (A) compliments the skill of one of Cooper's protagonists
    (B) derides Bumppo's characteristic braggadocio
    (C) indicates his own deep reverence for nature
    (D) reveals the impact of Cooper's familiarity with artillery
    (E) implies that much of Cooper's narrative is contrived

51. The phrase "…but that particular statement needs to be taken with a few tons of salt…" (lines 70-72) is primarily intended to reveal Twain's

    (A) deft control of hyperbole
    (B) deliberate mirroring of Matthews' "extraordinary fulness" (line 67)
    (C) concurrence with Matthews' high opinion of Cooper's creativity
    (D) cynicism toward Matthews' laudatory assessment of Cooper
    (E) feeling that Matthews' literary criticism is extremely bland

52. All of the following exemplify the admirable restraint Twain shows in articulating his opinion of Cooper's writing EXCEPT

   (A) "…Cooper's gift in the way of invention was not a rich endowment…" (lines 1-2)
   (B) "He prized his broken twig above all the rest of his effects, and worked it the hardest" (lines 17-19)
   (C) "I am sorry there is not room to put in a few dozen instances of the forest, as practiced by Natty Bumppo and some of the other Cooperian experts" (lines 30-34)
   (D) "If Cooper had any real knowledge of Nature's ways of doing things, he had a most delicate art in concealing the fact…." (lines 61-64)
   (E) "We must be a little wary when Brander Matthews tells us that Cooper's books 'reveal an extraordinary fulness of invention'" (lines 65-67)

Section II

Question One

(Suggested time–40 minutes. This question counts as one-third of the total essay section score.)

In the following passage a writer reflects on the qualitities which made Abraham Lincoln a great statesman. Read the passage carefully. Then, in a well-organized essay, identify the attributes that made Lincoln an effective leader and analyze the rhetorical strategies that author uses to convey them.

      Mr. Lincoln is sometimes claimed as an example of a ready-made ruler. But no case could well be less in point; for, besides that he was a man of such fair-mindedness as is always the raw material of wisdom, he had in his profession a training precisely the opposite of that to which a partisan is subjected. His experience as a lawyer compelled him not only to see that there is a principle underlying every

(5)   phenomenon in human affairs, but there are always two sides to every question, both of which must be fully understood in order to understand either, and that it is of greater advantage to an advocate to appreciate the strength rather than the weakness of his antagonist's position….His wisdom was made up of a knowledge of things as well as of men; his sagacity resulted from a clear perception and honest acknowledgment of difficulties, which enabled him to see that the only durable triumph of political

(10)   opinion is based, not on any abstract right, but upon so much of justice, the highest attainable at any given moment in human affairs, as may be had in the balance of mutual concession. Doubtless he had an ideal, but it was the ideal of a practical statesman,—to aim at the best, and to take the next best, if he was lucky enough to get even that….The cautious, but steady, advance of his policy during the war was like that of a Roman army. He left behind him a firm road on which public confidence could follow; he took

(15)   America with him where he went; what he gained he occupied, and his advanced posts became colonies. The very homeliness of his genius was its distinction. His kingship was conspicuous by its workday homespun. Never was ruler so absolute as he nor so little conscious of it; for he was the incarnate common-sense of the people….He seems to have had but one rule of conduct, always that of practical and successful politics, to let himself be guided by events, when they were sure to bring him out where

(20)   he wished to go….
      Undoubtedly, the highest function of statesmanship is by degrees to accommodate the conduct of communities to ethical laws, and to subordinate the conflicting self-interests of the day to higher and more permanent concerns. But it is on the understanding, and not on the sentiment, of a nation that all safe legislation must be based….The course of a great statesman resembles that of navigable rivers,

(25)   avoiding immovable obstacles with noble bends of concession, seeking the broad levels of opinion on which men soonest settle and longest dwell, following and marking the almost imperceptible slopes of national tendency, yet always aiming at direct advances, always recruited from sources near heaven, and sometimes bursting open paths of progress and fruitful human commerce through what seem the eternal barriers of both. It is loyalty to great ends, even though forced to combine the small and opposing

(30)   motives of selfish men to accomplish them; it is the anchored cling to solid principles of duty and action, which knows how to swing with the tide, but is never carried away by it,—that we demand in public men, and not obstinacy in prejudice, sameness of policy, or a conscientious persistency in what is impracticable….

Question Two

(Suggested time—40 minutes. This question counts as one-third of the total essay section score.)

"If a great man could make us understand him, we should hang him."

—George Bernard Shaw

This aphorism, taken from "The Revolutionist's Handbook" (the appendix to George Bernard Shaw's play *Man and Superman*), makes a strong statement about how human beings respond to people with vision. Discuss the implications inherent in the citation and, using your reading, studies, experience and/or observation, explore the validity of Shaw's claim.

<u>Question Three</u>

Reading Time: 15 minutes
Suggested Writing Time: 40 minutes

(This question counts as one-third of the total essay section score.)

Directions:

The following prompt is based on the accompanying six sources.

This question requires you to integrate a variety of sources into a coherent, well-written essay. *Refer to the sources to support your position; avoid paraphrase or summary. Your argument should be central; the sources should support this argument.*

Remember to attribute both direct and indirect citations.

Introduction:

Concerns in the United States about the cost and availability of oil have led to some high-risk ventures, including a relatively new procedure called "fracking." While these attempts to uncover new sources of oil are intended to reduce American dependence on the oil-rich but politically unstable countries of the Middle East, they have been rumored to trigger serious environmental issues that offset their financial benefits. Though it is widely affirmed that the United States government and its citizenry must become more committed to developing and using alternate sources of energy and propulsion, such solutions remain many years off or place stringent economic demands on consumers. This begs the question, which is the wisest path toward oil independence: the path of exploration or the path of conservation? Uncovering new sources of oil, or reducing our dependence upon it?

Assignment:

Read the following sources (including any introductory information) carefully. **Then, in an essay that synthesizes at least three of the sources for support, take a position that defends, challenges or qualifies the claim that reducing American dependency on the oil-rich countries of the Middle East is more reliant upon uncovering new domestic sources of oil than upon exploring alternate sources of energy and propulsion.**

Document A

White, Kathleen Hartnett. "The Fracas About Fracking." *National Review* 63.11 (June 20, 2011): 38-41.

A major boom in domestic oil and gas production is underway, brought about by breakthrough refinements of a 1940s technology known as hydraulic fracturing, or "fracking."

Hydraulic fracturing involves pumping water, sand, and some trace chemicals under high pressure into a completed wellbore to create fissures in relatively impermeable geologic formations such as shale. The fissures allow oil or natural gas to flow into the well. The sand props the fissures open, preventing the resealing of pathways. Combined with horizontal drilling at depths of one to more than two miles below the earth's surface, hydraulic fracturing has unlocked vast stores of natural gas.

Fracking is also now widely used in vertical and horizontal drilling in oil reservoirs with low permeability. Conventional oil reservoirs with permeable geologic formations allow oil to flow to the wellbore as a result of natural pressure. But in many wells, as much as 75 percent of the oil and gas may be left in place. Fracking is one of several new ways to get at the ample resources remaining after natural pressure subsides.

In these ways, human ingenuity, catalyzed by market dynamics, has foiled predictions of irreversible decline in domestic oil and natural-gas resources. Official estimates of the amount of recoverable oil and natural gas have soared. Last year, global natural-gas supplies rose 40 percent. From 2010 to 2011, the U.S. Energy Information Administration (EIA) doubled its estimate of recoverable natural gas in the U.S. The EIA increased its estimate of Texas's natural-gas reserves by 70 percent between 2005 and 2008, and Texas also is doing prolific fracking in oil. Producers now have access to 2 billion barrels in the Wolfberry formation in the Permian Basin. The Eagle Ford fields in South Texas increased oil production fourfold in the first ten months of 2010. And the Haynesville-Bossier fields, straddling Texas's border with Louisiana, increased reserves of natural gas by 9.4 trillion cubic feet while increasing production twelvefold.

The EIA also believes that natural gas in the Marcellus formation of New York, Pennsylvania, and West Virginia contains more BTUs of energy than do the oil reserves of Saudi Arabia. Drilling is well under way in Pennsylvania, where 141,000 new jobs in the "gas patch" have been created in the last few years…

Document B

Rauber, Paul. "Beyond Oil in 20 Years. *Sierra* 96.1 (Jan/Feb 2011): 32-37.

....Breaking an addiction is a wrenching process. And quitting oil certainly could be ugly, especially if we're cut off suddenly, as a result of another embargo by oil-producing states, say, or by stratospheric price hikes due to declining reserves. But a future without oil doesn't have to mean going cold turkey or fighting for fill-ups in a Mad Max world. Alternatives already exist for most uses of oil, and adopting them will improve our lives in many ways beyond slowing climate change.

....The no-brainer approach to reducing the amount of oil cars and light trucks consume is to drive our cars and trucks less. When gas approached $4 a gallon in 2008, consumption dropped by 900,000 barrels a day. People didn't stop going places; they just got there by public transit, cycling, or (gasp!) walking.

The other easy solution is to make vehicles that use less gas. Automobile fuel-efficiency basically remained unchanged from 1975 to 2007. (Auto engineering did improve in that period, but those advances overwhelmingly entailed increasing the horsepower, not the mileage, of cars and SUVs.) Last April, Obama signed a new fuel-efficiency standard mandating that light-duty vehicles average 35 miles per gallon by 2016. It will save, over the life of cars built between 2012 and 2016, 1.8 billion barrels of oil.

Much bigger reductions are to come in the years after 2016. Last October, the Obama administration announced that it wants to see an annual decrease in car and truck emissions of between 3 and 6 percent from 2017 to 2025. This would result in vehicles averaging 47 to 62 mpg by 2025 and could be accomplished, says a report by John DeCicco of the University of Michigan, through the use of lightweight steel, hybrid drives, efficient diesels, and aerodynamic styling. The Sierra Club and other groups in the Go60mpg campaign (go60mpg.org) are urging the EPA to adopt the highest possible standard, noting that a 60-mpg level would save 44 billion gallons of fuel by 2030. DeCicco, in fact, believes that an average of 74 mpg is achievable by 2035....

Of course, drivers don't have to wait 25 years for super-fuel-efficient vehicles. They can go to the dealer today and buy a standard Prius (50 mpg, according to the EPA), a Smart car (36 mpg), a Honda Civic (42 mpg), or any of a dozen other models achieving 30-plus mpg. By the time you read this, Chevy will have begun selling its gas-electric Volt (not yet rated) and Nissan its Leaf, the first mass-market car for which miles per gallon of gas no longer makes sense as a measurement, because it's all-electric....

Document C

© Cartoonstock.com

Document D

Marsh, Gerald E. "Can the Clash of Civilizations Produce Alternate Energy Sources?" *USA Today Magazine* (Jan 2007): 10-13.

...."Peak oil" theorists assert that there will be growing conflict over the remaining oil resources and a high probability of a worldwide economic collapse. Such claims, however, show a misunderstanding of the meaning of "oil reserves." These reserves depend on price and are not a direct measure of the amount of oil physically available in the ground. There is plenty of oil, perhaps as much as the 7.2 trillion barrels estimated by ExxonMobil, but these reserves cannot be brought to market as cheaply as oil from the Persian Gulf, and the economics of oil dictate that cheaper oil will be used first. Moreover, these sources cannot begin production immediately; there is a ramp-up period of years. If the phasing in of such reserves does not match the decline of current oil fields, rising prices and conflict over resources are inevitable.

The members of OPEC recently agreed to cut production to show their determination to defend $60 per barrel as a minimum international price. This is high enough to allow a good profit to be made on oil from shale or tar sands, of which North America has enormous quantities. However, the Saudis know full well that it is unlikely anyone will invest the many billions of dollars needed to produce enough oil from these sources to threaten OPEC dominance. OPEC is a cartel and, if such an investment were to be made, OPEC would pump enough oil to drop world prices to the point where the investment would be threatened.....

Many hope that America can avoid the clash of civilizations by finding a new source of energy, one that not only sidesteps the issue of dependence on Gulf oil, but is far more environmentally benign. Perhaps the time is ripe for a heavy investment in windmills or solar power. However, these sources only are capable of providing limited amounts of electric power compared to projected demand. All such sources of energy are unlikely to comprise more than two percent of the total energy mix by 2030.

There is a major government initiative underway to use hydrogen to power the country's vast transportation system. Hydrogen, though, like electricity, is not a source of energy; rather, it is a means of delivering energy from one point to another. In addition, hydrogen use has a built-in inefficiency, since the laws of physics dictate that it takes more energy to produce hydrogen than is given back from its use. Yet, it remains an attractive transfer medium since its sole waste product when burned is water.

In time, it is quite possible that hydrogen will replace oil, but only after less expensive production and handling methods are developed....

Document E

Marsa, Linda. "Fracking Nation." *Discover* 32.4 (May 2011): 62-70.

To comprehend the long-term implications of hydraulic fracturing, you need to visit the region where gas drilling first boomed. It sits above the Barnett Shale, a formation that underlies 5,000 square miles surrounding Fort Worth, Texas. Large-scale fracking began here in 2002. There are now about 14,000 gas wells in the area, and it is there that the environmental fallout of fracking has been most pronounced. Residents have complained for years of contaminated water, poor air quality, and unexplained health problems such as headaches, dizziness, blackouts, and muscle contractions.

Drilling operations have turned some of Texas's most affluent communities into industrial wastelands. In towns like Argyle and Bartonville, where drill rigs have been erected within a mile of schools, children complain of nosebleeds, dizziness, and nausea. Parents worry about the release of the cancer-causing chemical benzene in the air above gas fields from processing plants and equipment.

Fracking in the Marcellus Shale has not been going on as long as it has in Texas, but residents have already begun to experience its dark side. Just ask Craig and Julie Sautner. When the cable technician and his wife moved to Dimock, an agricultural community of about 1,500 nestled in the rolling hills of northeastern Pennsylvania, they had no inkling they were sitting on top of a mother lode of natural gas—that is, not until an agent from Cabot Oil & Gas, a Houston-based natural gas producer, knocked on their door in May 2008. He offered them $10,000 to lease the mineral rights on their four acres, with the promise of even more in royalties if Cabot struck pay dirt. "You might as well sign it because all your neighbors are," the man said, according to Craig. "If you don't, you'll miss out."

In August 2008, the company started drilling less than 1,000 feet from the Sautners' water well. By mid-September the family's tap water was undrinkable. "I noticed the toilet water was murky, and when I used the water in the sink in the kitchen, it was brown," Craig recalls. He called Cabot Oil & Gas to complain, but representatives insisted there was no way that Cabot's drilling process could have contaminated the Sautners' well water....

Tests conducted soon after by the Pennsylvania Department of Environmental Protection revealed that the Sautners' water contained high levels of methane, the main component of natural gas. Although methane is not normally harmful to drink in concentrations below 10 milligrams per liter, it can evaporate from the water. If it collects in enclosed spaces like basements, it can become flammable and explode or suffocate those who inhale it. The Sautners, who have joined with a group of neighbors and filed a lawsuit against Cabot, worry that the methane could explode at any time. "My son asks every night," Craig says, with no small measure of gallows humor, "'Do you think we'll wake up in the morning?'"....

Document F

Wagoner, Rick. "Charging Ahead." *Vital Speeches of the Day* 73.1 (Jan 2007): 19-23.

....Since 2001, a series of geopolitical, natural, and economic realities—from extraordinary economic growth in China and India, to regional conflicts in the Middle East, to population growth, global climate change, and natural disasters in the Gulf of Mexico—have combined to drive home the fact that we face an increasingly uncertain energy future on a global basis....

For the global auto industry, this means that we must—as a business necessity—develop alternative sources of propulsion, based on alternative sources of energy, in order to meet the world's growing demand for our products....

At GM, we believe that the biofuel with the greatest potential to displace petroleum-based fuels in the U.S. is ethanol, and so we have made a major commitment to vehicles that can run on E-85 ethanol....

At GM, we're partnering with government, fuel providers, and fuel retailers across the U.S. to help grow the E-85 ethanol fueling station infrastructure. Since May of 2005, we've helped add 175 E-85 fueling stations in 11 states, with more to come....

What are the other fuel options available to us?

Well, despite its success on the sands of Daytona Beach 100 years ago, steam is not one of the technologies we're pursuing today. But we are very serious about the third option that was big in 1906—that is, electrically driven vehicles.

In fact, I'm announcing today that GM is significantly expanding and accelerating our commitment to the development of electrically driven vehicles beyond what we have already committed to with our fuel cell and hybrid programs.

Why electricity?

First, electricity offers outstanding benefits, beginning with the opportunity to diversify fuel sources "upstream" of the vehicle. In other words, the electricity that is used to drive the vehicle can be made from the best local fuel sources—natural gas, coal, nuclear, wind, hydroelectric, and so on. So, before you even start your vehicle, you're working toward energy diversity.

Second, electrically driven vehicles, when operated in an all-electric mode, are zero-emission vehicles. And when the electricity, itself, is made from a renewable source, the entire energy pathway is emissions free. Third, electrically driven vehicles offer great performance, with extraordinary acceleration, instant torque, improved driving dynamics, and so on....

I should point out that GM's commitment to improving fuel economy, reducing vehicle emissions, and developing electrically driven vehicles is not a short-term strategy. We're in this game for the long term. We see energy and environmental leadership as a critical element of GM's ongoing turnaround plan, a key part of our future business strategy, and we intend to bring our substantial global resources to bear on this issue starting yesterday....